Fasttrack to America's Past

An interactive study guide and review of U.S. history

David Burns

www.fasttrackteaching.com

*Our free Internet support site is like an on-line "Teacher's Edition"
that is always available to help users of this workbook!*

Completed Maps	Finished Timelines
Names and Terms Glossary	Famous Quotes Identified
Charts Completed	Links to Historic Sites
Plus: Practice tests for all sections!	

Copyright Notice

Illustrations appearing in this publication are taken from sources in the public domain and from private collections used by permission. Sources include: the Dover Pictorial Archive, the Library of Congress, the U.S. Bureau of Printing and Engraving, Art Direction Book Company, The Hart Publishing Co., Corel Corporation and its licensors, Nova Development Corporation and its licensors, and others. Maps were created or adapted by the author using reference maps from the United States Geological Survey, the Library of Congress, and Cartesia Software.

International Standard Book Number

ISBN 1-893742-05-9

Fifth Edition - 2003

Every effort has been made to research the copyright status of historical selections appearing in this publication. Many have been condensed by the author from material in the public domain. Others are used with the permission of the publisher. The author welcomes information from legitimate copyright holders who have been overlooked, so that corrections can be made in future editions. In many cases, the full text of speeches and other historical documents can be easily found with a search engine like Google on the Internet. Sources include:

"The English Meet the Native Americans" is condensed from: *A Brief and True Report of the New Found Land of Virginia*, by Thomas Harriot. (Dover Publications, Inc. reprint of the 1590 edition held by the Library of Congress)

"The Mystery of the Lost Colony" is condensed from *The Principal Navigations, Voyages, Traffiques, & Discoveries of the English Nation*, vol. 8, by Richard Hakluyt. (1904)

"Capt. John Smith's Tale" is condensed from *The Generall Historie of Virginia, New-England, and the Summer Isles.* (Johnson Publishing Co. reprint of the 1624 edition)

"Planting a Sense of Community" is condensed from several Internet sites containing various sections of the text of William Bradford's journal, *Of Plymouth Plantation*; also, from sites with the text of John Winthrop's "A Model of Christian Charity."

"A Visit to the Middle Colonies" is condensed from *Travels into North America*, by Peter Kalm. (Dover Publications reprint of the 1770 English edition.)

"Patrick Henry Calls for a Fight" is condensed from *The World's Great Speeches*, ed. by Lewis Copeland and Lawrence W. Lamm. (Mineola, N.Y.: Dover Publications, 1986.)

"Thomas Paine's Common Sense" is condensed from *Common Sense*, the expanded 1776 edition of the pamphlet published anonymously by Thomas Paine.

"Abigail Adams' Plea for Women" is condensed from several Internet public domain sources. The original documents can be found in *Familiar Letters of John Adams and His Wife Abigail Adams During the Revolution* (New York: 1876), as well as many anthologies.

"First Impressions of a New Nation" is condensed from *Travels in the Confederation*, by Johann Schoepf. Trans. and ed. by Alfred J. Morrison. (Philadelphia: William J. Campbell, 1911)

"Red Jacket's Response" is condensed from *The World's Great Speeches*.

"An Immigrant's Letter" is condensed from *America's Immigrants: Adventures in Eyewitness History*, by Rhoda Huff. (N.Y.: Henry Z. Walck, Inc., 1967.) Source: *Land of Their Choice*, ed. by T.C. Blegen. (Minneapolis: U. of Minn. Press, 1955.) Used by permission.

"A Growing City and Its People" is condensed from *A Pioneer in Northwest America*, vol. 2, by Gustaf Unonius. Translated by Jonas Oscar Backlund. (Minneapolis: The University of Minnesota Press, 1960.) Used by courtesy of the Swedish-American Historical Society.

"A Call for Factory Reform" is condensed from *A Documentary History of American Industrial Society*, ed. by John R. Commons, et al. (Spokane: The Arthur H. Clark Co., 1910.) Original document: *The Harbinger*, Nov. 14, 1846.

"Dorothea Dix Pleads for the Mentally Ill" is condensed from *Memorial to the Massachusetts Legislature.* http://www.civnet.org/ teaching/basic/part 3/15.htm) Original document: *Memorial to the Legislature of Massachusetts*, 1843.

"Frederick Douglass on Slavery" is condensed from *The World's Great Speeches*.

"Abraham Lincoln Against Slavery" is condensed from Lincoln's speeches made in 1854 and 1858, which are available at http://www.speaker.gov/documents.asp

"Lincoln's Gettysburg Address" is reprinted from *The World's Great Speeches*.

"The Freed Slaves Tell Their Stories" is taken from interviews conducted by the WPA Writers Project, now collected at the Library of Congress.

"Voices of Reconstruction" selections are condensed from *The World's Great Speeches* and other public domain sources.

"Big Industry and Labor Unions" is condensed from several Internet sites containing public domain works by Andrew Carnegie, Ida Tarbell, and Samuel Gompers.

"Jane Addams Works for Better Cities" is condensed from several Internet sites containing public domain works by Addams.

"Jacob Riis Exposes Child Labor" is condensed from "Children of Immigrants" by Jacob Riis (1891) contained in *America's Immigrants: Adventures in Eyewitness History*. Used by permission.

"Why Women Should Vote" is condensed from *The World's Great Speeches* and other public domain sources.

"Mother Jones for the Miners" is condensed from Internet sites containing public domain selections from her autobiography.

"The Progressive Party Calls for Changes" is condensed from party platform records at the Library of Congress.

"FDR Attacks the Depression" is condensed from *The World's Great Speeches*.

"American Values Against Fascism" is condensed from *The World's Great Speeches*.

"FDR and World War Two" is condensed from *The World's Great Speeches*.

"The Struggle of the Cold War Begins" is condensed from Winston Churchill's *"The Sinews of Peace"* available at http://www.winston churchill.org. Also, from President Harry S. Truman's March 1947 speech before Congress expressing the Truman Doctrine, at http://www.tamu.edu/scom/ pres/ speeches/hstaid.html.

"Eisenhower on the Issues of the 1950s" is condensed from presidential speeches at http://www.tamu.edu/scom/ pres/ speeches/ikechance.html and http://www.tamu.edu/scom/ pres/ speeches/ikefederal.html.

"John F. Kennedy's Inaugural Address" is condensed from *The World's Great Speeches*.

"LBJ Calls for Racial Justice" is condensed from *Lyndon B. Johnson Address to Congress: We Shall Overcome* (http://history.hanover.edu/20th/johnson.htm, 1996).

"Ronald Reagan Speaks for Freedom" is condensed from the collection of speeches at http://www.cqc.com/ ~ barryt/ farewell.html, 1996.

"Hillary Clinton on Child Care" is condensed from *Remarks by the First Lady on Child Care* (http://www.whitehouse.gov/ , 1997)

"George W. Bush and the War on Terrorism" is condensed from the president's 2002 State of the Union Speech (http://www. whitehouse.gov)

*This study guide is dedicated to my parents
and teachers, who opened paths to
America's past for me.*

Acknowledgments

My thanks go first to my former students in the Fairfax County Public School system, who served as tireless classroom reviewers of these pages. Also, to my wife Jeanne, whose encouragement and support kept the project moving forward during the many years of development and revisions. In addition, I am grateful for the encouragement of teachers and administrators in the FCPS system, especially Don Majeske, Carol Marshall, Mike Wildasin, and Jay Pearson.

About the Author

David Burns is a native of Newport News, Virginia, and is currently a social studies teacher in the Fairfax County Public School system. He is a graduate of the University of Virginia (B.A., 1974) and Columbia University (M.S., 1978). Before becoming an educator, he worked as a reporter and documentary producer for television stations in Virginia and New York. His work has appeared nationally on PBS and CNN.

Table of Contents

Getting Started   vii

---

1   DISCOVERY AND EXPLORATION: 1400 - 1600

Section Page and Study Checklist	1 - 1
Timeline	1 - 3
New Worlds Discovered	1 - 5
Map - Trade Routes Before Columbus	1 - 7
Map - Native American Origins and Lands	1 - 9
Map - Early Voyages of Discovery	1 - 11
When Cultures Collided	1 - 13
The English Meet the Native Americans	1 - 15
The Mystery of the Lost Colony	1 - 17
Charting Golden Crops	1 - 19

---

2   COLONIAL AMERICA: 1600 - 1775

Section Page and Study Checklist	2 - 1
Timeline	2 - 3
Jamestown and Virginia	2 - 5
Capt. John Smith's Tale	2 - 7
Pilgrims and Puritans in Massachusetts	2 - 9
Planting a Sense of Community	2 - 11
Map - Early English Colonies	2 - 13
Map - The Spread of the Slave Trade	2 - 15
Map - Colonial America in 1754	2 - 17
The Colonial Heritage	2 - 19
A Visit to the Middle Colonies	2 - 21
Charting Colonial Statistics	2 - 23
Heading for Independence	2 - 25
Two Views From the Printing Presses	2 - 27

---

3   REVOLUTIONARY YEARS: 1775 - 1800

Section Page and Study Checklist	3 - 1
Timeline	3 - 3
The Revolution Begins	3 - 5
The Battle of Bunker Hill	3 - 7
Patrick Henry Calls for a Fight	3 - 9
Thomas Paine's Common Sense	3 - 10
The Declaration of Independence	3 - 11
Map - The Revolution's Famous Places	3 - 13
Life and Thought in the Revolution	3 - 15
Charting Money and Trade	3 - 17
Abigail Adams' Plea for Women's Rights	3 - 19
A Revolutionary Defense	3 - 20
The Challenges of Victory	3 - 21
The Constitution	3 - 23
The Bill of Rights	3 - 25
The National Government Organizes	3 - 27
First Impressions of a New Nation	3 - 29
Charting the First Census	3 - 31

---

4   THE GROWING YEARS: 1800 - 1860

Section Page and Study Checklist	4 - 1
Timeline	4 - 3
The Growing Years: An Overview	4 - 5
Charting Population and Immigration	4 - 7
Red Jacket's Response	4 - 9
An Immigrant's Letter	4 - 10
Charting the Transportation Revolution	4 - 11
Growing West	4 - 13
Map - Land Areas and Expansion to 1860	4 - 15
Map - Growth to the Mississippi	4 - 17
Map - Growth to the Far West	4 - 19
Growing Capitalism, Industry, and Cities	4 - 21
Charting Inventions and Cotton	4 - 23
A Growing City and Its People	4 - 25
Growing Reform and Religion	4 - 27
A Call for Factory Reform	4 - 29
Dorothea Dix Pleads for the Mentally Ill	4 - 30
Growing Apart: North and South	4 - 31
Charting Statistics of Slavery	4 - 33
Frederick Douglass Speaks for the Slaves	4 - 35
Abraham Lincoln Against Slavery	4 - 36

---

5   CIVIL WAR AND RECONSTRUCTION: 1860 - 1877

Section Page and Study Checklist	5 - 1
Timeline	5 - 3
The Civil War	5 - 5
Charting Manpower and Resources	5 - 7

continued

Map - The Civil War's Famous Places   5 - 9
Lincoln's Gettysburg Address   5 - 11
The Freed Slaves Tell Their Stories   5 - 12
Reconstruction and Beyond   5 - 13
Voices of Reconstruction   5 - 15

6   THE GILDED AGE: 1865 - 1900

Section Page and Study Checklist   6 - 1
Timeline   6 - 3
The Gilded Age   6 - 5
Map - Railroads, Cowboys, and Indians   6 - 7
Map - America Grows Overseas   6 - 9
Big Industry and Labor Unions   6 - 11
Charting Economic Trends   6 - 13
Jane Addams Works for Better Cities   6 - 15
Jacob Riis Exposes Child Labor   6 - 17
Why Women Should Vote   6 - 18

7   BECOMING A WORLD LEADER: 1900 - 1950

Section Page and Study Checklist   7 - 1
Timeline   7 - 3
Decade: 1900s   The Progressive Era   7 - 5
Mother Jones for the Miners   7 - 7
The Progressive Party Calls for Changes   7 - 8
Charting 20th Century Vital Statistics   7 - 9
Decade: 1910s   World War One   7 - 11
Ford's Progressive Wage Plan   7 - 13
Charting Automobile Use   7 - 14
Map - World War One: Who's Who   7 - 15
Decade: 1920s   The Roaring Twenties   7 - 17
Talk of the Twenties   7 - 19
Charting the Crash of 1929   7 - 21
Decade: 1930s   The Great Depression   7 - 23
FDR Attacks the Depression   7 - 25

Charting the New Deal and Unemployment   7 - 27
Decade: 1940s   World War Two   7 - 29
FDR and World War Two   7 - 31
Map - Axis Aggression in Europe   7 - 33
Map - The Japanese Empire   7 - 35
The Struggle of the Cold War Begins   7 - 37

8   MODERN AMERICA: 1950 - PRESENT

Section Page and Study Checklist   8 - 1
Timeline   8 - 3
Decade: 1950s   Post-War Prosperity   8 - 5
Charting the Affluent Society   8 - 7
Map - Cold War Alliances   8 - 9
Eisenhower on the Issues of the 1950s   8 - 11
Map - Civil Rights Hot Spots   8 - 13
Decade: 1960s   New Frontiers   8 - 15
John F. Kennedy's Inaugural Address   8 - 17
LBJ Calls for Racial Justice   8 - 18
Map - Vietnam and Southeast Asia   8 - 19
Charting Women and Jobs   8 - 21
Charting the Fight Against Poverty   8 - 22
Decade: 1970s   The Watergate Scandal   8 - 23
Charting Trends of the Seventies   8 - 25
Map - Israel and the Middle East   8 - 27
Decade: 1980s   The Reagan Years   8 - 29
Charting the Computer Revolution   8 - 31
Ronald Reagan Speaks for Freedom   8 - 33
Decade: 1990s   The Cold War Ends   8 - 35
The Federal Budget & The Federal Debt   8 - 37
Charting Welfare Reform   8 - 39
Hillary Clinton on Child Care   8 - 40
Decade: 2000s   A New Millennium   8 - 41
George W. Bush and the War on Terrorism   8 - 43

Appendix

Declaration of Independence
Blank Maps - U.S.A. and the World

A Note About The Reading Selections

Most of the reading selections in this book are condensed or excerpted from the originals. The selections use the original author's own words except where condensation or modern usage requires very slight editing. The full text of the selections can be found in the sources cited in the copyright pages of this publication.

Getting Started

Dear Students and Teachers,

This workbook and its Internet support site at *www.fasttrackteaching.com* were created to help all students find their way successfully into America's past. It grows from the author's experience that students truly are interested in America's story, but want to be active travelers on the journey.

Students, think of this workbook as a personal guidebook or road map for your journey into America's past. Guided by your teacher, we will concentrate on the most impressive and important features. You will be involved on every single page of the journey. For example, there are timelines throughout the book that you will complete. The finished timelines are shown on our Internet support site - just click on the **Timelines** antique clock icon. (A set of timeline keys is also available for use on an overhead projector.) Work from the finished timelines at first, but later, your teacher may have students work in groups in the library to research the events and dates to complete some of the timelines.

The Eight Sections

Discovery and Exploration
Colonial America
Revolutionary Years
The Growing Years
Civil War and Reconstruction
The Gilded Age
Becoming a World Leader
Modern America

The workbook is organized into eight sections. A **Section Title Page** with historical pictures and famous quotations starts each time period. See how many you or your classmates already know or can guess, and jot short notes down if you like. By the time your class finishes a section, you should be able to explain the meaning and context of each of the quotations. Help is available on the **Famous Quotes** section of the Internet support site.

A **Study Checklist** is at the start of each section to give you a good sense of what is expected. To check your progress, you can also take the practice tests on the Internet support site.

Always keep your pens and pencils at hand, and use a highlighter. Each section has interesting reading selections that will help you engage more deeply the issues and challenges Americans have faced. Make margin notes and highlight key points - your teacher will expect you to participate in the class discussion. Your teacher will also probably ask you to write out your responses to the questions before or after the class discussion.

The Civil War

Abraham Lincoln, Jefferson Davis, [F]
Robert E. Lee, Ulysses S. Grant,
Copperheads, Sherman's March,

All of the sections contain pages like this one that summarize a particular topic. Words listed at the top of these pages are the key names and terms you will meet on your journey. Visit them in more depth with your teacher, your textbook, or by using the **Names and Terms** section of our Internet support site.

By 1860, the year
and the South had
was changing into
and wage labor. The S
with _____ labor
especially policies to
of the country had

South Carolina
The election of
almost entire

You can also make index cards for these names and terms to help you remember them - see the example below!

If any page has blanks for you to fill in, look at the bottom of that page - or the bottom of the facing page - for a list of word choices.

Each word is used just once. Use a pencil so you can change your choice if necessary!

Use these terms to fill in the blanks: Booth, deadly, divide, Gettysburg, high, in, leave, northern, Richmond, slave, Virginia, war

Civil War and Reconstruction   5 - 6

Columbian Exchange   *p. 1 - 5*

- The <u>exchange</u> of previously unknown plants and animals between the Old World and the New World after <u>Columbus</u> crossed the Atlantic in 1492.

Ex: - corn and potatoes went back to Europe

- cows and horses spread to the Americas

- a big impact on both sides   * germs were part

To help get a firm grasp of the basic names and terms, it's a good idea to create a set of vocabulary cards. 4 x 6 inch lined cards are best. Here is an example of a study card you might create for "Columbian Exchange," a term from Section 1, page 5.

You can also make these in a "flash card" style with the term on one side and your notes on the other. (If you prefer, you can start a vocabulary notebook rather than use index cards.)

Each section contains one or more partially completed maps. You will complete the labeling and coloring. For example, on this map in Section 4, you are asked to add routes used by travelers to the West, such as the Oregon Trail.

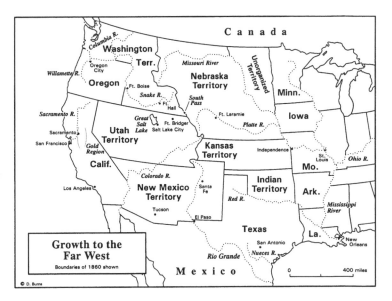

 As your guide, use the finished maps on the **Maps** section of our Internet support site. Your teacher may also have our matching set of transparencies, *Overhead Maps of America's Past*.

Here are some tips for finishing the maps:

- Color rivers - shown by dotted lines - with a blue pencil.
- Color all other bodies of water with a light blue pencil.
- Color land areas, if the directions call for shading, <u>very lightly</u> with color pencils so map labels and lines are not obscured.
- Print labels on the maps neatly with a #2 pencil. Regular color pencils usually are not very good for small lettering - use them only for larger letters like state names, etc. (Ink pens make good labels, but use them only if you work very carefully!)

 Keep your color pencils handy when you work on the charts and graphs pages. If you wish, you can see them finished on the Internet support site - just click on the icon for **Charts / Graphs** and select the ones you want.

Think of our Internet site as an on-line "Teacher's Edition" that is always available whenever you need help. Take some time now to visit the site at *www.fasttrackteaching.com* and explore the resources it contains. Good luck as you begin your own journey with *Fasttrack to America's Past*!

- David Burns

Supply List for Students: #2 pencils, color pencil set, highlighter, ruler, small pencil sharpener, index cards or notebook for vocabulary terms.

---

1 | Discovery and Exploration: 1400 - 1600

"I have always read that the world, both land and water, was spherical, as the authority and researches of Ptolemy and all the others who have written on this subject demonstrate and prove, as do the eclipses of the moon and other experiments that are made from east to west, and the elevation of the North Star from north to south."

"At two hours after midnight appeared the land, at a distance of two leagues. They handed all sails and set the treo, which is the mainsail without bonnets, and lay-to waiting for daylight Friday, when they arrived at an island of the Bahamas that was called in the Indians' tongue Guanahani."

"We have an illness only gold will cure."

Study Checklist

When you have completed this section, working with the Internet support site at *www.fasttrackteaching.com* or other resources, you should be able to:

 Identify and explain the context of the **Famous Quotes** shown on the Section Title Page.

 Identify and explain the importance of the **Famous Names and Terms** listed on the topic summary pages in this section.

 Identify on a map and explain the importance of the **Famous Places** shown on the maps in this section.

 Explain the general sequence of events in this period and tell from memory the **Famous Years**:

- Columbus discovered the New World (**1492**).
- Magellan left on his world voyage (**1519**).
- The Aztecs were overthrown (**1521**).
- The Lost Colony was started (**1587**).

Take a Practice Test!

A multiple-choice practice test for this section can be found on the Internet support site at:

www.fasttrackteaching.com

Textbook Page References:

 Discuss or write briefly on such questions and topics as these:

1. Explain why Spain and Portugal took the lead in the search for a sea route to the Far East in the 1400s.

2. What new approach did Columbus take to try to reach the Far East? What were his beliefs about the shape and size of the Earth? Describe the path his ships sailed on his first expedition in 1492.

3. Describe the leading theory about the origin of Native Americans. Compare and contrast the culture and lifestyle of at least one Indian group with that of Europeans in the early 1500s.

4. What were the main reasons the Spanish were so eager to conquer the land and people of the New World? Which reason seemed to motivate them the most?

5. Describe the impact of the Spanish conquest on native populations. What moral or philosophical issues did contact with the Indians raise for Europeans?

6. Explain how the geographic patterns of exploration and conquest by Spain, Portugal, and France are still visible today in North and South America.

Timeline 1400 - 1600

Find when these events occurred, fill in the blanks, and place them on the main timeline. The thin timeline shows some of the most famous English monarchs of this period.

Portuguese begin explorations - Prince Henry the Navigator began organizing voyages for _____ of the Atlantic.

Printing press invented - It helped spread _____ about the world.

Dias rounds Africa - Sailing for Portugal, Bartholomew Dias proved that ships could sail around the southern _____ of Africa and on to the Orient.

1st voyage of Columbus - Christopher Columbus thought he had reached the islands of the Far _____ by sailing west in a Spanish expedition.

Cabot reaches North America - Sailing for England, John Cabot was the _____ explorer of this era to reach the mainland of North America.

Vespucci explores Brazil - A map maker used Vespucci's first name, _____, to call the new land America.

Magellan begins world voyage - Ferdinand Magellan himself was _____ in the Philippines, but one of his five ships made it back to Spain.

Cortes conquers the Aztecs - Hernando Cortes, a Spaniard, defeated the Aztec ruler _____ in what is now Mexico City.

Pizarro conquers the Incas - Francisco Pizarro, like Cortes, was fighting for _____.

Cartier explores Canada - Sailing for _____, Jacques Cartier explored the area that is now eastern Canada.

de Soto finds the Mississippi - Hernando de Soto explored the _____ region of what is now the United States.

St. Augustine founded - It was a Spanish _____ that became the oldest continuous settlement by Europeans in what is now the United States.

The Lost Colony - The fate of the people of this English colony is still a _____.

Spanish Armada destroyed - The attempt by Spain to invade England failed, clearing the way for the English to start _____ colonies in North America.

Use these terms to fill in the blanks: Amerigo, city, East, exploration, first, France, killed, knowledge, Montezuma, mystery, new, southeastern, Spain, tip

---

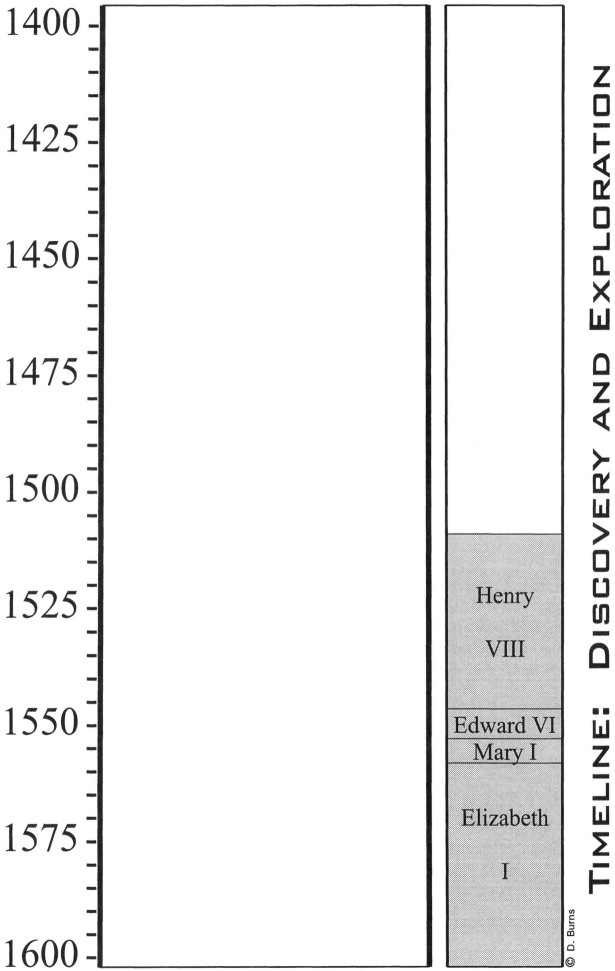

1400

1425

1450

1475

1500

1525

1550

1575

1600

Henry

VIII

Edward VI

Mary I

Elizabeth

I

TIMELINE: DISCOVERY AND EXPLORATION

NEW WORLDS DISCOVERED

Renaissance, Spice Islands, Christopher Columbus, Ferdinand Magellan, *conquistadors*,

Aztec, Inca, Hernando de Soto, Columbian Exchange, smallpox, Lost Colony

By the year 1400 Europe was growing out of the Middle Ages, and was entering a period of cultural rebirth and world discovery called the Renaissance. This development was caused in part by growing trade, both within Europe itself and with more distant lands. For example, after about 1100 the Crusades brought contacts with the Muslim Arabs, who had developed a rich civilization in the Middle East. The travels of Marco Polo started a brief period of direct contact with _____ in the distant land of Asia around 1300. Spices, silk, and other rare products from Asia, India, and the Spice Islands were especially valued by the nobility and the new merchant class growing in Europe.

But the journey to the lands of the Orient was extremely difficult. Developments in China and in the Muslim world gradually made the trip all but impossible for Europeans. Some trade continued along the almost forgotten paths. But most of the profits went to the Arabs controlling the middle of the trade routes, and merchants from Italian trading cities that controlled the European end.

Around 1420 the Portuguese, led by Prince Henry the Navigator, began an organized effort to explore the Atlantic. They carefully created new maps, and developed a new type of ship called a caravel to search further and further down the coast of _____. They hoped eventually to find a way around it to the lands of India and the Far East.

Christopher Columbus convinced Spain to bankroll a more daring plan. He would get to the Far East by sailing west! Instead, he hit the islands off North America in 1492. Like most people who studied navigation or astronomy, Columbus knew the Earth is shaped like a _____. But he badly under-estimated the size of the globe, and therefore, the distance to Asia. Even after four voyages, he apparently still believed the new land was either part of Asia or very close to it. Only later, in 1519, did Ferdinand _____ lead a Spanish expedition that circled the globe.

Spain took an early lead in colonizing the New World. The *conquistadors* (conquerors) were driven by greed for gold to explore Central and South America. They also wanted to convert natives to the religion of _____. Very quickly, the great civilizations of the Aztecs (in what is now Mexico) and the Incas (in what is now Peru) were overthrown. Not long after, Hernando de Soto led a small army through much of what is now the southeastern United States in search of gold and glory. He discovered the Mississippi River in 1541, but found no easy treasures.

Guns and horses gave the Spanish an advantage in all their conquests, together with help from native groups who opposed the ruling tribes. In addition, European _____ like smallpox, to which the natives had no immunity, killed millions of people.

The Portuguese also started colonies in the Americas. But early treaties that divided areas of exploration left Portugal only a small piece of the New World - the land that is now Brazil. Much of their interest remained on trade down the African coast and eastward to India.

The French got into the exploring act as well, mostly in North America. At first, they hoped to find a "Northwest Passage" or water route through the new land and on to Asia. They didn't find one. But their explorations of the Great Lakes area (and later the Mississippi River) led to profitable fur-trading settlements. The French language is often still heard in the Canadian province of _____. In fact, many American cities along the Mississippi River, like New Orleans, still have their original French names.

The English had bad luck at first. The Lost Colony was planted on Roanoke Island, in what is now North Carolina, in 1587. A war with Spain delayed the departure of re-supply ships. Three years later, the only clue left of the colonists' fate was the word *Croatoan* - the name of a nearby island - carved on the trunk of a tree. The colonists were _____ found. But about twenty years later, success finally came at Jamestown, Virginia. Other settlements up and down the coast quickly followed during the 1600s. The English colonies were ultimately the most successful in North America, mainly because settlers viewed the new land as a place to _____ and raise families.

The Age of Discovery opened fabulous opportunities to Europeans. Gold and silver flowed back to the Old World, along with previously unknown plants like corn and the potato. The contact also introduced many plants and animals to the New World, such as the _____ and cow. This two-way transfer is called the Columbian Exchange. It had a tremendous impact on both sides of the globe for centuries to come.

But generally, contact with Europeans was a _____ for the native groups. Some entire populations were wiped out by smallpox. Even for survivors, traditional culture and ways of _____ disappeared. Many were forced into slavery or near-slavery in mines and large farms. Only the French enjoyed generally good relations with Native Americans after the first contacts.

Use these terms to fill in the blanks: Africa, China, Christianity, disaster, diseases, horse, life, Magellan, never, Quebec, sphere, stay

MAP - TRADE ROUTES BEFORE COLUMBUS

Finish labeling and drawing the large globe map on the next page to show these:

GEOGRAPHICAL FEATURES

Mediterranean Sea	**Black Sea**
Caspian Sea	**Red Sea**
Persian Gulf	**Himalayas**
Indian Ocean	

MAJOR TRADING ROUTES AROUND 1450

Use different colors to show these routes that carried silk, spices, and other valuable products of the Orient to Europe. Be sure to complete the key.

Northern Route - From Beijing and elsewhere in China, caravans of merchants traveled overland to meet traders in central Asia. The goods continued on to the city of Constantinople. Italian traders carried the products by _____ to Europe. Venice and Genoa were the wealthiest and most famous of the Italian trading cities.

Middle Route - From China, the Spice Islands, and Ceylon, boats carried products to Calicut in India. Arab traders carried the goods on boats up the Persian Gulf, then overland to towns on the shore of the _____ Sea. Italian traders carried the products to Europe.

Southern Route - Branching off the Middle Route at India, Arab traders carried products from the Orient on boats up the Red Sea, then overland to the city of _____ in Egypt. Italian traders made their purchases, and took the goods for sale to Europeans.

CHRISTIAN AND MUSLIM AREAS OF CONTROL IN 1450

Color the small globe map and complete the key to show these areas of control in the year 1450. The shading of the map will help guide you.

Christian Europe - A large area, but the hodge-podge of kingdoms and small principalities was united only by the loose ties of the _____ Church. Italian trading cities had an effective lock on the European end of the trade routes.

The Muslim World - The Islamic lands stretched from North Africa through the Middle East and across to India. The Muslims controlled the _____ sections of the ancient trade routes, and even gained Constantinople in 1453.

Use these terms to fill in the blanks: Alexandria, boat, Catholic, Mediterranean, middle

---

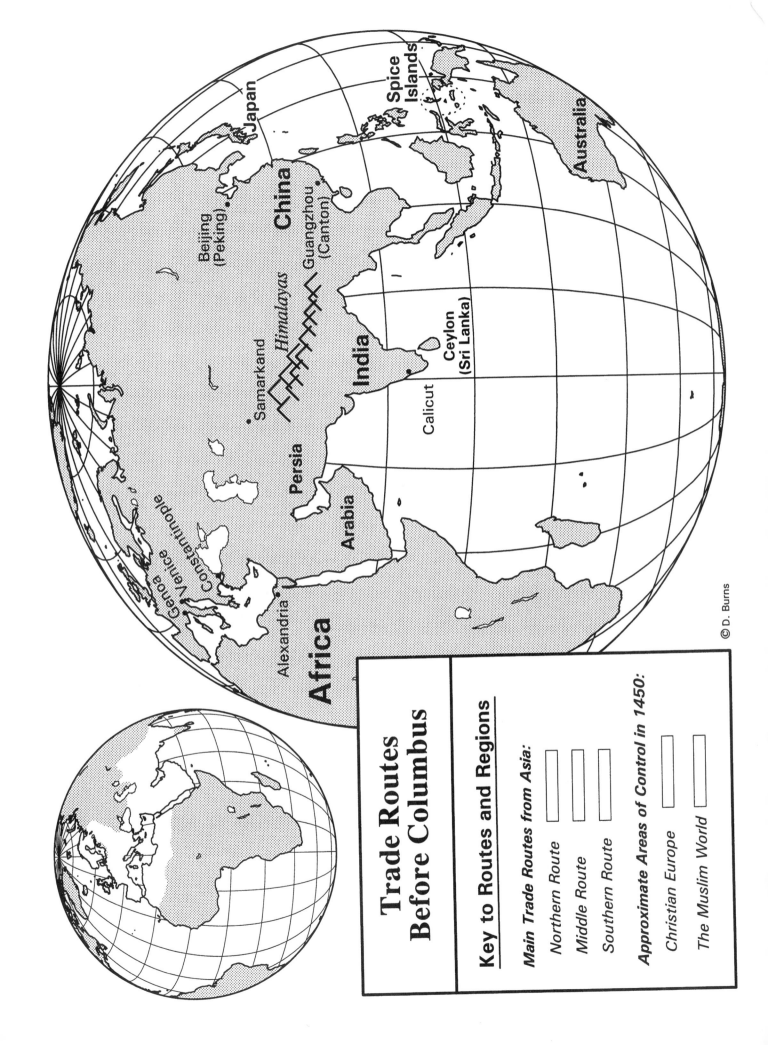

Trade Routes
Before Columbus

Key to Routes and Regions

Main Trade Routes from Asia:

Northern Route

Middle Route

Southern Route

Approximate Areas of Control in 1450:

Christian Europe

The Muslim World

Japan

Spice
Islands

Beijing
(Peking)

China

Guangzhou
(Canton)

Himalayas

Samarkand

Persia

India

Ceylon
(Sri Lanka)

Calicut

Australia

Arabia

Genoa

Venice

Constantinople

Alexandria

Africa

© D. Burns

MAP - NATIVE AMERICAN ORIGINS AND LANDS

Label and color the large globe map to show these:

Migration Route From Asia - The earliest
ancestors of the Indians crossed to North
America from northern Asia between
11,000 and 40,000 years ago.

  Today the Bering Strait separates the
continents. But during the last Ice Age,
when sea levels were _____, Asia
and North America were connected by land.

  *(Show the route from Asia on the small
North Polar Projection map also.)*

Pacific Ocean　　**Atlantic Ocean**　　**Route of Columbus in 1492**

*Label the large globe map as you complete these descriptions of selected Native American
groups and places:*

Aztec - The great civilization centered at
what is now Mexico City, called by the
Aztecs **Tenochtitlan**. They developed an
accurate calendar and a form of writing
with pictures. Their religion demanded
human sacrifice to the _____, which the
Aztecs considered to be a god.

Inca - The largest of the New World
empires, with _____ that stretched
thousands of miles in South America. The
Inca set up their capital at **Cuzco** in the
12th century.

Maya - A large civilization that rose on
the Yucatan Peninsula in _____
America, but faded after 900 A.D.

Pueblo - A group of Indian tribes in what
is now the southwest U.S. Descended
from the prehistoric **Anasazi** Indians, they
built multistory houses from sun-dried
bricks called _____.

Cahokia - The most important city of the
Mississippian civilization, famous for
building huge earth mounds topped by
religious _____. The civilization
collapsed by 1500 A.D.

Creek - A group of several tribes in what
is now the southeastern part of the U.S.
The Creeks lived in about 50 permanent
towns, and played the game now called
_____. Creek women raised
maize (corn), squash, and other crops.

Iroquois - A confederation, or alliance, of
five (later six) Native American groups
living in the woodlands of what is now
upper _____. The Iroquois
are famous for their "long houses," well-
kept villages, and system of government.

Inuit - Also known as _____,
they adapted in creative ways to the cold
and harsh environment of the far North.

Use these terms to fill in the blanks: adobe, Central, Eskimos, lacrosse, lower, New York, roads, sun, temples

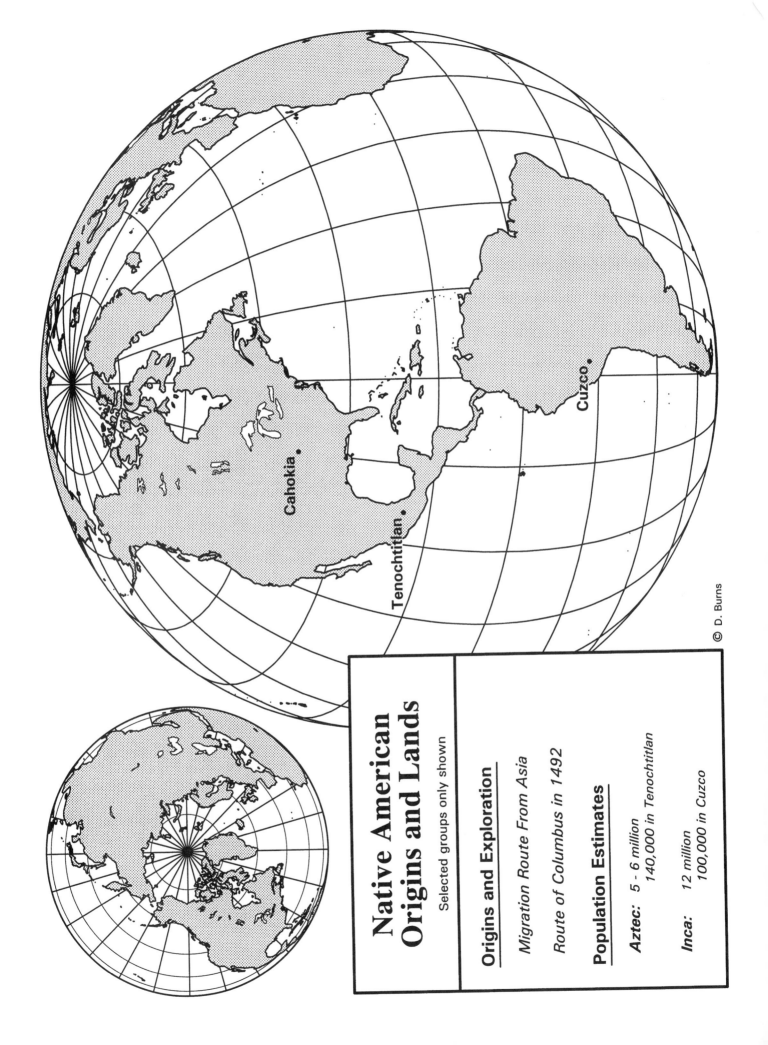

Native American Origins and Lands

Selected groups only shown

Origins and Exploration

Migration Route From Asia

Route of Columbus in 1492

Population Estimates

Aztec: 5 - 6 million
140,000 in Tenochtitlan

Inca: 12 million
100,000 in Cuzco

Cahokia

Tenochtitlan

Cuzco

© D. Burns

MAP - EARLY VOYAGES OF DISCOVERY

Finish labeling and drawing the large map on the next page to show these:

GEOGRAPHICAL FEATURES

Atlantic Ocean   **Pacific Ocean**

EARLY VOYAGES AND SPONSORING NATIONS

Choose one color for each country listed below. Color the four countries on the map, then carefully draw the selected voyage or voyages that each country sponsored. The explorers' names are already labeled on the map, but be sure to complete the color key.

Portugal	• **Bartholomew Dias** 1487 - 1488 • **Vasco da Gama** 1497 - 1499
Spain	• **Christopher Columbus** 1492 - 1493 • **Ferdinand Magellan** 1519 - 1522 *(Magellan was killed in the Philippines in 1521)*
England	• **John Cabot** 1497
France	• **Jacques Cartier** 1534

NEW WORLD AREAS COLONIZED BY 1600

Use the same colors to show where these countries had colonized the New World by 1600. The dotted lines will help guide you.

Portugal	**Brazil, along the eastern coast of South America.**
Spain	**Much of South America, the West Indies, Central America, Mexico, and Florida.**
England	**No successful permanent colonies before 1600.** *(East coast of North America after 1600.)*
France	**No successful permanent colonies before 1600.** *(Areas in North America after 1600.)*

THE LOST COLONY

The map shows the location of the famous English colony that disappeared around 1590. A map showing the area in more detail can be found on page 1 - 18.

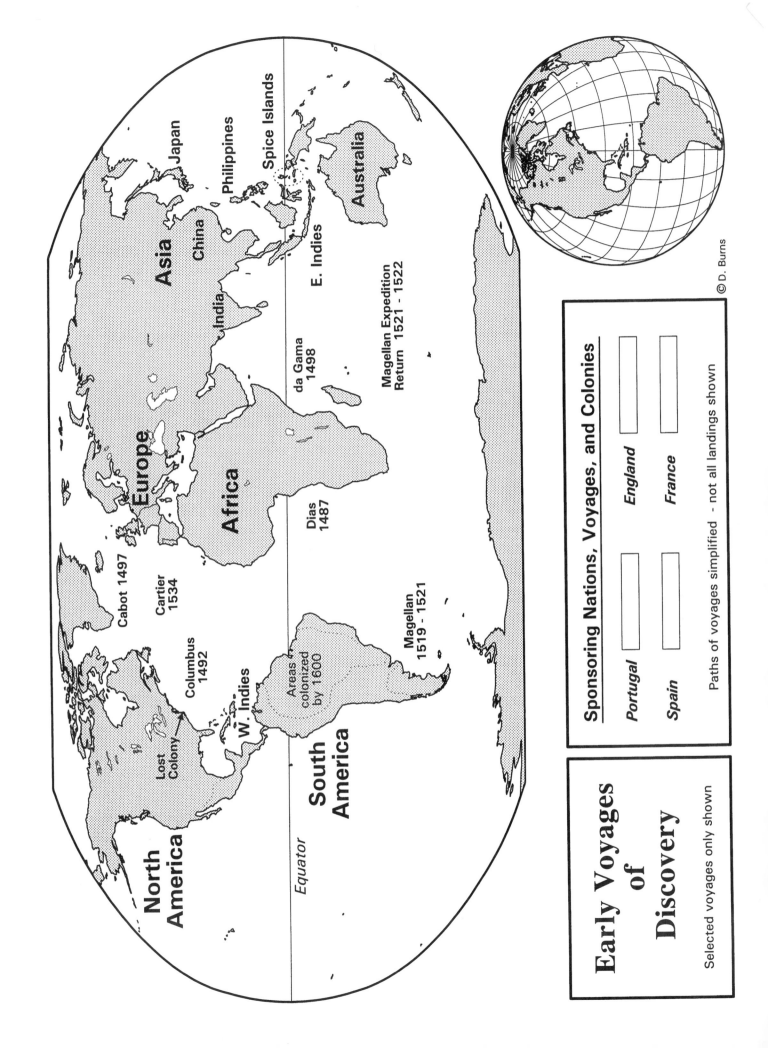

North America

Lost Colony

Columbus
1492

W. Indies

South America

Equator

Cabot 1497

Cartier
1534

Europe

Africa

Dias
1487

Areas colonized
by 1600

Magellan
1519 - 1521

Asia

China

India

Japan

Philippines

Spice Islands

E. Indies

da Gama
1498

Magellan Expedition
Return 1521 - 1522

Australia

© D. Burns

Sponsoring Nations, Voyages, and Colonies

Portugal		England	
Spain		France	

Paths of voyages simplified - not all landings shown

**Early Voyages
of
Discovery**

Selected voyages only shown

WHEN CULTURES COLLIDED

plantation, exploitation, Bartolome de Las Casas, Catholic Church, missions/missionaries

Think of tasty French-fried potatoes, pumpkins grinning at Halloween, corn on the cob, tomatoes in Spaghetti sauce, and _____ on the table at Thanksgiving. These are just a few of the plants and animals totally unknown to Europeans before the meeting of the Old World and New World in 1492. But the meeting of the worlds was not one of peaceful exchange of such treasures for Europe's horses or cows. Instead, it was usually a violent and tragic collision of cultures.

The cultures of the New World were as varied as those of the Old. The Anasazi, the ancestors of the Pueblo Indians, built stable democratic societies we might well envy. But the Aztecs, in what is now _____ City, conquered and oppressed neighboring tribes. (The Aztec priests ripped the hearts out of live prisoners captured for religious sacrifice.)

Columbus was startled by the friendliness and generosity of the natives he met when he first landed. But a nearby tribe ate human flesh, which horrified the Europeans. Near the Great Lakes in North America, the tribes of the Iroquois Confederacy developed an impressive political system to keep peace. Yet many Native American tribes _____ to death captives from other tribes with ferocious cruelty.

From the Indian perspective, the Europeans were equally strange. The best of them, the missionaries, talked of a strange new God who was to be worshiped in strange new ways. The worst Europeans were savagely cruel, and had much better _____ to force the natives into slavery on sugar plantations or in gold mines. Good or evil, the newcomers unknowingly carried the germs of Old World diseases like smallpox that killed millions of natives. Overwork or outright massacres by Europeans killed many others. For the native groups, old ways of life soon disappeared forever.

One important cultural difference helps explain the success of the Europeans as their colonies grew. To most Indians, land was something owned by the _____ as a whole, not by individuals. Europeans, however, had developed elaborate social and economic practices centered on individual ownership of land. Wealth and status were largely determined by land ownership. This fact, of land considered as one's own personal wealth, put a powerful drive behind the European conquest.

The collision of cultures confronted Europeans with a question that echoes to this day: *Are all the world's people equally human?*

Christianity, the religion of most Europeans, teaches that all men are brothers, as descendants of the same parents, Adam and Eve. But the discovery of such vastly different cultures made it easy for greedy colonists to argue that Indians were separate peoples who should work as _____ until they were "civilized."

A Spaniard named Bartolome de Las Casas, who took part himself in the bloody conquest of Cuba, later came to see many European actions in the New World as morally _____. For example, the Spanish practice of awarding settlers control over a group of natives and their land often led to brutal treatment of the Indians as laborers. Las Casas became a missionary priest, and pressed the Catholic Church and the Spanish king to proclaim the basic humanity of the Indians. Both did so, and an order was issued from Spain in 1542 to end the enslavement and abuse of Indians.

The exploitation of the native population did not end, however. The lure of _____ and silver was a far more powerful force than religion or law on many European colonists. In fact, the scramble for wealth in the colonies soon pulled a third group into the cultural collision: African slaves. Slavery had long existed in African societies. But it took a far more harsh form in the New World, starting with the sugar _____ of the Portuguese and the Spanish in South America and the West Indies.

The debate launched by Bartolome de Las Casas, however, advanced a vitally important principle in European thought: the common humanity of _____ groups of mankind. Picked up and spread by countless others, it eventually grew into a powerful idea shaping the history of the world.

_____ centuries have passed since 1492. Great empires - Spanish, Portuguese, French, and English - have grown, flourished, and then _____ in the New World. New systems of government have risen, and new definitions of human rights. Yet even today, the descendants of the three cultures that collided during the Age of Discovery still struggle to work out the real meaning of human equality in the New World.

Use these terms to fill in the blanks: all, disappeared, Five, gold, Mexico, plantations, slaves, tortured, tribe, turkey, weapons, wrong

THE ENGLISH MEET THE NATIVE AMERICANS

*In 1585 an English scientist named Thomas Harriot was aboard a ship exploring the coastal area of what is now North Carolina. His observations about the land and its native people were published and widely read. These are condensed selections from his book, **A Brief and True Report of the New Found Land of Virginia**.*

They are a people clothed with loose mantles [cloaks] made of deerskins, and aprons of the same round about their middles, all else naked. They have no edge tools or weapons of iron to offend us with, neither know they how to make any. Those weapons that they have are only bows made of witch hazel, and arrows of reeds.

Their towns are but small, some containing but ten or twelve houses, some twenty. Their houses are made of small poles, made fast at the tops in round form. In most towns these are covered with bark, and in some with mats made of long rushes [reeds].

In some places in the country, only one town belongs to the government of a *Wiroans* or chief Lord, in others some two or three, in some, six, eight, and more. The greatest *Wiroans* that yet we had been dealing with had but eighteen towns in his government.

Their manner of wars amongst themselves is either by sudden surprising one another, most commonly about the dawning of day, or moonlight, or else by ambushes. Set battles are very rare.

They seem very ingenious, for although they have no such tools, nor any such crafts, sciences, and arts as we, yet in those things they do, they show excellence of wit.

Some religion they have already, which although it is far from the truth, yet being as it is, there is hope it may be easier and sooner reformed.

They believe that there are many gods, which they call *Mantoac*, but of different sorts and degrees; one only chief and great God, which has been from all eternity.

For mankind they say a woman was made first, who by the working of one of the gods, conceived and brought forth children.

And in such sort they say they had their beginning. But how many years or ages have passed since, they say they can make no relation, having no letters or other such means as we to keep records of the particularities of time past, but only tradition [stories] from father to son.

They think that all the gods are of human shape, and therefore they represent them by images in the forms of men. Them they place in temples, where they worship, pray, sing, and make many times offerings unto them.

Most things they saw with us, as mathematical instruments, sea compasses, burning glasses, guns, writing and reading, and spring-clocks that seem to go of themselves, were so strange unto them, that they thought they were rather the works of gods than of men, or that they had been given and taught us by the gods.

Group Discussion: *Compare the Native American life described here with that of Europeans around 1590. What are the similarities and differences that you notice? What evidence is there that Thomas Harriot had respect for the Indians he met, in spite of their cultural differences?*

This drawing from Thomas Herriot's book shows an Indian town called Secota. It was on the mainland not far from the location of the Lost Colony. Make notes in the margins as you search for as much information as you can find about the life of the Indians shown here.

Group Discussion: *What can you discover from the picture about the life and culture of Native Americans living in this town? Be specific as you describe what you see.*

THE MYSTERY OF THE LOST COLONY

John White was a leader of the colonists who landed on Roanoke Island in 1587. He sailed back to England that same year to get more supplies. Even before he left, the colonists were seriously thinking of moving to the mainland. It was 1590 before White could finally return to Roanoke Island. As this condensed account shows, he found the colonists gone, apparently to another island called Croatoan.

Before we could get to the place where our planters [colonists] were left, it was so exceedingly dark that we overshot the place a quarter of a mile. At daybreak, we landed, and we walked through the woods, until we came to the place where I left our colony. In all this way we saw in the sand the print of the Indians' feet, and upon a tree were carved these letters, C R O.

These letters we knew to signify the place where I should find the planters, according to a secret agreement between them and me at my last departure from them. The agreement was that they should write or carve on the trees or posts the name of the place where they should be, for when I left they were prepared to move from Roanoke Island fifty miles into the main [mainland].

Therefore at my departure in 1587, I told them that if they should happen to be distressed [in trouble] that they should also carve over the letters a cross, but we found no such signs of distress.

And having well considered of this, we passed toward the place where they were left, but we found the houses taken down, and the place very strongly enclosed with a high palisade [fence] of great posts.

One of the chief trees or posts at the right side of the entrance had the bark taken off, and five feet from the ground in fair capital letters was graven [written] CROATOAN, without any cross or sign of distress.

We entered into the palisade, where we found many bars of iron, and such like heavy things, thrown here and there, almost overgrown with grass and weeds. We found five chests that had been carefully hidden, and of the chests three were my own. About the place many of my things lay spoiled and broken.

This could only be the deed of our enemies the Indians at Dasemunkepeuc, who must have watched the departure of our men to Croatoan, and as soon as they were departed dug up every place where they suspected anything was buried.

But although it grieved me to see such spoil of my goods, yet on the other side I greatly joyed that I had safely found a token of their being safe at Croatoan, which is the place where Manteo [an Indian] was born, and the Indians of the island were our friends.

When we had seen in this place so much as we could, we returned to our boats and departed from the shore towards our ships with as much speed as we could, for the weather began to overcast, and very likely that a foul and stormy night would ensue.

Therefore, the same evening, with much labor and danger, we got ourselves aboard, by which time the wind and seas were so greatly risen that we doubted our cables and anchors would scarcely hold until morning.

The next morning it was agreed to weigh anchor and go for the place at Croatoan where our planters were. But when the anchor was almost apeak [raised], the cable broke. It was therefore determined that we should go to the southward for fresh water.

The captain of White's ship refused to return to the area, and searches in later years found no sign of the colonists on Croatoan. They might have moved across to the mainland nearby. Since the colonists had originally hoped to settle in the Chesapeake Bay area, it is also possible they might have moved there. Their fate remains a mystery.

Lightly shade the map to the right with color pencils to show the land and water areas. Then compare it to the map below from 1590. (Notice that the old map is not oriented the way maps usually are today with North at the top.)

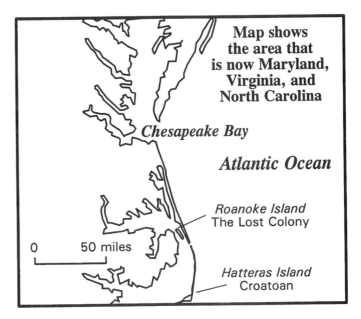

Map shows the area that is now Maryland, Virginia, and North Carolina

Chesapeake Bay

Atlantic Ocean

Roanoke Island
The Lost Colony

0   50 miles

Hatteras Island
Croatoan

Group Discussion: *Why is John White so sure the colonists had gone to Croatoan? Why does he think the colonists were not in any trouble or danger when they left? Why might Croatoan have been a good place to move? If you had been selected to lead the colony, what would you have recommended once the supply ship became long overdue?*

CHARTING GOLDEN CROPS

The Spanish conquistadors *took vast quantities of gold and silver from the New World. But New World plants like corn and the potato have surpassed in value all the precious metals they carried away. Complete these bar graphs to see why these plants are so valuable. The first chart compares the yield per acre of four crops grown on American farms 500 years after the Columbian Exchange began.*

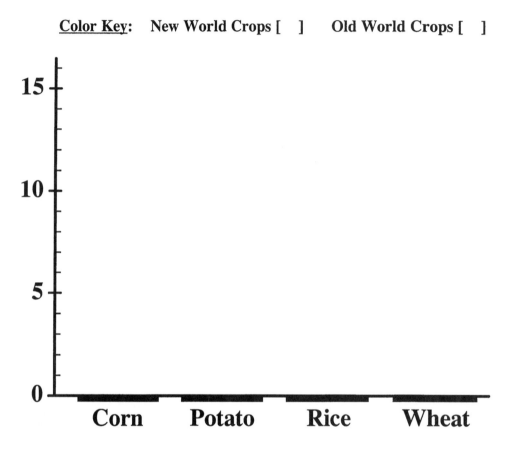

Color Key: New World Crops [   ]   Old World Crops [   ]

15

10

5

0

Corn   Potato   Rice   Wheat

Crop Yields (Tons per Acre) on U.S. Farms - 1992

Use the table below to find the information you need to complete the bar graph above. Draw a vertical bar for each crop, with the length corresponding to the yield of that crop. Then pick a color for each category in the key, and shade the bars with the appropriate colors.

"New World" Crops	Yield (Tons per Acre) U.S. Farms - 1992	"Old World" Crops	Yield (Tons per Acre) U.S. Farms - 1992
Corn	3.7	Rice	2.8
Potato	16.2	Wheat	1.2

source: *Statistical Abstract of the United States*

The bar graph below compares the monetary value of the same four crops in the United States in 1992. What reasons can you give to explain why the corn crop is so large and valuable in modern America?

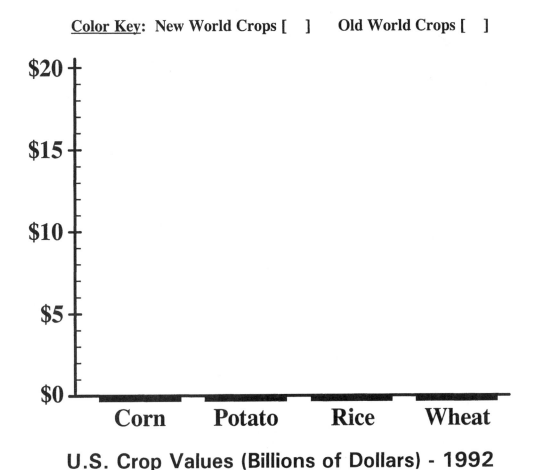

Color Key: New World Crops [   ]   Old World Crops [   ]

U.S. Crop Values (Billions of Dollars) - 1992

Use the table below to find the information you need to complete the bar graph above. Draw a vertical bar of the appropriate length for each crop. Then shade the color key with the same colors you used on the previous chart, and shade the bars with the appropriate colors.

"New World" Crops	1992 Value - U.S. Farms (Billions of Dollars)	"Old World" Crops	1992 Value - U.S. Farms (Billions of Dollars)
Corn	19.7	Rice	1.1
Potato	2.3	Wheat	8.0

source: *Statistical Abstract of the United States*

2 Colonial America: 1600 - 1775

"He that will not work shall not eat."

"For we must consider that we shall be as a city upon a hill. The eyes of all people are upon us."

JOIN or DIE

"Taxation without representation is tyranny."

"The distinction between Virginians, Pennsylvanians, New Yorkers, and New Englanders, are no more. I am not a Virginian, but an American."

Study Checklist

When you have completed this section, working with the Internet support site at *www.fasttrackteaching.com* or other resources, you should be able to:

 Identify and explain the context of the **Famous Quotes** shown on the Section Title Page.

 Identify and explain the importance of the **Famous Names and Terms** listed on the topic summary pages in this section.

 Identify on a map and explain the importance of the **Famous Places** shown on the maps in this section.

 Explain the general sequence of events in this period and tell from memory the **Famous Years**:

- The Jamestown colony was started (**1607**).
- The Pilgrims landed at Plymouth (**1620**).
- The Boston Tea Party occurred (**1773**).
- The First Continental Congress met (**1774**).

Take a Practice Test!

(A) (B) (C) (D)

A multiple-choice practice test for this section can be found on the Internet support site at:

www.fasttrackteaching.com

Textbook Page References:

 Discuss or write briefly on such questions and topics as these:

1. Compare and contrast the goals of the settlers who came in the early years to Virginia and Massachusetts. How do the differences help explain the pattern of settlement that developed in each region?

2. Explain why slavery became much more common in Virginia and the other Southern colonies than in New England. What role did climate and geography play?

3. How was the "holy experiment" of the Quakers in Pennsylvania similar to the Puritan idea of "The City Upon a Hill"? How did the two groups differ in their willingness to accept people with different beliefs?

4. Describe the role that each of these had in the government of the colonies: Colonial assemblies (such as the House of Burgesses); Royal Governors; town meetings.

5. How was the French and Indian War a result of the growth of the English colonies? How did the war end up causing the colonies to increasingly resent British rule?

6. Describe how the colonists' heritage of "the rights of Englishmen" led them, in the 1760s and 1770s, to begin challenging British authority over the colonies.

Timeline 1600 - 1775

Find when these events occurred, fill in the blanks, and place them on the main timeline. The thin timeline shows the English monarchs of this period.

Jamestown settled - It became the first successful _____ speaking colony in what is now the United States.

Pilgrims land at Plymouth - Many were part of a religious group in England called the _____ because they wanted to run their own churches separate from the official Church of England.

Puritans settle Boston - This group, which also had disagreements with the Church of England, was much _____ than the Pilgrims' colony.

Maryland settled - It was established as a colony for _____ from England.

England seizes New Amsterdam - The Dutch colony surrendered without a _____, and the English renamed it New York.

Carolina settled - Later, it split into _____ separate colonies.

Quakers settle Pennsylvania - Their big settlement was at _____.

English Bill of Rights - Drawn up by Parliament, it sharply _____ the power of English monarchs and listed the rights of Englishmen.

Salem witch trials - These were the _____ witchcraft trials in the colonies.

Georgia settled - It was a _____ against Spanish expansion in Florida.

French and Indian War - The British _____ this war, and gained vast territory.

George III becomes king - He wanted to get _____ control of the colonies.

Stamp Act - Colonists began shouting, "No _____ without representation."

Boston Massacre - No one really knows which side _____ the riot.

Boston Tea Party - In response, England ordered Boston harbor _____.

First Continental Congress - The colonies were now beginning to _____.

Use these terms to fill in the blanks: barrier, Catholics, closed, English, larger, last, limited, Philadelphia, Separatists, shot, started, taxation, tighter, two, unite, won

---

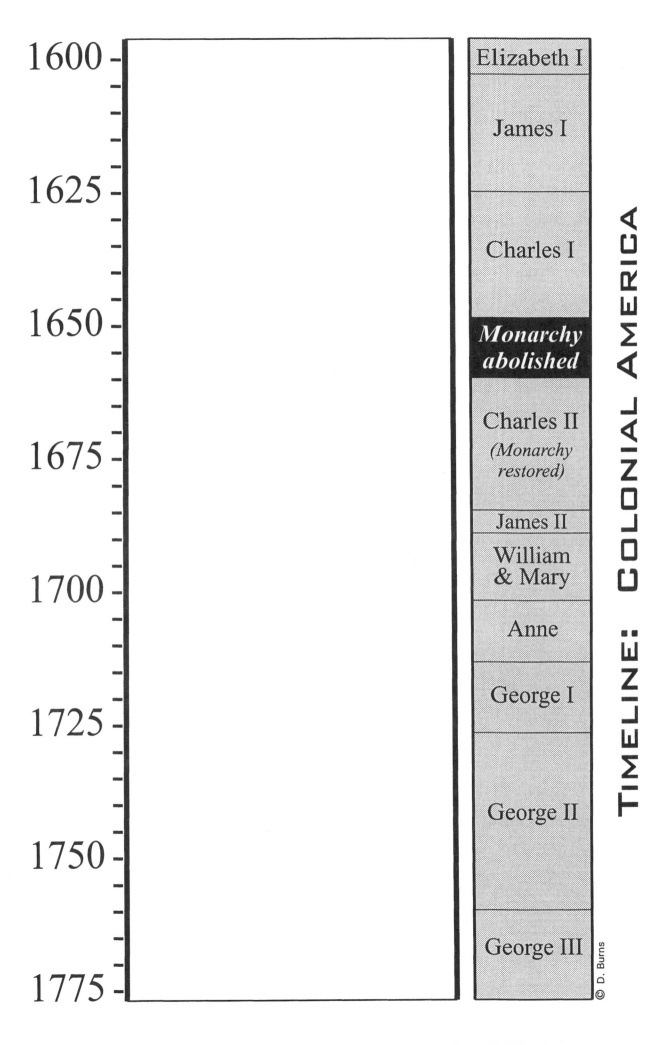

1600 —

1625 —

1650 —

1675 —

1700 —

1725 —

1750 —

1775 —

Elizabeth I

James I

Charles I

Monarchy abolished

Charles II
(Monarchy restored)

James II

William & Mary

Anne

George I

George II

George III

TIMELINE: COLONIAL AMERICA

© D. Burns

JAMESTOWN AND VIRGINIA

John Smith, Pocahontas, House of Burgesses, royal governor, indentured servant,

social mobility, gentry, Williamsburg

Jamestown, Virginia was settled in 1607. The expedition was organized and financed not by the English government, but by the Virginia Company of London. It was called a joint-stock company, and was similar to what we would call a corporation today. The company's investors put up the _____ to finance the colony in hope of making a profit. This kind of enterprise is an example of the commercial spirit growing in Europe (and especially in England) at the time.

But things went badly at Jamestown at first. The swampy location on the _____ River was very unhealthy. Most of the settlers had no idea how hard they would need to work to survive. In less than a year, many of the original 104 settlers were dead. More supplies and settlers arrived, but many of the new settlers were also soon _____. Still, the colony survived. Capt. John Smith took charge of the situation and issued a simple rule: "He that will not work shall not eat." Smith also obtained help from the Powhatan Indians in the area. (The chief's daughter, named Pocahontas, later married one of the settlers, but died on a visit to England.)

The colony was supposed to earn the investors in England a profit, and attempts were made to produce glass and other products. But it was a plant native to the New World, _____, that saved the venture. It had become enormously popular in Europe, and grew well in the Chesapeake Bay area. New settlements were soon spreading along the James River. As they did, a council of elected representatives from each settlement was set up in Jamestown. This colonial assembly, called the House of Burgesses, marks the start of representative government in the English colonies.

King James took over control of the colony when the Virginia Company fell into disputes, and appointed a _____ governor. But the Virginia House of Burgesses remained, and it had power over tax laws. This division of power, modeled after the system in England, would play a key role in later events.

Decade by decade, farmers spread up Virginia's _____, which served as highways. Typically, houses were very small, with few furnishings. Men outnumbered women, and the resulting lifestyle often had a rough and tumble frontier quality. There was a very high death rate, from disease and hard work. Deadly conflicts sometimes erupted with Indians. In spite of all this, however, people came for the promise of free or inexpensive land and a chance at wealth in the rich soil of Virginia.

Even poor Englishmen could come, if they were willing to promise five to seven years of labor to a colonist for the price of passage across the Atlantic. These were known as indentured servants, and were a big share of the immigrants arriving in all the English colonies.

Slavery developed more slowly. The first Africans, sold by other _____ to European traders, arrived at Jamestown in 1619. They were apparently treated by the colonists like other indentured servants at first. But over time, laws were written that set a permanent slave status for most Africans. After about 1670, the slave trade grew _____ to meet the labor needs of the tobacco planters in the Chesapeake region.

For most early arrivals, English or African, Virginia gave only an early grave. By 1700, however, a small gentry or upper class of prosperous planters had developed. By 1750 this class could be found on large but scattered plantations like _____, the home of George Washington's family. The gentry class (including people like Thomas Jefferson) would later play a big role in shaping the ideas of the American Revolution.

Other colonies around the Chesapeake Bay and down the southern coast also developed plantations and a gentry class. Because this kind of large-scale farming was so profitable, there was little incentive to promote the growth of commerce and trade that was typical further north.

In the mid-1700s the colonists were still happy to be Englishmen, under the _____ and his appointed governor in the colony. But thanks to the wide Atlantic, they were getting used to the idea of largely governing _____ through elected assemblies like Virginia's House of Burgesses. (In 1699 this assembly moved to the colony's new capital, Williamsburg, because a fire destroyed Jamestown.)

While the upper class was dominant, its position at the top was based mainly on wealth and personal accomplishment. This was an important difference from Europe, where a class called the nobility (the dukes, barons, etc.) sat at the top by right of birth. Another difference was that a large middle class of farmers grew in America. By our standards, their life was rough. But compared to England or any other country at the time, the average person had it pretty good. Social mobility - movement by individuals up the ladder of social class - was much higher in the colonies than anywhere in Europe. Living as they did, independent and _____-reliant, many of the colonists developed views that naturally led them to support the idea of independence when the break with England came after 1775.

Use these terms to fill in the blanks: Africans, dead, James, king, money, Mount Vernon, rapidly, rivers, royal, self, themselves, tobacco

CAPT. JOHN SMITH'S TALE

Captain John Smith left a remarkable history of the early years of the English settlement at Jamestown, Virginia. These are condensed excerpts from his account.

The temperature of this country agrees well with the English, being once seasoned to the country. The summer is as hot as in Spain, the winter as cold as in France or England. The winds here are variable, but with thunder and lightning I have seldom either seen or heard in Europe.

There is but one entrance by sea into this country, and that is at the mouth of a very goodly bay, 18 or 20 miles broad. Heaven and earth never agreed better to frame a place for man's habitation, were it fully inhabited by industrious people. Here are mountains, hills, plains, valleys, rivers, and brooks, all running most pleasantly into a fair bay.

Virginia does offer many excellent plants and living creatures, yet grass there is little or none, for all the country is overgrown with trees. The wood that is most common is oak and walnut, and many of the oaks are so tall and straight that they will bear good timber 20 yards long.

Of beasts, the chief are deer, nothing differing from ours. Their squirrels are near as great as our smallest sort of wild rabbits. Their bears are very little in comparison with those in parts of Europe.

Concerning the entrails of the earth [minerals and precious metals like gold], little can be said for certainty.

The land is not populous, for the men be few; their far greater number is of women and children. Within 60 miles of Jamestown, there are about 5,000 people, but of able men fit for their wars scarce 1,500.

The people differ very much in stature, but are generally tall and straight, of a comely [attractive] proportion, and of a color brown.

Their hair is generally black, but few have any beards.

They are very strong, of an able body and full of agility, able to endure to lie in the woods under a tree by the fire in the worst of winter. They are crafty and very ingenious. Some are of disposition fearful, some bold, most cautious.

For their apparel, they are sometimes covered with the skins of wild beasts, which  in winter are dressed with the hair, but in the summer without.

The better sort use large mantles [cloaks] of deer skins, some embroidered with white beads, some with copper, others painted after their manner. But the common sort have scarce to cover their nakedness but with grass, the leaves of trees, or such like.

Their houses are built of small young trees bowed and tied, and so close covered with mats, or the bark of trees very handsomely, that they are as warm as stoves, but very smokey, yet at the top of the house is a hole made for the smoke to go into right over the fire.

While Virginia appeared ideal to Smith for settlement, the attempt to start an English colony at Jamestown claimed hundreds of lives in the first few years. In just the first six months, nearly half the first group of 104 colonists died. The account below starts after the colonists' largest ship left Jamestown to sail back to England.

Being thus left to our fortunes, it fortuned that within ten days scarce ten amongst us could either go, or well stand, such extreme weakness and sickness oppressed us. And none should marvel at this, if they consider the cause and reason, which was this:

While our ships stayed, our ration was somewhat bettered by a daily proportion of biscuit which the sailors would pilfer [swipe] to sell, give, or exchange with us for money or furs. But when they departed, there remained neither tavern, beer-house, nor place of relief but the common kettle [the shared supply of food].

That was half a pint of wheat and as much barley boiled with water for a man a day, and this, having been some twenty-six weeks in the ship's hold, contained as many worms as grain. Our drink was water, our lodgings castles in the air [nothing but plans].

With this lodging and diet, our extreme toil in bearing and planting palisades [log fences] so strained and bruised us, and our continual labor in the extremity of the heat had so weakened us, as to have made us miserable.

From May to September [1607], those that survived lived upon sturgeon [a fish] and sea crabs. Fifty in this time we buried.

The disease faded away, and the surviving colonists were saved when Indians brought food to Jamestown at harvest time. But relations with the Indians were never certain, and at times became open war.

Smith himself was captured in December 1607 during an exploring trip. The Indians took their captive to Chief Powhatan. Historians still debate whether Smith's account of being saved by the 11 or 12 year old Pocahontas is fact or fiction.

At last they brought him to Werowocomoco, where Powhatan, their Emperor was. Before a fire upon a seat like a bedstead, he sat covered with a great robe made of raccoon skins and all the tails hanging by.

At his entrance before the King, all the people gave a great shout. The Queen of Appomattoc was appointed to bring him water to wash his hands, and another brought him a bunch of feathers, instead of a towel, to dry them.

Having feasted him after their best barbarous manner they could, a long consultation was held, but the conclusion was, two great stones were brought before Powhatan. Then as many as could laid hands on him [Smith], dragged him to them, and thereon laid his head.

They being ready with their clubs, to beat out his brains, Pocahontas, the King's dearest daughter, when no entreaty [pleas] could prevail, got his head in her arms, and laid her own upon his to save him from death.

Chief Powhatan released Smith, and he returned to Jamestown. He was elected leader of the colony in 1608 after a period of near chaos and bickering among the settlers. His strict rule for "idle loiterers" was: "He that will not work shall not eat."

A gunpowder explosion injured Smith in 1609, and he returned to England. That winter, hundreds of settlers died in what was soon called "the starving time."

Pocohontas, who often helped the colonists, later married one of the settlers. She died on a visit to England in 1617.

Group Discussion: *What did Smith think of Virginia as a location for the English to settle? Why? What impressions did Smith have of the Native Americans? What were the biggest problems the settlers faced as they tried to start their colony?*

PILGRIMS AND PURITANS IN MASSACHUSETTS

Church of England, Puritans, Pilgrims, Mayflower Compact, Squanto, town meetings,

Salem witch trials, Great Awakening

The early settlers of Massachusetts came from England, motivated mainly by religion. Most were Puritans. They were people who followed the official Church of England, but wanted it "purified" of all practices that resembled those of the Catholic Church. The most extreme Puritans were called Separatists. They had formed their own separate churches, and were considered disloyal troublemakers by English officials. At times they were harassed or even jailed.

One congregation of Separatists decided to go to Holland, because it had greater freedom of _____ at that time than England. They weren't happy there, however, so they began planning a voyage to America. The group that set sail on the *Mayflower*, called the Pilgrims, landed at Plymouth in 1620. Since no government controlled the area, they wrote and signed the Mayflower Compact. This document is famous as an early declaration of self-government by colonists in America. But winter set in, and within a few months over half the Pilgrims were dead. Help from Indians, including one named Squanto, saved the colony from being wiped out completely. After their first successful harvest they held a now famous feast of _____ in 1621.

In 1630 a much larger group of more moderate Puritans from England arrived nearby at Boston. They had been trying to change the Church of England from within, but were increasingly viewed with hostility by English leaders. Now they, too, decided to start a community of their own in America. These Puritans hoped that their settlement would become a shining _____ to England and the rest of the world of a good and godly society.

Over the next dozen years, about 18,000 more Puritans arrived. Each new community was centered on a town, its church, and its minister. The town meeting became the basic form of local government, although only _____ church members were allowed to vote.

Puritan society had no tolerance for anyone with different religious views. They watched each other closely for sinful behavior, which they punished swiftly. Still, in a harsh new world, the Puritans held together their families and grew in brotherhood. Since the ability to read the Bible was so important to them, Puritans began the first public _____ and the first college (Harvard) in the colonies. Puritans also believed that work was a kind of worship, and felt that wealth and prosperity won by work was a kind of blessing.

The other New England colonies trace back to the spread of Puritan settlements in the 1600s. The region was generally a much healthier place to be than Virginia. The small communities and the cooler climate promoted a rapid growth of the population. Women and families were much more numerous than in early Virginia settlements. Farms were usually small, and Virginia-style plantations rare. The generally _____ soil forced the Puritans to branch out into lumbering, shipbuilding, trade, and especially fishing for cod.

Growth and time soon brought changing values. For new generations, the emphasis on the strict religious code of the Puritans gradually weakened. The hysterical accusations made in the _____ witch trials in 1692 may have been caused in part by fear of this changing of values.

But times were changing. A new royal charter issued in England for Massachusetts at about the same time eliminated church membership as a voting requirement. In the 1740s, an important religious movement called the Great _____ led to the spread of new denominations and independent churches. By doing so, it promoted the idea that diversity of views was not necessarily a bad thing.

By the late colonial period the upper class in the New England colonies included a good number of wealthy _____ in cities like Boston. Their trade routes crossed the Atlantic to England, Africa, and the sugar plantations of the West Indies. The middle class was _____ in size, and included most of the small merchants, townspeople, and craftsmen. The lower class included indentured servants and slaves, as in the other colonies, although slavery was much less common than in southern colonies.

The growth of trade, and New England's tradition of citizen involvement in public affairs, put Boston at the _____ of events leading to the American Revolution. After about 1760 England decided it should tighten its control over the colonies. The descendants of the original Pilgrims and Puritans considered themselves Englishmen. They accepted the royal governor who represented the king. But as events unfolded, they refused to accept certain trade restrictions and new tax laws passed in England. They felt these laws stepped on their traditional _____ as Englishmen, especially since the colonists had no vote in the English Parliament.

Use these terms to fill in the blanks: Awakening, center, example, large, male, merchants, poor, religion, rights, Salem, schools, Thanksgiving

PLANTING A SENSE OF COMMUNITY

*Historians know very little about the **Mayflower**, the ship that carried the Pilgrims to their new home at Plymouth in 1620. But there are good records of that settlement and others that followed. The accounts below are condensed, and in some cases the text has been slightly modernized.*

The Pilgrims' "Starving Time"

*Delays in leaving England and poor navigation put the **Mayflower** in the Cape Cod area in the late fall. The result was described in an account by William Bradford, who served as governor for many years.*

But that which was most sad and lamentable was that in two or three months time half of their company died, especially in January and February, being depth of winter, and wanting [lacking] houses and other comforts. Also, they were infected with the scurvy and other diseases which this long voyage and their poor conditions had brought upon them.

There died sometimes two or three a day in those months, so that of one hundred and odd persons, scarce fifty remained.

And of these in the time of most distress, there were but six or seven healthy persons. These spared no pains night or day, but with abundance of toil [work] and hazard of their own health fetched them wood, made them fires, dressed [prepared] them meat, made their beds, washed their loathsome clothes, clothed and unclothed them.

In a word, they did all the homely and necessary things for them which dainty and queasy stomachs cannot endure to hear named; and all this willingly and cheerfully, without any grudging in the least, showing their true love for their friends and brethren.

Help From The Indians

With the arrival of spring, the surviving Pilgrims were helped by the Wampanoag Indians, including one named Squanto. Bradford's account of the settlers continues:

Afterward they (as many as were able) began to plant their corn, in which service Squanto stood them in great stead, showing them both the manner how to set it and after how to dress and tend it; also he told them, unless they got fish and set it with it in these old grounds, it would come to nothing.

All of which they found true by trial and experience. Some English seed they sowed, as wheat and peas, but it came not to good, either by badness of the seed or lateness of the season or both, or some other defect.

The Land And Property Question

At first the Pilgrims decided to share all work and chores together as a community. The fields and crops belonged to everyone, and the harvest was shared equally. But there were soon many complaints:

This was found to breed much confusion and discontent. For the young men that were most able and fit for labor and service did complain that they should spend their time and strength to work for other men's wives and children, without any extra payment.

The strong had no more in division of victuals [food] and clothes than he that was weak and not able to do a quarter the other could; this was thought injustice. And for men's wives to be commanded to do service for other men, as dressing their meat, washing their clothes, etc., they deemed it a kind of slavery. Neither could many husbands well brook it [accept it].

Within a few years, the colonists gave up the idea of sharing the work and harvest equally. Instead, a new plan gave each of the families a specific piece of land near the settlement and the ownership of whatever they could grow on it.

This had very good success, for it made all hands very industrious, so as much more corn was planted than otherwise would have been. The women now went willingly into the field and took their little ones with them to set corn, which before would allege [claim] weakness and inability.

The Puritan Ideal Of Community

The failure of the Pilgrim experiment of shared work and shared property showed that there was a practical limit to the power of community spirit. But the Pilgrims and Puritans never gave up the high value they placed on the shared sense of community in their towns and villages.

The lines below are condensed from a famous sermon by the Puritan religious leader John Winthrop. He spoke to his followers on a ship headed to Boston in 1630.

It is by a mutual consent, for the work we have in hand, to seek out a place to live under a form of government both civil and religious. In such cases as this, the care of the public must be counted above all private interests.

Whatsoever we did or ought to have done when we lived in England, the same must we do, and more also, where we go.

We must love one another fervently. We must bear one another's burdens. We must not look only on our own things, but also on the things of our brethren [neighbors].

Thus stands the cause between God and us. We have entered into a covenant [a sacred agreement] with Him for this work.

We must delight in each other, make other's conditions our own, rejoice together, mourn together, labor and suffer together, always having before our eyes our community as members of the same body.

For we must consider that we shall be as a city upon a hill. The eyes of all people are upon us, so that if we shall deal falsely with our God in this work we have undertaken, and so cause Him to withdraw His present help from us, we shall be made a story and by-word through the world.

Group Discussion:

1. As they began their settlement in 1620, how did the Pilgrims live up to their belief in sharing and placing the needs of the community first?

2. Within a few years, there was grumbling about the plan of sharing the work and harvest equally in the Pilgrim settlement. Explain what happened. Why did the new plan produce larger crops?

3. What values did John Winthrop tell his followers they should practice as they started their settlement in Boston? What do you think he is saying in the last paragraph?

MAP - EARLY ENGLISH COLONIES

Finish labeling and coloring the maps to show these:

GEOGRAPHICAL FEATURES

Chesapeake Bay   James River

Potomac River   Connecticut River

Hudson River   Cape Cod

Long Island   Delaware River *(Appears on both maps.)*

EARLY ENGLISH SETTLEMENTS

*This list shows, in chronological order, some of the most famous of the early English
settlements. Find the settlements on the maps, and
finish labeling them to show the dates.*

Roanoke Island, the
location of **The Lost
Colony (1587)**   Williamsburg (1633)

                          St. Mary's City (1634)

Jamestown (1607)   Hartford (1635)

Plymouth (1620)   Providence (1636)

Salem (1626)   New Haven (1638)

Boston (1630)   Richmond (1644)

Map Skills: Finding Distances

The scale of miles is shown on both maps. To use it easily, line the edge of a small piece of
paper just under the scale, and duplicate the scale marks. Slide and turn your new scale to
line up with these locations on the maps, then estimate the straight-line distances.

From **Jamestown** to **Richmond**: _____ miles.

From **Plymouth** to **Boston**: _____ miles.

From **Providence** to **New Haven**: _____ miles.

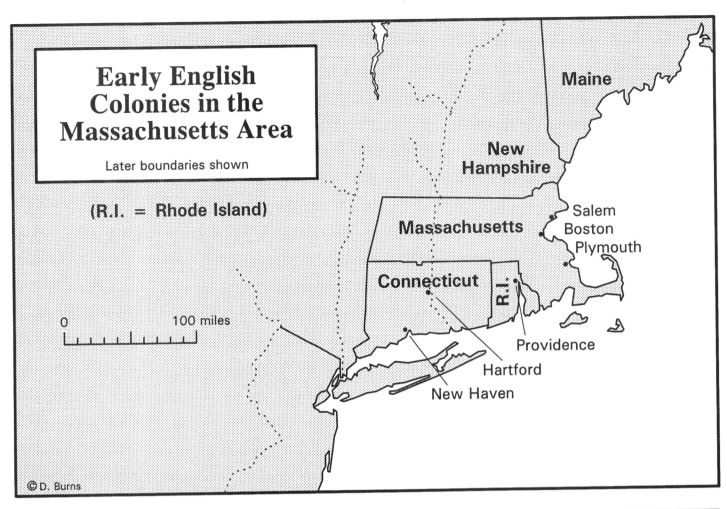

Early English Colonies in the Massachusetts Area

Later boundaries shown

(R.I. = Rhode Island)

0   100 miles

Maine

New Hampshire

Massachusetts

Salem
Boston
Plymouth

Connecticut

R.I.

Providence

Hartford

New Haven

© D. Burns

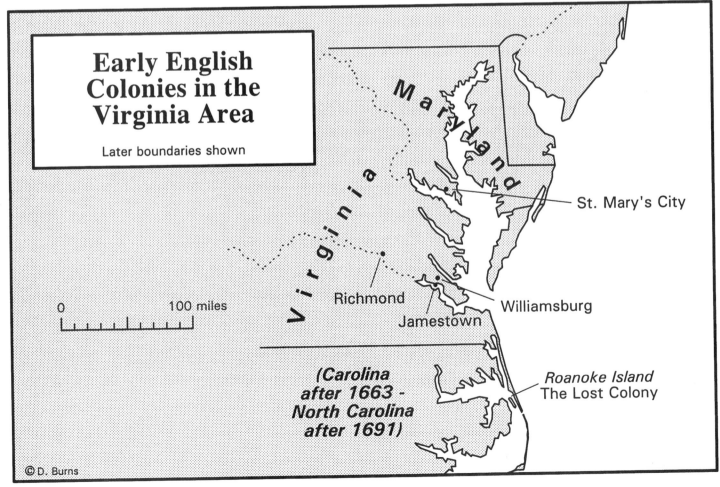

Early English Colonies in the Virginia Area

Later boundaries shown

0   100 miles

Maryland

Virginia

St. Mary's City

Richmond

Williamsburg

Jamestown

(Carolina after 1663 - North Carolina after 1691)

Roanoke Island The Lost Colony

© D. Burns

MAP - THE SPREAD OF THE SLAVE TRADE

Finish the map, using color to highlight the European countries and their colonies. The dotted lines will help guide you in showing some of the areas.

Show a **triangular trade route** across the **Atlantic Ocean** connecting **Boston, Africa,** and the **West Indies.**

Africa, where slavery and a slave trade involving Arab merchants existed for _____ centuries before Europeans began exploring the continent. The area called the **Slave Coast** was a leading source of slaves sold by African tribal chiefs to European traders, although slaves came from many other areas as well.

Portugal, which began exploring the African coast around 1400. Slaves purchased from African tribes were brought back as workers and servants. By 1500 the Portuguese were using slaves to work on their _____ plantations on **Madeira** and the **Canary Islands.**

Brazil, a large colony of Portugal in South America. The practice of using African slaves to work on sugar plantations spread there in the 1500s as the desire for sugar _____ in Europe.

Hispaniola, also called Santo Domingo after the capital city. It was an early colony of **Spain** in the islands of the **West Indies.** As the native Indian population _____, Spanish settlers also began using African slaves. Sugar plantations were growing, and the slave trade spread through the West Indies. Some of these islands were later controlled by other European countries.

Jamestown, the English colony where the first Africans were taken on a Dutch ship in 1619. Since the English did not have a slave system at that time, the early arrivals were treated as indentured servants at first. But by 1670, new laws modeled after those in the West Indies established a _____ slave status. The labor of slaves was especially valuable on the tobacco plantations spreading in the **Chesapeake Bay** area.

Charles Town, in the colony of South Carolina. It became a center of trade, including the slave trade, for many of the Southern colonies. Tobacco, rice, and indigo plantations in the area were all _____ users of slave labor.

Boston, a center of ship building and trade in the New England colonies. Its ship captains often sailed a profitable "trading triangle" that carried rum and iron to trade for slaves in Africa, then returned home with a stop in the West Indies to trade the slaves for sugar and _____.

England, home to merchants and ship owners who grew rich in the slave trade in the 1700s. The Anti-Slavery Society formed there in 1823, and England freed the slaves in its colonies ten years later. Slavery in the _____ ended in 1865.

Use these terms to fill in the blanks: declined, heavy, many, molasses, permanent, soared, sugar, U.S.

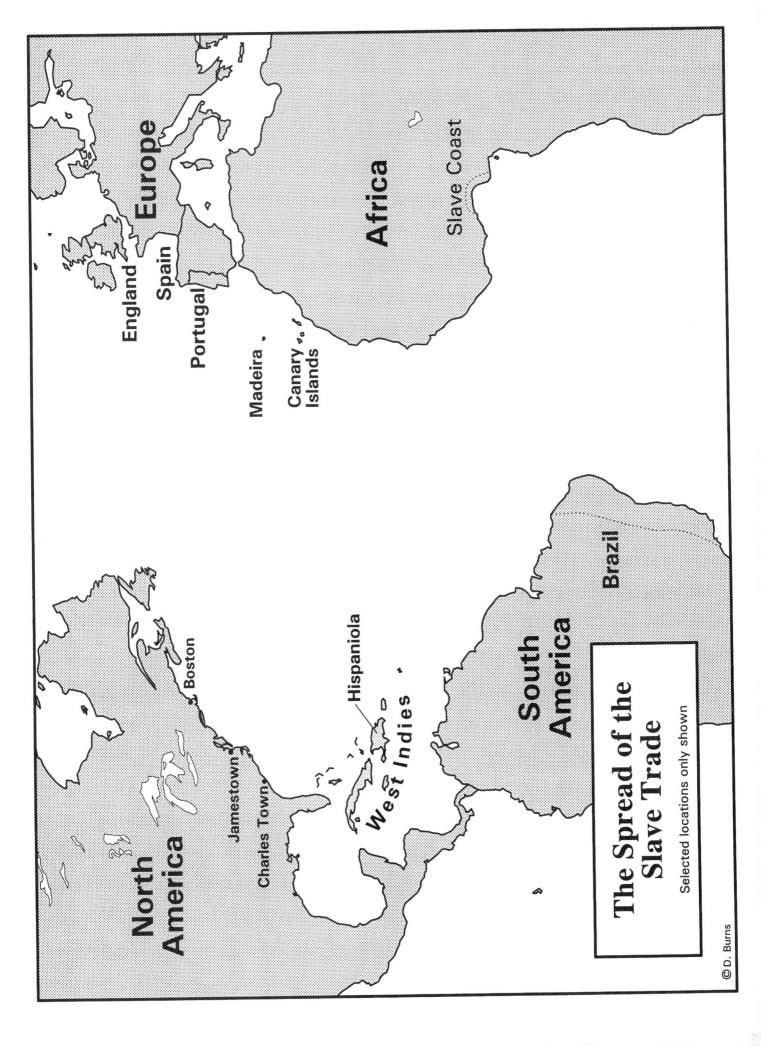

The Spread of the
Slave Trade

Selected locations only shown

© D. Burns

MAP - COLONIAL AMERICA IN 1754

Finish labeling and coloring the map to show these:

The 13 Colonies *(Use red letters and abbreviations to label each of the 13 English colonies and Maine, which was part of the colony of Massachusetts.)*

Chesapeake Bay - Around this bay and nearby rivers were many of the oldest settlements of England's American colonies, including _____ in Virginia.

Appalachian Mountains - This range marked the western edge of settlement of the American colonies around 1750. But a few colonists were beginning to explore and claim land _____ of the mountains.

The Great Lakes - These were explored by the French, and were important routes for trade with _____ tribes in the region. The trade, mostly in animal furs, helped keep relations between the French and the Indians generally peaceful.

New France - This was the main area of French settlements around the Great Lakes and the St. Lawrence River, including _____ and Montreal.

Louisiana - This area along the Mississippi River was claimed and settled by the _____. The total French population in North America, however, was very much smaller than the population of the English colonies.

Mississippi River - Near the mouth of this great river stood the important French colonial city of _____.

Ohio River - Beside this river the French built Fort _____ in 1754 as a warning to the English colonists to stay out of French claimed territory. (The name is pronounced "Dew-kane.") Fighting between the French and the English near this fort helped start the conflict called the French and Indian War that same year.

Hudson's Bay Company - This area well north of the French settlements in Canada was claimed by the _____, based on their early exploration of the region.

Spanish Florida - This area included the city of _____, the oldest continuous settlement in what is now the United States.

Finally, use light yellow shading to show the area on the map claimed by the French. Use light green shading to show the area claimed by the Spanish. The thin dotted lines on the map will help guide you.

Use these terms to fill in the blanks: Duquesne, English, French, Indian, New Orleans, Quebec, St. Augustine, west, Williamsburg

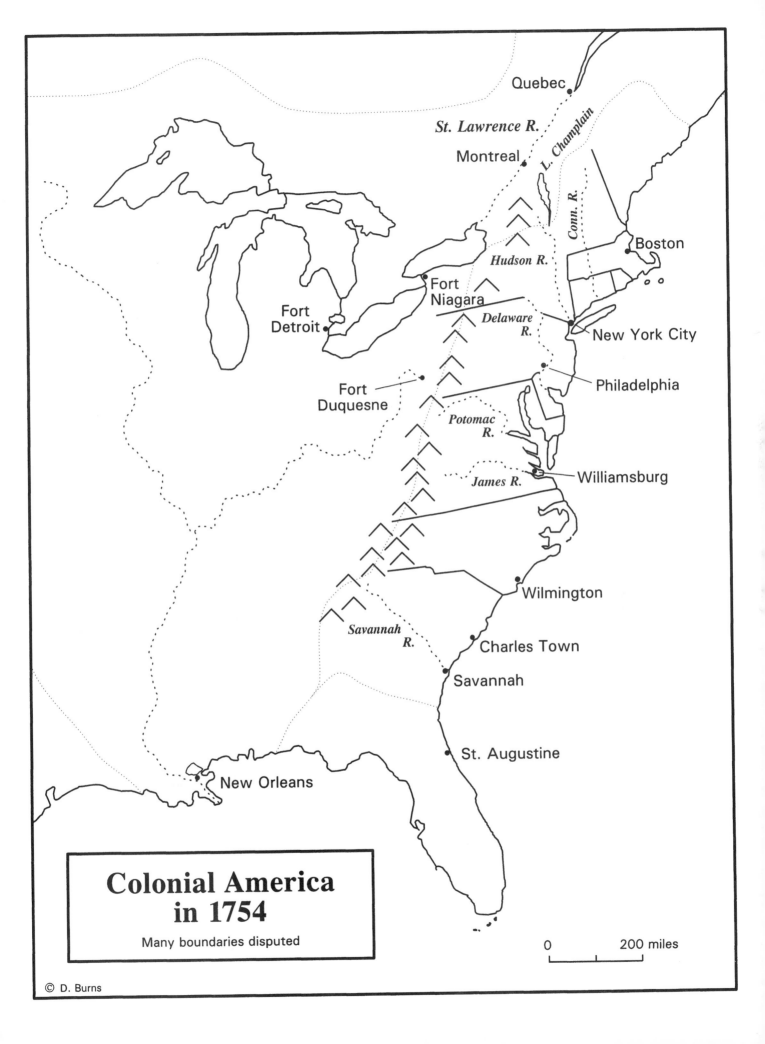

Quebec

St. Lawrence R.

Montreal

L. Champlain

Conn. R.

Hudson R.

Boston

Fort
Niagara

Fort
Detroit

*Delaware
R.*

New York City

Fort
Duquesne

Philadelphia

*Potomac
R.*

Williamsburg

James R.

Wilmington

*Savannah
R.*

Charles Town

Savannah

St. Augustine

New Orleans

Colonial America
in 1754

Many boundaries disputed

0   200 miles

© D. Burns

THE COLONIAL HERITAGE

Quakers, pluralistic society, open/closed society, Benjamin Franklin

Have you ever noticed how much a child is like its parents, even long after he or she has grown up? Consider the colony of Virginia, and the other colonies that soon followed in the South. The people who went there went for personal opportunity, in the face of real hardship and danger. Over time, plantation owners and back-woods farmers created a lifestyle with a great emphasis on self-reliance and individual liberty. Even _____ of years later, most people consider those ideas to be key parts of American life and culture.

In the New England colonies, small towns dotted the countryside. Settlers there placed a high value on the communities in which they lived. Morality - trying to do the _____ thing - was a constant part of the Puritans' religious consciousness. The Puritans believed they had a mission to show the rest of the world the way to build a good and godly society. Even today, these attitudes can be seen in American political life and in the belief that America has a special obligation to live up to its values and ideals.

Pennsylvania was settled in 1682 by a religious group from England called the Society of Friends, or Quakers. This group, like the Puritans, saw their colony as a kind of "holy experiment" to build a good society. But the Quakers had a very different religion than the Puritans. Each person, they felt, was guided by an "inner light." There was no need for the church to rigidly control its members. They believed in the freedom to worship God in one's own way. They believed all men are _____ in the sight of God, and they rejected distinctions of social class. They refused to fight in wars.

Their leader, William Penn, invited to the new colony people of all religious beliefs and national origins. Indians, he insisted, were to be treated fairly. Philadelphia was the main city. (The name means "City of brotherly _____.") The colony was very successful, and the Scotch-Irish and Germans flocked there in large numbers. As so many different groups arrived, Quaker beliefs were _____ always followed. Even so, Pennsylvania set a pattern for a pluralistic or open society that accepted people of different views and national origins.

It is certainly no accident that the Declaration of Independence was written in the city of _____ many years later. By the late colonial era it had become the largest and most prosperous of colonial cities, with a population of about 30,000. Over time, many of the ideas that once led some people to call the

Quakers crazy became basic American principles. Benjamin _____, a printer, writer, and patriot who helped push America toward independence, made it his home.

Ever since King Henry VIII left the Roman Catholic Church and formed the Church of England, a Protestant church, Catholics in England were frequently harassed. Lord Baltimore organized an expedition to create Maryland as a safe haven for Catholics. Protestants were welcome too, and an early law called the _____ Act provided for freedom of worship, which all Americans enjoy today.

Another colony, New York, was originally named New Amsterdam, because the _____ settled there first. A well-known story says that Manhattan itself was bought from an Indian tribe for 24 dollars worth of trade goods. Some Dutch families later began moving up the Hudson River, and some of their homes and barns can still be seen. But in 1664 the English took over the colony, and renamed it. It was from the earliest days a trading city, and it accepted people from many nations and religious backgrounds. It is still world famous as a business center, and is still a city of many ethnic groups that usually try to get along so everyone can try to get _____.

The last of the original thirteen colonies was Georgia, settled in 1733. The colony's organizers set it up in part to help poverty-stricken Englishmen who faced debtors' prison at home. Most Americans today take pride in the fact that for hundreds of years, our nation has given millions of down-and-out immigrants a chance to climb back on their feet.

It's important not to oversimplify the reality or heritage of the English colonies. Remember that while our national character began forming in those times, _____ people then could have imagined our current form of democracy. Only men could vote. Ordinary citizens didn't expect to hold positions of real political power. That was for their "betters" in higher social positions. Most colonists felt a king was needed to ensure a strong and stable government. Many accepted slavery as "natural," even as they began shouting about their own rights and _____. Yet almost any social pattern or political idea in modern America can be traced back into colonial times. The changes along the way make up some of the most compelling stories in American history.

Use these terms to fill in the blanks: ahead, Dutch, equal, few, Franklin, hundreds, liberties, love, not, Philadelphia, right, Tolerance

Colonial America 2 - 20

A VISIT TO THE MIDDLE COLONIES

This account of life in the middle colonies is by a Swedish visitor named Peter Kalm. He traveled through New Jersey, Pennsylvania, and New York in 1748. These are condensed excerpts.

The country through which we passed was for the greatest part level, though sometimes there were long hills. Some parts were covered with trees, but by far the greater part of the country was without woods.

On the other hand, I never saw any place in America, the towns excepted, so well populated. An old man who lived in this neighborhood assured me that he could well remember the time when, between Trenton and New Brunswick, there were not above three farms. He reckoned that was about 50-some odd years ago.

 During the greater part of the day we had very extensive cornfields on both sides of the road. Near almost every farm was a large orchard full of peaches and apple trees. In some of them the fruit was fallen from the trees in such quantities as to cover nearly the whole surface.

Part of it they left to rot, since they could not take it all in and consume it. Whenever we passed by, we were always welcome to go into the fine orchards and gather our hats and pockets full of the choicest fruit, without the possessor so much as looking after it.

The country, especially all along the coasts in the English colonies, is inhabited by Europeans. In some places they are already so numerous that few parts of Europe are more populous. The Indians have sold the country to the Europeans, and have retired further up. In most parts you may travel 120 English miles from the seashore before you reach the first houses of the Indians.

It is very possible for a person to have been at Philadelphia and other towns on the seashore for half a year without so much as seeing an Indian.

Besides the different sects of Christians, there are many Jews settled in New York, who possess great privileges. They have a synagogue and houses, and their own property in the countryside, and are allowed to keep shops in town. They have likewise several ships, which they send out with their own goods.

In truth, they enjoy all the privileges common to the other inhabitants of this town and colony.

New York, the capital of the colony of the same name, is about 97 English miles from Philadelphia. The situation is extremely advantageous for trade. The town stands upon a point which is formed by two bays, into which the Hudson River discharges itself. New York is therefore on three sides surrounded with water. The place is generally reckoned very wholesome.

The port is a good one. Ships of the greatest burden can lie in it. Its water is very salty, as the sea continually comes in upon it, and therefore is never frozen, except in extraordinarily cold weather.

New York probably carries on a more extensive commerce than any town in the English North American colonies; at least it may be said to equal them. Boston and Philadelphia, however, come very near to it.

Every year they build several ships here, which are sent to London, and there sold. Lately they have also shipped a quantity of iron to England. In return for these, they import from London every article of English growth or manufacture, together with all sorts of foreign goods.

England, and especially London, profits immensely by its trade with the American colonies. Not only New York, but likewise all the other English towns on the continent, import so many articles from England that all their money must go to Old England in payment.

 The goods with which the colony of New York trades are not very numerous. They chiefly export the skins of animals, which are bought from the Indians, great quantities of boards, timber, and lumber from the area around the Hudson River, and lastly, wheat, flour, barley, oats, and other kinds of corn.

New York likewise exports some flesh [meat] and other provisions. Iron, however, may be had more plentifully, as it is found in several parts of this colony, and is of a considerable goodness.

No manufactures of note have as yet been established here. At present they get all manufactured goods, such as woolen and linen cloth, etc., from England, and especially from London.

The Hudson River is very convenient for the commerce of this city, as it is navigable for near 150 English miles up the country, and falls into the bay not far from the town, on its western side. During eight months of the year this river is full of boats of all sizes, either going to New York or returning from there, laden either with inland or foreign goods.

The country people come to market in New York twice a week, much in the same manner they do at Philadelphia.

The governor of the colony of New York resides here, and has a palace in the fort. An assembly of delegates from all the districts of the colony is held in the city of New York once or twice every year. Everything relating to the good of the colony is here debated. The governor calls the assembly, and dissolves it [ends its meeting] at his pleasure.

The King appoints the governor according to his royal pleasure, but the inhabitants of the colony make up [provide] the governor's salary. Therefore, a man entrusted with this office has greater or lesser revenues according as he knows how to gain the confidence of the inhabitants.

There are examples of governors in this and other colonies of North America who, by their disagreements with the inhabitants, have lost their whole salary, the King having no power to make them pay it.

If a governor had no other resource in these circumstances, he would be obliged either to resign his office, or to be content with an income too small for his dignity, or else to agree in everything with the wishes of the inhabitants.

Group Discussion:

1. What did Peter Kalm see that shows that farmers settled in the middle colonies were doing very well in 1748?

2. What indication is there that religious tolerance was already fairly common in New York at the time Kalm made his visit?

3. What are the main points Kalm makes about trade and commerce between the colonies and England?

4. What are the main points Kalm makes about the system of colonial government in New York?

CHARTING COLONIAL STATISTICS

Complete the pie charts below to show the relative size of the white and black population living in the colonies listed. (The size of each pie is proportional to that colony's total population.) What do you think best explains the patterns shown by the charts?

White and Black Population of the Colonies in 1750

<u>Color Key:</u> White [   ]   Black [   ]

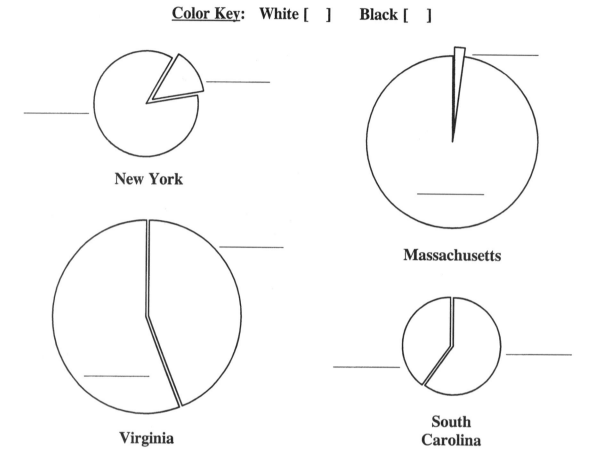

New York

Massachusetts

Virginia

South Carolina

Use the table below to find the information you need to complete the charts above. Label each pie to show the <u>percent</u> of white and black residents for that colony. Be sure to add the "%" sign. Finally, pick a color for each category in the key, and shade the appropriate segments.

Colony	Total Population in 1750	White Residents		Black Residents	
		Population	Percent	Population	Percent
Massachusetts	188,000	184,000	98	4,000	2
New York	77,000	66,000	86	11,000	14
Virginia	231,000	130,000	56	101,000	44
South Carolina	64,000	25,000	40	39,000	60

source: *Historical Statistics of the United States*

During this period, the colonists produced most of their own food and other products, but also produced a steadily growing surplus for export. Create a bar graph below to show the value of leading exports in 1770. What was the most valuable export?

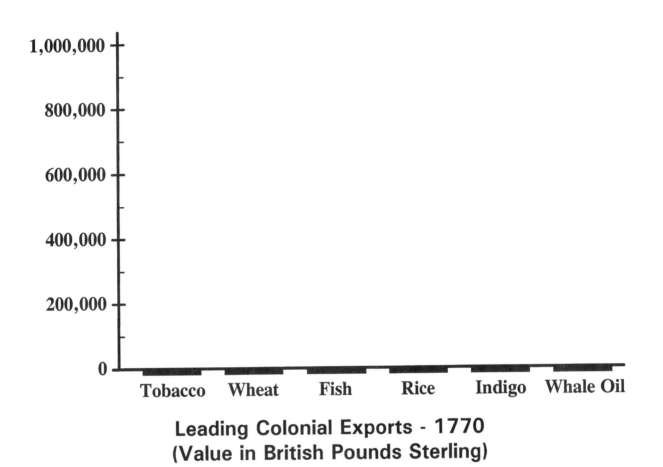

**Leading Colonial Exports - 1770
(Value in British Pounds Sterling)**

Use the table below to find the information you need to complete the bar graph. Draw a vertical bar for each product, with the length corresponding to the value of exports of that product.

Product	Exports - 1770 Value in British Pounds Sterling	Product	Exports - 1770 Value in British Pounds Sterling
Tobacco	906,638	Rice	340,693
Wheat (including flour and bread)	636,020	Indigo (a blue dye)	131,552
Fish	397,945	Whale Oil	85,013

source: *Historical Statistics of the United States*

HEADING FOR INDEPENDENCE

Parliament, mercantilism, French and Indian War, King George III, Proclamation of 1763,

Stamp Act, Sons/Daughters of Liberty, boycott, Boston Massacre, Tea Act,

Boston Tea Party, Coercive/Intolerable Acts, First Continental Congress, militia

By 1750 the population of the English colonies was over one million and was rapidly growing. They considered themselves British subjects under the king and Parliament, and maintained all the traditional "rights of Englishmen." These included the right to trial by a _____, the right to elected representation in the government, and the right of those elected to approve all taxes.

The colonists actually had more say in their own government than the English back home. It's true that the king appointed royal governors to manage most of the colonies, and the governors had wide powers over laws passed by the elected colonial assemblies. It's also true that Parliament, following a policy known as mercantilism, passed laws that controlled or limited colonial trade. But England was _____ away. The colonists got used to having many things their own way, and most importantly, controlled taxes through their colonial assemblies.

But things changed after 1750, especially after a war with the French and their Indian allies. The colonists were starting to spread across the _____ Mountains into the rich land of the Ohio River valley. The French also claimed that area, however, and many Indian tribes in the region were equally unhappy about the spread of the colonists.

In 1754 the British sent a young Virginia man named George _____ to check out the situation. He and his troops were captured, but later released. The British sent over more troops, and the French and Indian War began. After years of fighting, England won almost all the French territory in North America.

Defending the colonies cost money, and the British wanted the colonists to pay a fair share. They also wanted no more trouble from the Indians. In the Proclamation of 1763, King George III declared that the area west of the Appalachians was reserved for the Indians only. That was very unpopular with the colonists. Next, Parliament passed new taxes on the colonists to help pay the cost of maintaining British soldiers in the colonies. These taxes included the Sugar Act (1764) and the Stamp Act (1765). A kind of "hidden tax" was the Quartering Act, which forced colonists to provide food and _____ for British troops stationed in the colonies.

All these measures angered the colonists. The cry of "No taxation without representation" went up from leaders like Virginia's Patrick Henry. Colonists, after all, were _____ allowed to elect representatives to sit in the British Parliament.

Many colonists believed the new laws proved that the king and Parliament considered them "second class" Englishmen. Delegates from nine colonies met, and demanded that England _____ both the Sugar Act and the Stamp Act. Groups like the Sons of Liberty organized boycotts of British goods in the colonies to protest the laws. Another effective protest came from mob action by citizens. Crowds threatened British tax collectors, and forced them to resign.

The Stamp Act was quickly repealed, but Parliament declared it had a right to tax the colonists. The colonists still insisted that right was _____ alone. Trouble erupted again when Parliament passed new taxes on certain goods like glass and paint imported into the colonies. These were the Townshend Acts. Another boycott of British goods was organized by the colonists. In Boston, Samuel Adams was a well-known face in the movement. He and many others also objected to the presence of so many British troops stationed there in peacetime. In 1770 a confrontation between some British soldiers and a group of Boston townspeople turned deadly. It was dubbed "The Boston Massacre" by many of the colonists, although the British felt the _____ themselves started the fight.

By that time England was trying to calm things down. Parliament repealed all the taxes except the one on tea. That seemed to satisfy most colonists. But in 1773 another problem erupted. Parliament passed the Tea Act to boost profits for the (British) East India Company. The new law gave the company an exclusive right to import and sell tea in the colonies. Tea, of course, was a very _____ drink at the time.

Colonists were outraged by the law, which would have hurt colonial merchants in the tea business. Worst of all, the tea carried a small British tax. In many colonies, protests forced the shipments of tea to be sent back to England or left unsold on the docks. In Boston, however, colonists raided the tea ships and dumped the cargo in the water. Parliament responded with the Coercive (or "Intolerable") Acts, which among other measures ordered Boston harbor closed. The other colonies began to make shipments of supplies to help the city's residents. This effort for a common cause _____ the colonies as nothing ever had before.

The crisis in Boston led colonists to organize and meet at the First Continental Congress in Philadelphia (1774). The delegates voted to declare that Parliament had no right to pass tax laws for the colonies. They also urged the colonies to form armed militia units of citizens for defense. Most delegates still hoped England would try to reach a compromise, but already some voices were calling for _____.

Use these terms to fill in the blanks: Appalachian, colonists, far, housing, independence, jury, not, popular, repeal, theirs, united, Washington

TWO VIEWS FROM THE PRINTING PRESSES

Printing presses became powerful tools on both sides of the Atlantic for influencing public opinion as the dispute grew between the colonies and Great Britain. These pages show two examples of how each side attempted to influence the public's perception of events. The picture below of the Boston Massacre (March 5, 1770) was drawn by Paul Revere and circulated widely in the colonies.

Group Discussion: *Eyewitness accounts of the Boston Massacre show that the assembled crowd was harassing and threatening the British soldiers. It included waterfront "toughs" carrying clubs and throwing rocks. Some eyewitnesses also said the soldiers were not ordered to "aim and fire," but fired in panic and fear. Does the picture depict those facts? What impression of the event would this picture probably give to most colonists who saw it?*

The political cartoon below was printed in London, and shows the view many people in England had of the American colonists. The figure in the center is a British tax collector being "tarred and feathered" by a group of American colonists. Write short notes in the margins to identify each part of the picture that would probably leave a bad impression of the colonists and their cause.

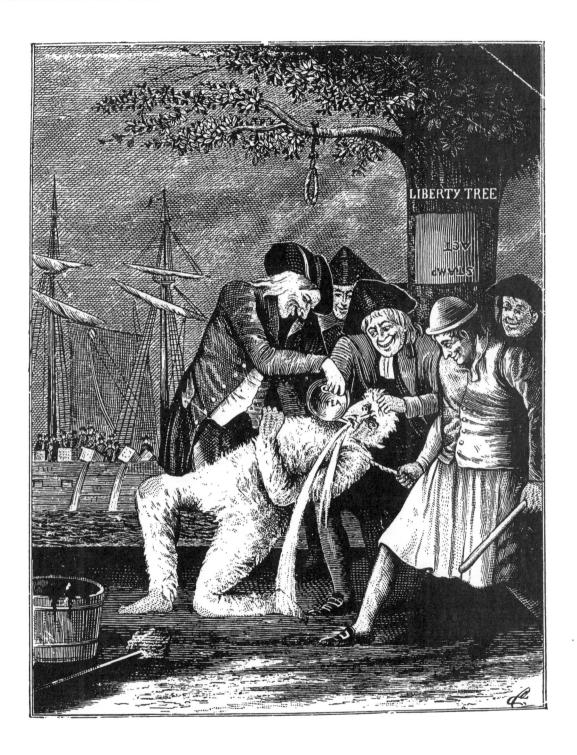

Group Discussion: *What is the picture saying about the loyalty of the American colonists to English law? How does it portray the American colonists themselves? What does it seem to be predicting will be the likely result of the colonists' push for greater self-government?*

<table>
| 3 | Revolutionary Years: 1775 - 1800 |
</table>

3

Revolutionary Years: 1775 - 1800

"I know not what course others may take; but as for me, give me liberty, or give me death!"

"We hold these truths to be self-evident, that all men are created equal, that they are endowed by their Creator with certain unalienable Rights, that among these are Life, Liberty, and the pursuit of Happiness. - That to secure these rights, Governments are instituted among Men, deriving their just powers from the consent of the governed. - That whenever any Form of Government becomes destructive of these ends, it is the Right of the People to alter or to abolish it...."

"We the People of the United States, in Order to form a more perfect Union, establish Justice, insure domestic Tranquility, provide for the common defense, promote the general Welfare, and secure the Blessings of Liberty to ourselves and our Posterity, do ordain and establish this Constitution for the United States of America."

Study Checklist

When you have completed this section, working with the Internet support site at *www.fasttrackteaching.com* or other resources, you should be able to:

Identify and explain the context of the **Famous Quotes** shown on the Section Title Page.

Identify and explain the importance of the **Famous Names and Terms** listed on the topic summary pages in this section.

Identify on a map and explain the importance of the **Famous Places** shown on the maps in this section.

Explain the general sequence of events in this period and tell from memory the **Famous Years**:

- The Declaration of Independence was signed (**1776**).
- The Americans won at Yorktown (**1781**).
- The Constitution was written (**1787**).
- The Bill of Rights was ratified (**1791**).

Take a Practice Test!

 (A) (B) (C) (D)

A multiple-choice practice test for this section can be found on the Internet support site at:

www.fasttrackteaching.com

Textbook Page References:

Discuss or write briefly on such questions and topics as these:

1. Describe how each of these laws and events pushed the colonies closer to breaking with England: the Tea Act; the Boston Tea Party; the Intolerable Acts; the British march to Lexington and Concord; the Second Continental Congress.

2. How did the geographic pattern of fighting during the Revolution reflect the strengths and weaknesses of each side? How was the American victory finally achieved?

3. How revolutionary was the American Revolution? What aspects of life did it change? What aspects of life remained relatively unchanged?

4. What were the main problems in the years after the Revolution that led to the decision to write the Constitution?

5. Describe several of the ways the Constitution tries to deal with the fact that governments often tend to become too powerful or to abuse power.

6. Describe the differences in the political views of Thomas Jefferson and Alexander Hamilton. Explain how these differences led to the formation of the first political parties in the U.S.

Timeline 1775 - 1800

Find when these events occurred, fill in the blanks, and place them on the main timeline. Space has been left at the top to show a few items from the late Colonial era.

Late Colonial era items: **Boston Tea Party** - December 1773

Intolerable Acts - May 1774

First Continental Congress - September 1774

Lexington/Concord fighting - The British went to seize weapons and rebels from these towns near the city of _____.

Second Continental Congress - It sent the Olive Branch Petition to King George III, in hope that war with Great Britain could be _____.

Common Sense **published** - It swung public opinion toward _____.

Independence declared - The Declaration was written by Thomas _____.

Valley Forge Camp - About one _____ of the 10,000 man army died that winter.

Victory at Yorktown - The French _____ was a key factor in the victory at this town beside the York River in Virginia.

Treaty of Paris - It put the western border of the U.S. at the _____ River.

Constitutional Convention - It decided to toss out the Articles of _____.

Constitution ratified - The Constitution sets up the rules the government _____ follow.

George Washington inaugurated - He is often called the _____ of our country.

Bill of Rights ratified - This list gives solid _____ from government power.

Proclamation of Neutrality - Washington wanted to avoid being dragged into a war that had erupted between Great Britain and _____.

John Adams elected - One of his accomplishments was avoiding _____ with France.

Sedition Act - It was a law that tried to make criticism of government officials a _____.

Jefferson elected - He and his supporters were loud _____ of the Sedition Act.

Use these terms to fill in the blanks: avoided, Boston, Confederation, critics, crime, father, France, independence, Jefferson, Mississippi, must, navy, protection, quarter, war

---

1775 -

1780 -

1785 -

1790 -

1795 -

1800 -

George III
*(King in
England
to 1820)*

**American
Revolution
in
progress**

*Articles
of
Confed-
eration*

Constitution

George
Washington

*(Elected as
president
under the
Constitution)*

John
Adams

TIMELINE: REVOLUTIONARY YEARS

THE REVOLUTION BEGINS

minutemen, Lexington & Concord, Paul Revere, Second Continental Congress,

George Washington, Thomas Paine, Patrick Henry, tyrant/tyranny, Thomas Jefferson

The first fighting of the American Revolution came in 1775, as the dispute over the Tea Act and the Boston Tea Party came to a boil. England had ordered Boston Harbor closed in 1774, and suspended the right of colonists in Massachusetts to elect officials and hold town meetings. A military governor was appointed to run the colony. These measures were quickly dubbed the "Intolerable Acts" by colonists. The colonies began to unite as never before to _____ Boston and resist England.

The First Continental Congress of the colonies met in Philadelphia in 1774 to coordinate a response to the Intolerable Acts. It called for the formation of citizen militia units for _____, and set up a new boycott of British goods. (Some delegates, but not a majority at this time, wanted a total break with England.)

The British, of course, considered all this to be rebellion, especially the armed militia groups in Massachusetts known as minutemen. When spring arrived (1775), the British set out from Boston with about 700 soldiers to flush out "trouble-makers" and seize weapons kept by the rebel colonists in the town of Concord. On the way, the soldiers ran into a group of armed colonial minutemen in the town of Lexington, and the shooting began. (This is where Paul _____ made his famous ride to warn the townspeople.) The British Redcoats didn't find much to grab in Concord. But on the march back to Boston, they fell by the dozens to the angry fire of colonial _____.

The very next month, in May 1775, delegates of the colonies met again in Philadelphia. This was the Second Continental Congress. It named George Washington as commander of the militia units camped in the Boston area that were to become the Army of the United Colonies. It also sent a message to King George III stating that the colonies did not really want to break away, but simply wanted the colonists' basic _____ recognized. This was called the Olive Branch Petition. But King George refused to consider negotiating with the colonists. The revolt, he felt, had to be stopped cold, and English authority over the colonies _____.

Events, meanwhile, were already sweeping ahead. In June there was another much more deadly fight between colonists and the British. This was the battle of _____ Hill, just outside Boston. (The British actually won, but lost so many men it almost seemed a colonial victory.) By the time the year of 1775 ended, Virginians had chased their _____ governor out of the colony and defeated his troops. In retaliation, the governor ordered English ships to fire their guns on Norfolk.

Talk of outright revolution was in the air as 1776 began. It got a big boost when Thomas Paine published a pamphlet or slim book that winter titled *Common Sense*. In powerful language, he urged independence for the colonies. It was absurd, he wrote, for a vast continent like America to be ruled forever by a small nation on an _____.

Paine also argued that independence would create a chance to build a new and better kind of government, without kings or nobility. Ordinary citizens, he argued, could run their own government. The spread of this idea is what made the fight truly _____, and more than just a tax revolt. *Common Sense* became enormously popular, and helped push public opinion toward the idea of a break with England. Other colonists, like Patrick Henry in Virginia, were adding their own voices for independence. More and more dared to call the English king a "tyrant."

It was now spring of 1776. The British pulled out of Boston, but only because colonists set up cannons in the hills overlooking the city and its harbor. In June a Virginia delegate at the Second Continental Congress in Philadelphia made a motion (a call for a vote) on the question of independence. But some delegates _____, and debate continued. A committee

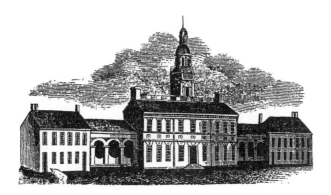

was then set up to prepare a document for the delegates to consider. A young delegate from Virginia, Thomas _____, was asked to pull the committee's ideas together in writing.

Finally, on July 4th, 1776, the final break with the mother country was made. The Declaration of Independence was adopted by a unanimous vote. The fighting had already begun, and now there could be no turning back.

Use these terms to fill in the blanks: Bunker, defense, help, island, Jefferson, muskets, resisted, Revere, revolutionary, rights, royal, upheld

THE BATTLE OF BUNKER HILL

The Battle of Bunker Hill (June 17, 1775) is among the most famous in American History. Bunker Hill sits on the Charlestown Peninsula, just across the Charles River from the city of Boston. Study the map below to answer the questions on the next page.

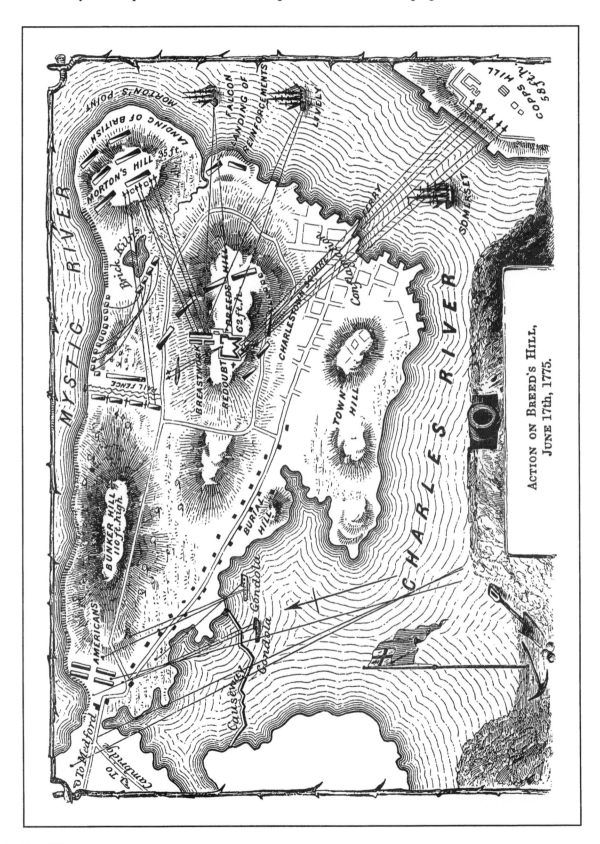

ACTION ON BREED'S HILL, JUNE 17th, 1775.

1. The American militia forces were camped outside Boston in June of 1775 because British forces occupied the city of Boston itself. American forces snuck under cover of darkness onto the Charlestown Peninsula, intending to fortify Bunker Hill. Instead, they built their "redoubt" or small dugout fort on Breed's Hill. Did that put the American position closer to or farther away from the British cannon position on Copps Hill in Boston?

2. Where did the British first land their soldiers on the Charlestown Peninsula as they prepared to attack the American position?

3. The British made several attacks up Breed's Hill. The American forces had limited gunpowder, and a legend says the Americans were ordered not to fire on the British troops until they saw "the whites of their eyes." What was the height of Breed's Hill that the British had to climb as they attacked?

4. The Americans repulsed two major British attacks and inflicted heavy casualties before being forced to retreat during a third attack. What risk would the Americans have faced if they had stayed on the Charlestown Peninsula instead of retreating back to the mainland?

The Outcome: The American forces did retreat successfully, and rejoined the other militia units gathered in the Boston area. Almost half the British troops involved were killed or wounded. The event proved to both sides that the Americans could fight effectively. Although most of the fighting took place on Breed's Hill, the event is always called the Battle of Bunker Hill, and inspired Americans in all the colonies.

Group Discussion: Later in 1775 the Americans printed handbills like the one shown below to encourage British soldiers holding Bunker Hill to desert and come over to the American side ("Prospect Hill.") What does it tell about the life of a British soldier at the time?

PROSPECT HILL. | BUNKER's HILL.

PROSPECT HILL.

I. Seven Dollars a Month. — —

II. Fresh Provisions, and in Plenty. — —

III. Health. — — — —

IV. Freedom, Ease, Affluence and a good Farm.

BUNKER's HILL.

I. Three Pence a Day.

II. Rotten Salt Pork.

III. The Scurvy.

IV. Slavery, Beggary and Want.

PATRICK HENRY CALLS FOR A FIGHT

Boston harbor was closed by the Intolerable Acts, but no fighting had yet occurred when Patrick Henry delivered his famous speech in March of 1775. The presence of British troops in the colonies and the years of conflict over British rule, however, convinced him that war was coming. He made the speech (condensed here) at a convention of Virginia's leaders called to consider what action should be taken.

The question before the House is one of awful moment [importance] to this country. For my own part I consider it as nothing less than a question of freedom or slavery.

I ask gentlemen, sir, what means this martial array [the British military force], if its purpose be not to force us into submission? Has Great Britain any enemy in this quarter of the world, to call for all this accumulation of navies and armies?

No, sir, she has none. They are sent over to bind and rivet upon us those chains which the British have been so long forging.

And what have we to oppose them? Shall we try argument? Sir, we have been trying that for the last ten years.

Sir, we have done everything that could be done, to avert the storm which is now coming on.

There is no longer any room for hope. If we wish to be free, we must fight! I repeat it sir, we must fight! An appeal to arms and to God is all that is left to us!

They tell us, sir, that we are weak; unable to cope with so formidable an adversary. But when will we be stronger? Will it be the next week, or the next year? Will it be when we are totally disarmed, and when a British guard shall be stationed in every house?

Sir, we are not weak, if we make a proper use of the means which the God of nature has placed in our power. Three millions of people, armed in the holy cause of liberty, and in such a country as that which we possess, are invincible by any force which our enemy can send against us.

Besides, sir, we shall not fight our battles alone. There is a just God who presides over the destinies of nations, and who will raise up friends to fight our battles for us.

The battle, sir, is not to the strong alone. It is to the vigilant, the active, the brave.

Besides, sir, we have no election [no choice]. If we were base [coward] enough to desire it, it is now too late to retire from the contest. There is no retreat, but in submission and slavery!

Our chains are forged! Their clanking may be heard on the plains of Boston! The war is inevitable - and let it come! I repeat it, sir, let it come!

It is in vain, sir, to extenuate [delay] the matter. Gentlemen may cry peace, peace - but there is no peace. The next gale that sweeps from the north will bring to our ears the clash of resounding arms!

Our brethren are already in the field! Why stand we here idle? What is it that gentlemen wish? What would they have? Is life so dear, or peace so sweet, as to be purchased at the price of chains and slavery? Forbid it, Almighty God! I know not what course others may take; but as for me, give me liberty, or give me death!

Group Discussion: *What does Patrick Henry claim is the choice that confronts the colonies in 1775? What arguments does he make to persuade his listeners that the colonies could win against the far superior forces of Great Britain?*

THOMAS PAINE'S COMMON SENSE

Thomas Paine immigrated to America from England after failing there at business and marriage. In January, 1776, he published Common Sense, *which instantly became a "best seller" in the colonies. The booklet helped convince many Americans to embrace the idea of independence. These are condensed excerpts.*

In the following pages I offer nothing more than simple facts, plain arguments, and common sense.

I challenge the warmest advocate for reconciliation to show a single advantage that this continent can reap by being connected with Great Britain.

But the injuries and disadvantages we sustain by that connection are without number. Any submission to, or dependence on, Great Britain tends directly to involve this continent in European wars and quarrels, and sets us at variance [at odds] with nations who would otherwise seek our friendship.

Everything that is right or natural pleads for a separation. Even the distance at which the Almighty has placed England and America, is a strong and natural proof that the authority of the one over the other was never the design of Heaven.

As to government matters, it is not in the power of Britain to do this continent justice. The business of it will soon be too weighty and intricate to be managed with any tolerable degree of convenience by a power so distant from us and so very ignorant of us. To be always running three or four thousand miles with a tale or petition, waiting four or five months for an answer, will in a few years be looked upon as folly and childishness.

Small islands not capable of protecting themselves are the proper objects for kingdoms to take under their care; but there is something very absurd in supposing a continent to be perpetually governed by an island.

O ye that love mankind! Ye that dare oppose, not only the tyranny, but the tyrant, stand forth!

Every spot of the old world is overrun with oppression. Freedom has been hunted around the globe. Asia and Africa have long expelled her. Europe regards her like a stranger, and England has given her warning to depart. O! receive the fugitive, and prepare in time an asylum [a safe place] for mankind.

We ought to reflect, that there are three different ways by which independence may be established; and that one of those three will, one day or another, be the fate of America: by the legal voice of the people in [the Continental] Congress; by a military power; or by a mob.

Should independence be brought about by the first of those means, we have every opportunity before us, to form the noblest, purest constitution on the face of the earth.

We have it in our power to begin the world over again. The birthday of a new world is at hand.

Group Discussion: *What do you think is Paine's best argument for breaking the colonies away from Great Britain? What does he think is happening around the world to the idea of freedom? What possibilities does he see for America if it becomes an independent country?*

THE DECLARATION OF INDEPENDENCE

The Enlightenment, social contract theory, Benjamin Franklin, John Hancock

In the spring of 1776, the Second Continental Congress was still debating whether to break completely with England when Thomas Jefferson was put on a committee to draw up a Declaration of Independence. The document included the ideas of many people, but Jefferson pulled it all together in brilliant language and form. The final version was approved on July 4, 1776, at the Pennsylvania State House in the city of _____. (The building is now called Independence Hall.) The Declaration can be divided into three main parts:

Part I. The first section says that the colonists want to explain why they are making the break with England. It also spells out a political theory that justifies such a break. This section draws on ideas about government that developed in an intellectual movement of that time called the Enlightenment. The English philosopher John Locke, for example, had written of the "natural rights" of individuals, and even suggested that people have a right to overthrow their government when their rights are _____. Find the copy of the Declaration in the Appendix, and complete the famous lines in this section which declare:

A. That individuals have "unalienable" rights that cannot be taken away:

"We hold these truths to be self-evident, that all men are created equal, that they are

_____

_____

_____ *of Happiness."*

B. That the only legitimate source of a government's power to rule and make laws is the consent or approval of the people themselves:

"That to secure these rights, Governments are instituted among Men, deriving their just

_____ *the governed."*

C. That if a government becomes abusive of the people's rights, the people have a right to abolish that government and form a new one:

"That whenever any Form of Government becomes destructive of these ends, it is the

_____ *abolish it ..."*

Part II.   The next section is a long list of specific complaints about King George III and the British Parliament. The delegates wanted to convince leaders in England and in other nations that the Americans were justified in their actions, and deserved support. For example, this part of the Declaration criticizes the King and Parliament:

"For cutting off our _____ with all parts of the world."

"For imposing _____ upon us without our Consent."

"For depriving us in many cases, of the benefits of Trial by _____."

Thomas Jefferson also wrote a passage critical of slavery in this section. But some colonies objected, and the passage was _____ to keep as much support for the document and the independence movement as possible. The delegates knew the vote for independence, when it came, had to be unanimous.

Part III.   The final section states that the colonists have tried to resolve or settle their differences with England, but without success. Therefore, the Declaration boldly announces in this section, *"these United Colonies are, and of right ought to be, _____*
_____."

The men who signed the Declaration were _____ wild-eyed radicals aiming for a complete overhaul of society. Many were quite prosperous men like John Hancock and Benjamin Franklin. Most simply objected to the idea that a far-away King or Parliament could arbitrarily make the _____ for the colonies. To protect what they considered their traditional English liberties, they were ready to endorse some very *untraditional* political language and action. But the American Revolution never slipped into the extreme radicalism that plagued so many later revolutions around the world.

In the last line of the Declaration, the signers pledged to each other *"our Lives, our Fortunes, and our sacred _____."* Some, in fact, lost their lives and fortunes before it all ended. But the document they signed remains famous as one of the _____ most powerful and most important political statements. Its ideas were laid out so clearly and forcefully that it often helped steer later events toward goals that might not even have been imagined in 1776.

Use these terms to fill in the blanks: abused, Free and Independent States, Honour [honor], Jury, laws, not, Philadelphia, removed, Taxes, Trade, world's

MAP - THE REVOLUTION'S FAMOUS PLACES

Draw three <u>lightly shaded</u> ovals on the map to show the three main stages of fighting in the Revolution. The list is divided to help you. For clarity, include in your ovals only places on the eastern half of the map. Finally, show the route of Gen. Cornwallis from Charleston to Yorktown and complete the key.

Lexington and **Concord,** the small towns outside Boston where the first shots of the Revolution were fired in April of 1775.

Fort Ticonderoga, a British outpost that the colonists captured in 1775.

Boston, where the Battle of Bunker Hill was fought in 1775. The British pulled out of Boston early in 1776 and sailed to their base in eastern Canada.

Montreal and **Quebec,** British cities the Americans attacked late in 1775. While victorious at Montreal, they could not take the more important city of Quebec.

New York City, where a British attack in July 1776 forced the Continental Army to retreat to Pennsylvania.

Trenton, where General Washington led a daring Christmas night raid across the Delaware River in 1776. The victory at Trenton boosted morale and kept the Revolution alive.

Philadelphia, which the British seized and held in 1777.

Saratoga, where American forces defeated one part of the British army in 1777. This victory became a turning point in the war, as France declared itself an ally of U.S.

Valley Forge, where the Continental Army under Washington camped late in 1777. The army suffered through a terribly cold winter with inadequate food and supplies.

Savannah, taken by the British in 1778 as they shifted their war effort to the South.

Charleston, where the American forces had their worst defeat of the war in 1780.

Cowpens and **Guilford Courthouse,** where the strength of the American forces early in 1781 sent British General Charles Cornwallis retreating to **Wilmington,** then into Virginia.

Yorktown, where the British under Gen. Cornwallis were trapped on a peninsula and defeated in October 1781 by the combined American and French forces.

Other important places:

Vincennes, where Americans seized an important British outpost in 1779.

New Orleans, in Spanish territory. When Spain joined the war as an ally of France, this port city became available for the American ships to use as a base.

West Point, a key American fort on the Hudson River. Benedict Arnold, a hero early in the Revolution, tried to betray the fort to the British in 1780.

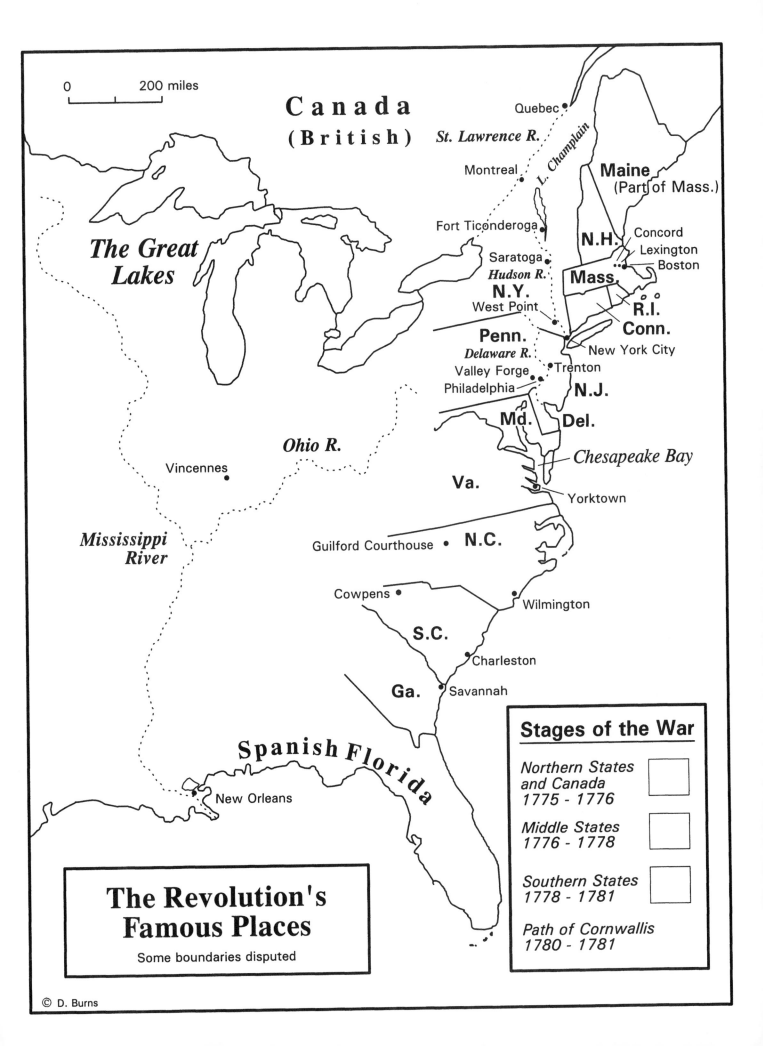

Canada
(British)

Quebec

St. Lawrence R.

Montreal

L. Champlain

Maine
(Part of Mass.)

0   200 miles

*The Great
Lakes*

Fort Ticonderoga

N.H.   Concord
         Lexington
Saratoga   Boston
Hudson R.
N.Y.   **Mass.**
West Point   **R.I.**
         Conn.
Penn.   New York City
Delaware R.
Valley Forge   Trenton
Philadelphia   **N.J.**

Ohio R.

Md.   **Del.**

Chesapeake Bay

Vincennes

Va.

Yorktown

*Mississippi
River*

Guilford Courthouse • **N.C.**

Cowpens •

Wilmington

S.C.

Charleston

Ga.   Savannah

S p a n i s h   F l o r i d a

New Orleans

Stages of the War

*Northern States
and Canada
1775 - 1776*

*Middle States
1776 - 1778*

*Southern States
1778 - 1781*

*Path of Cornwallis
1780 - 1781*

**The Revolution's
Famous Places**

Some boundaries disputed

© D. Burns

LIFE AND THOUGHT IN THE REVOLUTION

Loyalist/Tory, Patriots, Continental Army, Hessians, inflation, idealism,

Virginia Declaration of Rights, rule of law, legislature, constitutional government, republic

As the Revolution began, Americans faced a tough question: *Which side am I on?*

Perhaps one-third of the people were Loyalists (also called Tories) who did not want to break with England. Perhaps one-third were Patriots who were committed to the fight. Some of the rest might swing back and forth, depending on whose troops were in the neighborhood. In some areas, Loyalists were harassed into fleeing. In a few places, Loyalists organized and took up arms to _____ against the Patriots.

A revolutionary soldier's life was often very rough. At first, enthusiasm was high, and men of all social classes volunteered. But as the war dragged on, enlistment quotas in the Continental Army were often filled by poorer men who were paid bonuses to sign on for three years. Pay and bonuses, however, often were long overdue. Supplies ran short almost constantly. At the winter encampment at Valley Forge, many soldiers lacked the most basic items, like shoes and blankets. The British armies were far _____ equipped, and used hired German soldiers called Hessians as well. The remarkable thing is that George Washington was able to hold together an army at all under the circumstances.

One way or another, the Revolution affected everyone. Women often had to run the family _____ or business while their husbands were away. Some followed their husbands, and sometimes even joined the fighting itself, like the famous Molly Pitcher.

Blacks generally saw England in a different light than most whites as the fighting began. The English commanders promised freedom to all slaves who escaped and came to fight on the British side. Many did. Later, however, many blacks also served in the Continental Army. Indians generally sided with the _____.

Whatever their position, everyone was affected by the economic crisis. The volume of both imports and exports fell to almost nothing. People involved in trade often lost their businesses. Farmers who grew crops like _____ for export were hurt. Some of the unemployed people went into the army. On the other hand, craftsmen and women who could make guns, _____ cloth, or produce other needed items could easily sell them.

Money itself, however, quickly became unstable. The government borrowed money, but also met the expenses of war by simply printing more _____ money. The result was a rapid inflation of prices that ruined many people financially.

Yet alongside these problems, a powerful change was taking place in the average citizen's way of thinking about government. Before, people accepted the idea that political authority started at the _____ with a king. A colonist might vote, but he felt the "better" classes had the right to sit in the colonial assemblies and make decisions. Events of the Revolution, however, often brought ordinary people directly into the action. A spirit of idealism grew, and the old lines of social _____ and traditional authority seemed less important. Groups of citizens formed committees, discussed issues and took action, often without waiting for any official backing.

As the Revolution spread, citizens and leaders were thrilled by the job of creating the new state governments. Virginians meeting in 1776 to write their state constitution even added a breathtaking Declaration of Rights. This document, which later became the model for the U.S. Bill of Rights, describes virtually all of the principles of government that Americans live by even today. Political equality, free elections, freedom of the press, the free exercise of _____, the rule of law - all are listed as the basic foundation of the new state government formed by "the good people of Virginia."

The various state constitutions reveal a practical side, as well as idealism. Most set forth a system with a governor and a legislature, the pattern familiar since early colonial days. The legislature (the law-making branch) itself was typically divided into two separate parts or "houses." One house (often called the Assembly) would represent the average citizen. The other part (usually called the Senate) would represent the _____, who were better educated and more experienced in governmental affairs. Each center of power would serve to balance the others.

But the idea that political authority ultimately resides in "the people" got a powerful push forward as the Revolution unfolded. It became accepted that the new state constitutions should be written, not by existing government bodies, but by special conventions of citizens. The resulting documents had to be approved by a vote of the people. Only then did a legitimate government truly spring to life, with its rules and especially its _____ clearly listed. This concept of constitutional government was one of the most important results of the Revolution, and survives to this day as the cornerstone of liberty in our republic.

Use these terms to fill in the blanks: *better, British, class, farm, fight, limits, paper, religion, tobacco, top, wealthy, weave*

The Revolution created a large and sudden need for money to pay soldiers and buy supplies. The Continental Congress met that need in part by printing paper money called Continentals. Complete the bar graph below to show how the value of the new money fell as more and more of the paper dollars were issued.

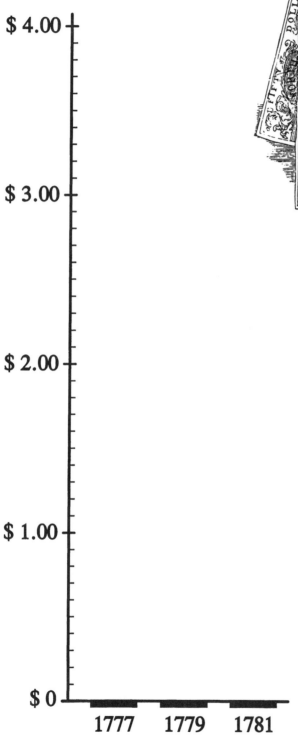

Use the table below to find the information to complete the bar graph on the left. Draw a vertical bar for each year, with the length corresponding to the actual value of $10.00 in the Continental paper currency.

Year	Actual Value of $10.00 Continental Paper Currency*
1777	$ 3.33
1779	$ .25
1781	$ .07

* approximations based on exchange rates, which could vary widely

Actual Value of $10.00 Continental Paper Currency

The war with Great Britain ended most American trade with British merchants for the duration of the conflict. In fact, the war made trade of any kind very difficult to conduct. Complete the bar graph below to show the impact on America's exports. What groups would have been hurt most by the trends shown on these pages?

Use the table below to find the information to complete the bar graph on the right. Draw a vertical bar for each year, with the length corresponding to the value of exports.

Year	Exports (Value in British Pounds Sterling)
1774	1,373,846
1776	103,964
1778	17,694

source: *Historical Statistics of the United States*

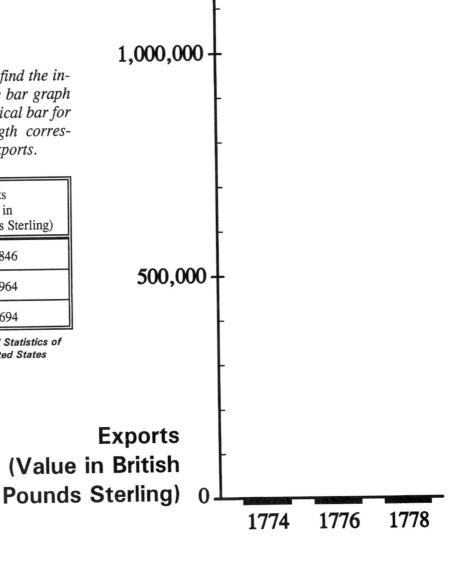

ABIGAIL ADAMS CALLS FOR WOMEN'S RIGHTS

The start of the rebellion against British rule led colonists to think in fresh ways about liberty. Abigail Adams began thinking about the fact that English laws often put women in a very disadvantaged position. (Divorce was almost impossible, for example, and husbands held legal power over property in a marriage.)

In March of 1776 Abigail wrote a now famous letter to her husband, John Adams, who was in Philadelphia meeting with other leaders at the Continental Congress. These condensed excerpts use the spelling found in the original letters.

I long to hear that you have declared an independancy -- and by the way in the new Code of Laws which I suppose it will be necessary for you to make I would desire you would Remember the Ladies, and be more generous and favourable to them than your ancestors.

Do not put such unlimited power into the hands of the Husbands. Remember all Men would be tyrants if they could.

If perticuliar care and attention is not paid to the Laidies we are determined to forment [begin] a Rebellion, and will not hold ourselves bound by any Laws in which we have no voice, or Representation.

That your Sex are Naturally Tyrannical is a Truth so thoroughly established as to admit of no dispute, but such of you as wish to be happy willingly give up the harsh title of Master for the more tender and endearing one of Friend.

Why then, not put it out of the power of the vicious and the Lawless to use us with cruelty and indignity. Men of Sense in all Ages abhor [despise] those customs which treat us only as the vassals [servants] of your Sex. - *Abigail Adams*

John wrote back from Philadelphia to his wife in a partly serious and partly joking style. He agrees that the legal system favors males. But he makes the bold claim that in practice (as opposed to legal theory) women actually have great power over men. Changing the laws, he argues, would give women ("the Petticoat") complete power ("Despotism") over men.

As to your extraordinary Code of Laws, I cannot but laugh.

Depend upon it, We know better than to repeal our Masculine systems. Altho they are in full Force, you know they are little more than Theory. We dare not exert our Power in its full Latitude.

We are obliged to go fair, and softly, and in Practice you know We are the subjects [the ones who are ruled].

We have only the Name of Masters, and rather than give up this, which would compleatly subject Us to the Despotism of the Petticoat, I hope General Washington, and all our brave Heroes would fight.

- *John Adams*

Abigail was not convinced by John's arguments. From their home near Boston, she sent her husband a letter predicting (correctly) that someday the laws that limited women's rights would be changed.

Group Discussion: *What is the main argument Abigail uses to justify women's right to rebel against laws that put them at a disadvantage? How is her argument similar to the arguments used by the colonists against British rule? What do you think of John's arguments?*

A REVOLUTIONARY DEFENSE

Defending the new nation against the powerful British army and navy forced the Americans to try new ideas and adopt new tactics. One famous example is shown here. It was the world's first combat submarine, built by a Connecticut man in 1776.

It was sent against a British warship in the harbor of New York City. The submarine's drill bit could not penetrate a metal plate on the ship's hull, however, so the torpedo could not be attached. The submarine headed back to the shore, and released the torpedo.

An hour later, the torpedo exploded on the water's surface, giving the British a very bad scare and prompting them to move their ships to a safer location.

Study both drawings, then label the parts of the submarine with the letters shown.

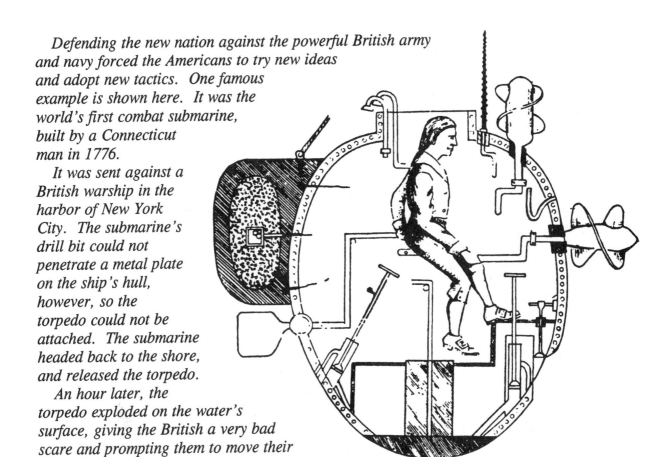

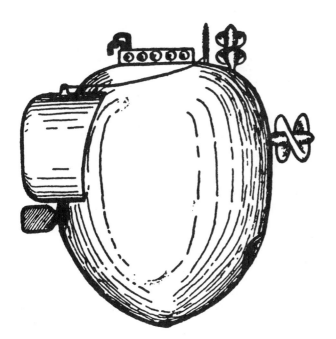

Design of the *Turtle*

A - Propellers

B - Rudder

C - Torpedo (*Filled with gunpowder, it is carried on the back of the submarine. A clockwork timer sets it off an hour after it is attached to an enemy ship.*)

D - Drill bit (*It is cranked into a ship's wooden hull, and holds the torpedo in place with a rope. The drill bit and the torpedo detach from the submarine.*)

THE CHALLENGES OF VICTORY

Articles of Confederation, James Madison, Federalists, Anti-Federalists

The victory at Yorktown won independence from England. The peace treaty signed in 1783 vastly expanded the new nation's territory all the way out to the Mississippi River. But Americans discovered that winning independence didn't automatically settle everything.

Many Americans had died in the cause, perhaps 25 thousand or more. Many farms and towns had been _____ by raids and fighting. Trade, especially exports, had been badly hurt. The paper currency issued by the Continental Congress to finance the fight was worth only a small fraction of its original value. No one had a clear idea what the future might bring.

Loyalists, who had sided with England, were in an especially ticklish situation. Fortunately, there were few violent attacks or reprisals against them. But tens of thousands decided to emigrate to Canada or England when the British troops sailed away.

The Revolution led to laws ending slavery in many of the northern states. Slavery, these states said, was not at all compatible with the ideas of liberty on which the Revolution itself was based. (Of course, it helped that these states never had very many slaves to begin with.) Southern states did not follow their lead, but some, like Virginia, made it much easier for owners to _____ their slaves. Communities of free blacks began growing more rapidly.

The Revolution also helped spread the spirit of religious tolerance. Visitors often remarked on the _____ of the churches and beliefs that could be found in American cities.

ARTICLES
OF
Confederation
AND
Perpetual Union
BETWEEN THE
S T A T E S

Of all the challenges of the years after the Revolution, the toughest was finding an answer to the question: *Just what is "The United States"?*

The nation was only a loose association of independent states under the Articles of Confederation when the Revolution ended. This system or form of government didn't work so well. The national level of government had too little power. For example, it could not regulate foreign trade, or even trade between states. It had no power to collect money directly with _____. It didn't even have a permanent place to hold meetings.

This early national government had some accomplishments. One was a decision to give the unsettled territories to the west the right to form into new states, and enter the Union on an equal footing with the original states. But within five years of the Yorktown victory, even the original states seemed to be falling _____. Luckily, some of the most capable leaders saw what was happening, and called for a special meeting or convention to be held in Philadelphia in the spring of 1787.

The convention's delegates soon realized that the problems in the Articles of Confederation system couldn't just be given a quick fix-up. James Madison, from Virginia, played a key role as they worked through the summer to develop something completely _____. The meetings were closed to everyone but the delegates themselves. It was an idea that people accepted only because _____ was named as the chairman of the meetings.

The delegates had a tough job designing a system that left the states with most of the power they wanted, but also created a stronger national government. By September, a compromise plan was worked out which _____ power among different branches and levels of government.

The proposed Constitution faced some stiff opposition from people who feared that a stronger national government might become as bad as King George. These opponents were called Anti-Federalists. They basically thought that a good government was a _____ sized government.

But supporters (called Federalists) campaigned hard for the new system. They wrote essays and articles in _____. They promoted the fact that many of the big names of the Revolution were supporting the change. (Alexander Hamilton was among the most famous of the Federalists, and his essays on the Constitution are widely read even today.) People who feared the new system might someday lead to a loss of individual liberty were promised that a _____ of Rights would soon be added to the document.

THE

FEDERALIST:

A COLLECTION

OF

E S S A Y S

WRITTEN IN FAVOUR OF THE

NEW CONSTITUTION

By the next summer, 1788, the Constitution was approved by nine states and went into effect. (The rest gave approval by the end of 1790.) George Washington was picked as the first president by a group of special electors chosen by the states. He took office in _____ City in 1789.

Use these terms to fill in the blanks: *apart, Bill, destroyed, diversity, divided, free, George Washington, new, New York, newspapers, small, taxes*

THE CONSTITUTION

federalism, separation of powers, checks and balances, branches of the federal government,

judicial review, House of Representatives, Senate, Electoral College, ratify, amendment

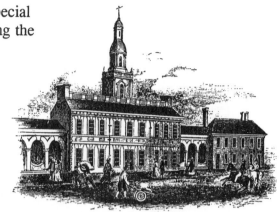

The Constitution was written by delegates to a special convention that met in the city of Philadelphia during the summer of 1787. The leaders who met there were concerned that the government formed during the Revolution by the Articles of Confederation was not working well. In fact, the nation was almost falling apart. Unable to propose an easy "fix" for that system, they wrote an entirely new document.

During the Revolution, many people believed that the struggle for independence would inspire citizens and state leaders to work selflessly for the good of the entire nation. But various conflicts that developed by 1787 showed that this expectation was not very realistic. The new government system designed at the Constitutional Convention assumes free people will often _____ about important issues and push for their own interests. It also recognizes the fact that anyone with too much _____ is likely to abuse it.

The Constitution the delegates wrote is based on three important principles: **federalism**, **separation of powers**, and a system of **checks and balances**. For example:

1. The document splits the big jobs of government between the national level and the state level. This split system is called federalism. The national level has control of matters like foreign relations and coining money. The states kept control of highways, education, marriage and divorce laws, punishment of most _____, etc.

2. The powers of the national (federal) government are further separated into three branches. Each branch is given certain specific powers to "check" or limit unwise actions by the other branches. The branches, and their basic functions, are these:

    A. _____ *Branch - makes the laws for the nation. The Congress is in this branch.*

    B. _____ *Branch - proposes policy; carries out the laws; makes treaties. The president is the head of this branch and also serves as commander in chief of the armed forces.*

    C. _____ *Branch - interprets the laws. It includes the Supreme Court.*

In a famous legal case in 1803 called *Marbury* v. *Madison*, the Supreme Court claimed for itself the right of "judicial review." That means the Supreme Court has the final say on whether laws and actions of the government are constitutional or unconstitutional.

3. Another important separation and balancing of power occurs within the legislative branch itself. A "two-house" or bicameral system was devised for the Congress. The House of Representatives was designed to bring in the views of the average American citizen and voter. The Senate was designed to bring in the views of the wealthier, better educated, and more experienced citizens. Proposed laws must pass _____ houses.

This two-house approach solved a big headache for the delegates. Should all states have the same number of representatives in the Congress, or should the big states have more? The "Great Compromise" gave each state _____ senators. But the number of seats each state gets in the House of Representatives is based on the population of that state. Senators serve six year terms, while members of the House face election much more often, every two years.

We the People of the
insure domestic Tranquility, provide for the common defense,
and our Posterity, do ordain and establish this Constitution for
Article I

The opening paragraph of the Constitution, called the Preamble, begins with the famous phrase "*We the People*." But many delegates feared that putting too much power directly into the hands of the people could be dangerous, and lead to mob rule. So a check was placed on the power of the people in the presidential election. The president is elected by an indirect or two-step process. The citizens' vote - called the _____ vote - selects the members of a group called the Electoral College. That group then casts the ballots that actually elect the president. (The details are a bit complicated, but the system has proven to be a good one.)

Remember that the Constitution does not offer a guarantee that everyone will live or act the way we might want them to. It recognizes that citizens must first be _____ who think and act freely within the law. In such a society there will always be disagreements about public policy. On most matters the Constitution does not dictate, but rather forces all sides to talk and reach a _____ as part of the political process.

At the same time, the Constitution sets up an open, free society in which citizens can steadily improve their own lives and the character of the nation. Despite some opposition, the Constitution was ratified (formally approved) by the states in 1788. It was amended to add a Bill of Rights a few years later. That listing provides additional limits or checks on the powers of the government in order to protect citizens' rights. Other amendments have been made since, as Americans tackled important issues like ending slavery (the 13th Amendment), problems created by _____ (the 18th), and women's voting rights (the 19th).

Use these terms to fill in the blanks: alcohol, both, compromise, crimes, disagree, Executive, individuals, Judicial, Legislative, power, popular, two

THE BILL OF RIGHTS

search warrant, due process, grand jury, "take the fifth," civil lawsuit, common law, bail

The Bill of Rights was added to the U.S. Constitution in 1791 to satisfy people who had questioned the wisdom of creating a much stronger federal government. At the time, many people feared that a strong national government might eventually grow out of control and try to grab too much power. But the idea of a list of limits on government power wasn't entirely new. Many states had listings of basic rights in their own state constitutions. In fact, the Bill of Rights is largely modeled on the Virginia Declaration of Rights, adopted in that state in 1776.

Here are some of the key rights protected by these first ten amendments to the Constitution:

1. Your first amendment rights include freedom of religion, freedom of speech, and freedom of the press. They also include the right to assemble or _____ together with other citizens. You have a right to petition the government for the "redress of grievances." That means you have a right to have your concerns heard by government officials.

2. This amendment guarantees that you have a right to "keep and bear arms," so that citizen militia units could be organized if necessary to _____ the nation. The debate over gun safety and crime in recent decades has often put this amendment in hot controversy.

3. Remember the Quartering Act that sometimes required the American colonists to provide a room in their homes for British soldiers? This amendment states that in peacetime the government cannot house troops in a private home without the owner's _____.

4. This amendment says that the government cannot search you or your _____ without a search warrant issued by a judge. The judge will first require reasonable evidence, called "probable cause," to justify the search.

5. If the government takes any action against you, they must follow due process of law. That means they must follow all the legal rules. You cannot be put on trial for a crime unless a group of citizens, serving on a grand jury, agrees that there is enough _____ to proceed. You cannot be made to testify against yourself - you can "take the fifth" and remain silent. The government cannot try you twice for the same crime. This amendment also says that the government cannot take your property without fair payment.

6. If you are charged with a crime, you have a right to a speedy and public trial before a jury of your fellow citizens. The government has to tell you exactly what law you have broken. If there are witnesses, their testimony must be made in _____ of you, so you know exactly what is going on. Since the workings of law can be pretty complicated, you have a right to a lawyer to help you make your defense.

7. If a civil lawsuit involving over twenty dollars is brought against you by another citizen or group, you have a right to a trial by a _____. The court must follow the customary legal practices and court rulings that have been made in previous cases, called the common law.

8. If you are charged with a crime, the bail can't be set excessively high. (Bail is the term for money you may be required to put up to guarantee you will show up for the trial.) If you are convicted, the punishment cannot be _____ or unusual. The amendment doesn't specify exactly what this means, so some disputes still exist on issues like the death penalty.

9. Citizens have _____ rights other than those specifically listed in the Constitution and Bill of Rights. Even though they may not be listed, the government can't step on them.

10. The federal government can only claim powers that are specifically listed in the Constitution. All other powers belong to the _____ level of government or to the people themselves. In spite of this amendment, the power of the federal government has grown enormously in modern times, prompting considerable political debate.

The Bill of Rights did not automatically end all danger of abuse by government power. Slavery, of course, was a direct affront to the principles it contains. Native Americans were often _____ of their rights as the nation expanded. In a few cases, laws have been passed which trampled even more broadly on basic rights. In 1798 a law called the Sedition Act was passed by Congress, which was angered by criticism in certain newspapers. The new law declared criticism of government officials a crime. The Sedition Act was widely protested, and enforcement of it was soon stopped. But the attempt remains a good example of the reason why specific written _____ on government power are needed.

Today the Bill of Rights is still constantly cited in courthouses across America whenever disputes involving citizens' rights and government power are decided. For more than 200 years, it has remained a powerful shield for people in America working to protect their basic civil rights.

Use these terms to fill in the blanks: cruel, defend, deprived, evidence, front, home, jury, limits, many, meet, permission, state

THE NATIONAL GOVERNMENT ORGANIZES

Cabinet, Whiskey Rebellion, Alexander Hamilton, John Adams, Sedition Act

George Washington was cheered nationwide when he took office as the country's first president in New York City in 1789. There the great task of transforming a paper constitution into a working government began under his leadership and that of vice-president John Adams.

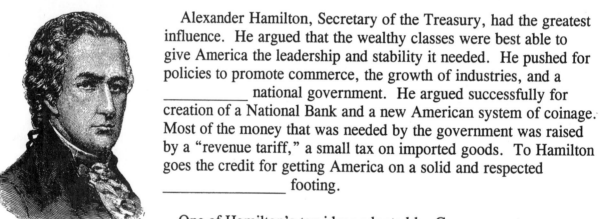

The new Congress was also ready to begin work. One of their first tasks was creating several "executive departments." These were the Department of State (to handle foreign affairs), the Department of the Treasury (to handle money matters), and the Department of War (to manage the military). An Attorney General was named to handle legal matters. The men Washington chose to head these departments and offices became his closest _____, and were called his Cabinet. Their influence on issues and events in these early years was enormous, and remains visible to this day.

Alexander Hamilton, Secretary of the Treasury, had the greatest influence. He argued that the wealthy classes were best able to give America the leadership and stability it needed. He pushed for policies to promote commerce, the growth of industries, and a _____ national government. He argued successfully for creation of a National Bank and a new American system of coinage. Most of the money that was needed by the government was raised by a "revenue tariff," a small tax on imported goods. To Hamilton goes the credit for getting America on a solid and respected _____ footing.

One of Hamilton's tax ideas adopted by Congress, a tax on whiskey production, led to a small but historic conflict. Farmers in western Pennsylvania refused to pay the tax, and even threatened federal tax collectors. Washington sent in troops to put down this "Whiskey Rebellion." The fact that order was quickly restored without bloodshed solidified the power and prestige of the _____ government at a critical time.

Thomas Jefferson, Secretary of State, often opposed Hamilton's vision of America's future. America should be built on a foundation of small farms and virtuous, freedom-loving farmers, he believed. That would best protect the Revolutionary ideals of liberty and _____. Growing cities, industry, and commerce would lead, he feared, to great inequality of conditions, and eventually kill the spirit of democracy. Jefferson also resented Hamilton's policies that favored the wealthy. Events in later decades moved America _____ from Jefferson's vision. But his faith in the wisdom of ordinary citizens, democracy, and open discussion of all issues remains a vital part of American life.

Next to finance, the biggest domestic issue was trouble on the western frontier. Fighting by settlers and Native Americans over land was killing thousands of people. In the area south of the Ohio River, treaties were signed with the Cherokee (1791) and other tribes. This accelerated settlement of lands that soon became the new _____ of Kentucky and Tennessee. Further north, resistance by Indians caused Washington to send in troops. By 1795 Native Americans were forced to surrender most of present-day Ohio. Settlers poured into the region, which officially became a state in 1803.

Some of the most difficult decisions in these early years concerned foreign relations. When war broke out between Great Britain and France in 1793, at the end of the French Revolution, American leaders faced a real dilemma. The French had helped America win its own Revolution, and now expected _____ in return. But America was in no shape to oppose the British navy on the seas, and could not afford losing its profitable trade with British merchants. George Washington, urged by Hamilton, issued a Proclamation of Neutrality. This kept America _____ of the war, in spite of some troublesome incidents provoked by both sides in the European conflict.

Washington was re-elected with no opposition in 1792. But with the approach of the election of 1796, he decided to step down. Now a new development appeared: political parties. Followers of Jefferson organized into a group that called itself the Republicans, and later, the Democratic-Republican Party. Followers of Hamilton also organized, and called themselves Federalists. (It was the same name used by those who pushed for approval of the _____ some years earlier.)

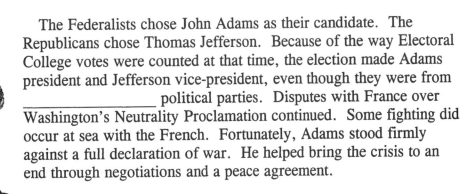

The Federalists chose John Adams as their candidate. The Republicans chose Thomas Jefferson. Because of the way Electoral College votes were counted at that time, the election made Adams president and Jefferson vice-president, even though they were from _____ political parties. Disputes with France over Washington's Neutrality Proclamation continued. Some fighting did occur at sea with the French. Fortunately, Adams stood firmly against a full declaration of war. He helped bring the crisis to an end through negotiations and a peace agreement.

The Federalists actually planted the seeds of their own political decline in these years. In Congress, they pushed through several laws that were blatant attempts to unfairly undermine their political opponents. The Sedition Act was one. This law made it a crime to speak or publish criticism of the federal government or its officers. Jefferson and the Republicans rallied public anger _____ the law, and against the snobby attitude that seemed to motivate many of the Federalists. The election of 1800 gave Thomas Jefferson the presidency. He was the first president inaugurated (sworn into office) in the new capital built beside the Potomac River: Washington, D.C.

Use these terms to fill in the blanks: advisors, against, away, Constitution, different, equality, federal, financial, help, out, states, strong

FIRST IMPRESSIONS OF A NEW NATION

These condensed excerpts are from a book by a German visitor, Johann Schoepf. He was a surgeon with the Hessian troops who fought on the side of the British. With peace established in 1783, he decided to take a trip through the new nation before returning home. He gave an especially complete account of Philadelphia.

Who in the fatherland [Germany] has not heard of Philadelphia? William Penn, well known in history, founded the city in 1682, and in the space of 100 years it has grown to a notable size. The city, if not greatly beyond others in America in wealth and number of houses, far surpasses them all in learning, in the arts, and public spirit.

Throughout the city the streets are well paved and well kept. At night the city is lit by lanterns placed on posts. The streets are kept clean and in good order by the householders themselves. Appointed night-watchmen call out the hours and the state of the weather.

Behind each house is a little court or garden, where usually are the necessaries [out-houses]. The kitchen, stable, etc., are all placed in buildings at the side or behind, kitchens often underground.

In the matter of interior decorations the English style is imitated here as throughout America. The taste generally is for living in a clean and orderly manner, without the continual scrubbing of the Hollanders or the frippery and gilt [fancy style] of the French. The rooms are in general built with open fire-places.

The number of inhabitants at present is placed at thirty to forty thousand - with what certainty I am not prepared to say. A strict numbering of the inhabitants is difficult in America, where people are continually moving about, leaving a place or coming in.

Pennsylvania, and in consequence Philadelphia, assures freedom to all religious sects. Men of all faiths, and many of none, dwell together in harmony and peace. The spirit of tolerance has gone so far that different religious sects have assisted one another in the building of houses of worship. At the present time there are in Philadelphia more than thirty such buildings.

A college in Philadelphia founded for the instruction of the young was raised to a University in the year 1780. The University consists of two departments, the Academy or lower preparatory schools for younger students, and the University proper, where the higher sciences, Philosophy, Mathematics, and Medicine are taught.

The science of Medicine has the most Professors. None of them has a fixed salary, but they earn considerable sums, according to the number of those attending their lectures. Candidates for the degree of Doctor in Medicine, it is said, are exactly and strictly examined. But with the degree the practitioner has no advantage over other practitioners and bunglers, except as he himself chooses to make much of his diploma.

In America every man who is in the curing trade is known without distinction as Doctor, as elsewhere every person who makes verses is a poet, so there are both bad doctors and quacks [deliberate frauds] in abundance.

Libraries also Philadelphia possesses. A taste for reading is pretty wide-spread. People of all classes use the library on Carpenter Street. Benjamin Franklin, supported particularly by Quakers, began this library as early as 1732 by the creation of a Reading

Society. The rooms are open to the public twice a week in the afternoon, but the members of the society have access every day. In an adjoining room several mathematical and physical instruments are also kept, as also a collection of American minerals.

There are eight to ten newspapers, weekly sheets in large folio [folded paper]. Of them all the *Independent Chronicle* is the favorite on account of its freedom in regard to public affairs. Liberty of the press was one of the fundamental laws which the states included in the design of their new governments.

It arouses the sympathies to see how often the Congress is mistreated in these sheets. The financier, Bob Morris, recently found himself slandered [falsely criticized] by an article in the *Independent Chronicle* and began a lawsuit. But the public supported the printer and as free citizens asserted their right to communicate to one another their opinions regarding the conduct of public officials. But it must be said that through the misuse of so special a privilege great harm may arise. How many upright and innocent characters are roughly treated under the shield of the freedom of the press!

People think, act, and speak here precisely as it prompts them. The poorest day-laborer on the bank of the Delaware River holds it his right to advance his opinion, in religious as well as political matters, with as much freedom as the gentleman or the scholar. And as yet there is to be found as little distinction of rank among the inhabitants of Philadelphia as in any city in the world.

No one admits that the Governor has any particular superiority over the private citizen except in so far as he is the right hand of the law, and the law equally regards and deals with all citizens. Riches make no difference, because in this regard every man expects at one time or another to be on a footing with his rich neighbor. Rank of birth is not recognized, and is resisted with a total force.

The Philadelphia market deserves a visit from every foreigner. Astonishment is excited not only by the  extraordinary store of provisions but also by the cleanliness and the good order in which the stock is exposed for sale. On the evenings before the chief market days (Wednesdays and Saturdays) all the bells in the city are rung. People come into Philadelphia in great covered wagons. Numerous carts and horses bring in from all directions the rich surplus of the countryside. Everything is full of life and action.

Besides the customary sorts of meat, Europeans find in season several dishes new to them, such as raccoons, opossums, otters, bear-bacon and bear's foot, as well as many local birds and fishes. All sorts of melons and many kinds of pumpkins are seen in great quantity, and fruits also.

The war has left no sign of want [poverty or shortages] here. The inhabitants are not only well clothed but well fed, and comparatively, better than in Europe.

1. Highlight at least six sentences in this account that in your judgement make important or interesting observations about what Americans were like in the 1780s.

Group Discussion: *What were Americans like, and what did they value, in the 1780s? What aspects of American life described here have changed since this account was written? What aspects of American life have not changed?*

CHARTING THE FIRST CENSUS

The first official U.S. census was made in 1790, and a new census is made every ten years. Many census figures can be found in **Historical Statistics of the United States** *and* **Statistical Abstract of the United States**. *Both are government publications, and are available in many libraries. Complete the bar graphs below to show some of the basic population changes revealed by statistics from these sources.*

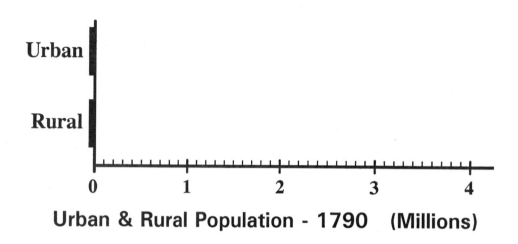

Urban & Rural Population - 1790   (Millions)

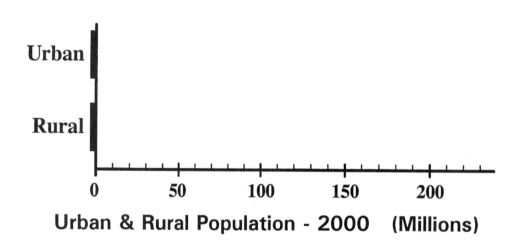

Urban & Rural Population - 2000   (Millions)

Use the table below to find the information to complete the bar graphs. Draw horizontal bars of the appropriate length to show the <u>urban</u> *and* <u>rural</u> *population for the years shown.*

Year	Total Population (Millions)	Urban Population (Millions)	Rural Population (Millions)
1790	3.9	.2	3.7
2000	281	226	55

sources: *Historical Statistics of the United States* and *Statistical Abstract of the United States.*

Complete the pie chart below to show the ethnic and national backgrounds of Americans in the census year 1790. How has the pattern changed in the years since that time?

Ethnic and National Backgrounds of Americans - 1790
Total Population: 3.9 Million

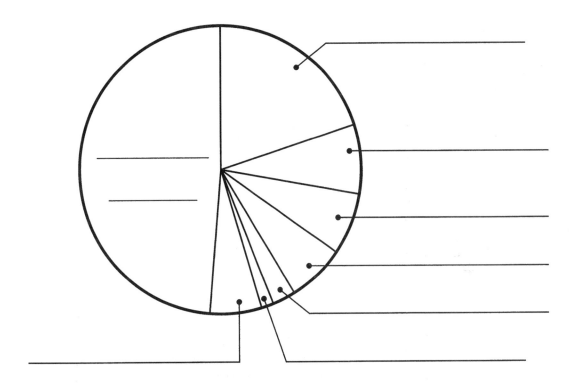

Use the table below to complete the pie chart. Show each group and its percent of the total American population on the lines provided. Be sure to add the "%" sign. The pie chart starts with the English on the left, and moves clockwise in order, ending with "Other" at the bottom.

Group	Percent of Total	Group	Percent of Total
English	48.7	Scottish	6.6
African	20	Dutch	2.7
Irish	7.8	French	1.4
German	7	Other	5.8

source: *Historical Statistics of the United States*

4 | The Growing Years: 1800 - 1860

*"Oh, say, does that star-spangled banner yet wave,
O'er the land of the free and the home of the brave?"*

"Go West, young man!"

"We hold these truths to be self-evident: that all men and women are created equal."

"A house divided against itself cannot stand. I believe this government cannot endure permanently half slave and half free.

Study Checklist

When you have completed this section, working with the Internet support site at
www.fasttrackteaching.com or other resources, you should be able to:

 Identify and explain the context of the **Famous Quotes** shown on the Section Title Page.

 Identify and explain the importance of the **Famous Names and Terms** listed on the topic summary pages in this section.

 Identify on a map and explain the importance of the **Famous Places** shown on the maps in this section.

 Explain the general sequence of events in this period and tell from memory the **Famous Years**:

- Thomas Jefferson was elected president (**1800**).
- The Erie Canal was opened (**1825**).
- The California Gold Rush occurred (**1849**).
- Abraham Lincoln was elected president (**1860**).

Take a Practice Test!

A multiple-choice practice test for this section can be found on the Internet support site at:

www.fasttrackteaching.com

Textbook Page References:

 Discuss or write briefly on such questions and topics as these:

1. Explain what Manifest Destiny meant to Americans in the 1800s. What were the main reasons Americans moved westward in the years from 1800 to 1860?

2. How did improvements in transportation in the early 1800s contribute to the growth of America?

3. Explain why the factory system began growing rapidly in America in the decades after 1800. Describe the impact the Industrial Revolution had on American life and on workers.

4. Explain briefly the concerns and goals of social reformers working on each of these issues: women's rights; slavery; factory conditions; the mentally ill.

5. What opportunities did immigrants to America find between 1800 and 1860? What problems did they face?

6. Explain how the developments of this era tended to split the nation apart into two sections, North and South. Why did their differences finally reach the breaking point in 1860?

Timeline 1800 - 1860

Find when these events occurred, fill in the blanks, and place them on the main timeline. The thin timeline shows the presidents of this period.

Jefferson elected - Thomas Jefferson was the _____ president of the United States.

Louisiana Purchase - The U.S. got it from _____ for $15 million dollars.

Lewis and Clark expedition - They explored as far west as the _____ Ocean.

First steamboat - Called the *Clermont*, it was invented by Robert _____.

War of 1812 - It gave us our National _____, *The Star-Spangled Banner*.

Factories grow in Lowell, Mass. - It was one sign of the _____ Revolution.

Erie Canal opens - It opened an easy water route into the _____ Lakes area.

First railroad in U.S. - It was a short line built by the Baltimore and Ohio Railroad Company, and made history by using the first American built steam locomotive, named the _____.

Indian Removal Act - It encouraged the federal government to negotiate deals with Eastern Indians to move their tribes to areas _____ of the Mississippi.

***The Liberator* begins** - This newspaper fought to _____ slavery.

Texas declares independence - Within ten years, it _____ the U.S. as a state.

Telegraph demonstrated - It was invented by Samuel _____.

Mexican War begins - It forced Mexico to _____ the Mexican Cession to the U.S.

Women's Rights Convention - It was held in _____ Falls, New York.

California Gold Rush - Gold was discovered at _____ Mill.

***Uncle Tom's Cabin* published** - This book gave a horrifying picture of _____ life.

John Brown's raid - He intended to seize _____ and start a slave rebellion.

Lincoln elected - His election convinced _____ Carolina to leave the Union.

Use these terms to fill in the blanks: abolish, Anthem, France, Fulton, Great, guns, Industrial, joined, Morse, Pacific, sell, Seneca, slave, South, Sutter's, third, Tom Thumb, west

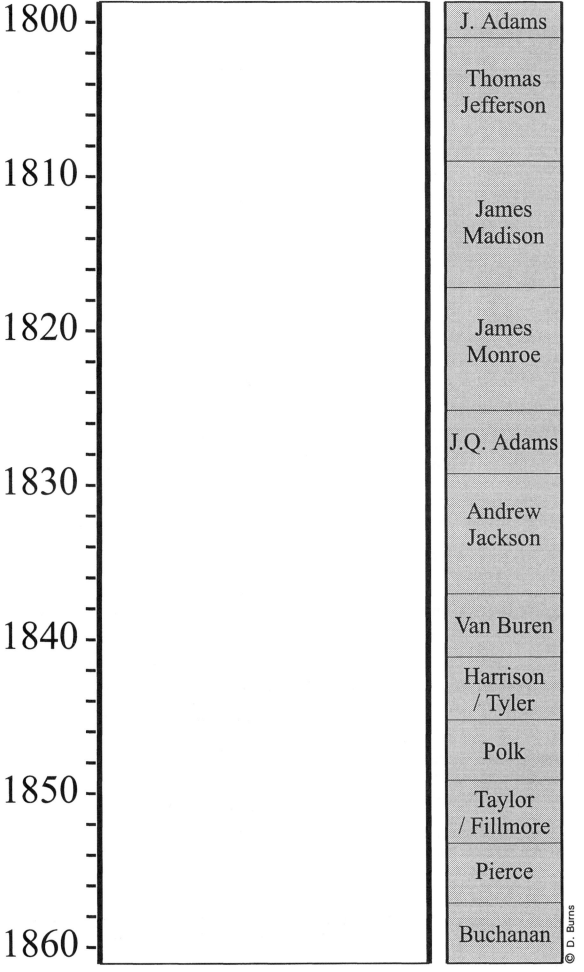

1800 —

1810 —

1820 —

1830 —

1840 —

1850 —

1860 —

J. Adams

Thomas Jefferson

James Madison

James Monroe

J.Q. Adams

Andrew Jackson

Van Buren

Harrison / Tyler

Polk

Taylor / Fillmore

Pierce

Buchanan

TIMELINE: THE GROWING YEARS

© D. Burns

THE GROWING YEARS: AN OVERVIEW

Thomas Jefferson, War of 1812, Manifest Destiny, Industrial Revolution, telegraph,

cotton gin, Monroe Doctrine, Andrew Jackson, egalitarian

The decades after 1800 were years of incredible growth and change in America. As Thomas Jefferson was elected, most people farmed their land by hand with simple tools. Most still lived east of the Appalachian mountain range in the original 13 states. Manufacturing was done in small shops or at home. Craftsmen produced shoes, wagons, guns, or shirts one by _____. There were few big cities, and the small communities where most people lived would strike us as strangely quiet and isolated. All this would change dramatically by 1860.

Daniel Boone had marked a path into what is now Tennessee and Kentucky even before 1800. Further north, settlement by Americans of the area near the Great Lakes was one factor that helped provoke the War of 1812 with England. But that conflict was only a brief interruption to steady westward growth. There was the vast territory of the Louisiana Purchase beyond the Mississippi River, added in 1803. Within a few decades, many people were saying that the nation's "Manifest Destiny" was to stretch out to the Pacific Ocean. A war with Mexico, and the California _____ Rush of 1849, cinched the matter. But as the nation spread west, Indians steadily lost their lands.

This era saw fantastic improvements in transportation. In 1800 most roads were poor. Soon, however, canals like the Erie Canal in New York State opened easier routes to the West. They also cut the cost of shipping farm crops and manufactured goods dramatically - in some cases by 90 percent. The steamboat quickly matched their success, because it could easily go _____ in rivers like the Mississippi and the Ohio, or navigate the Great Lakes. After about 1830 railroad tracks began to spread rapidly across the landscape.

Most of the changes of this era were linked to the Industrial Revolution, which is the change from hand production to production by _____. It was underway by 1820 and led to big changes in the lives of working people, and in society itself.

Cities and factory towns, mostly in the northern half of the country, grew very rapidly. Manufactured cloth and other products became less expensive. Experiments with electricity led to the invention of the telegraph, which sent messages almost instantly across wires. Improved printing methods made magazines, newspapers, and _____ much more widely available. Farms, too, felt the impact of the Industrial Revolution, as new steel plows and machines like Cyrus McCormick's reaper were developed.

But the Industrial Revolution brought some big problems, as well as many benefits. Factories themselves were often dangerous and hours were long. But the average worker's only choice was: take it or _____ it. The rapid growth of cities created conditions of poverty and often, political corruption. In the South, there were fewer factories than in the North. But a machine called the cotton gin was invented in 1793. It simplified the task of removing _____ from cotton. Very quickly, the cotton crop became large and important in the South. This greatly expanded the demand for slaves.

There were, however, many hopeful signs for the young republic. An attitude of progress and inventiveness was widespread. One sign of America's growing confidence was the Monroe Doctrine. Issued by President James Monroe in 1823, it warned the European nations that they must not attempt to interfere with the nations in the Western Hemisphere.

The election of Andrew Jackson in 1828 marked a new surge of "the common man" in the nation's democratic system. He was the first president born west of the Appalachian Mountains, and had risen from poverty. His presidential campaign and success helped create the lively free-wheeling style of American _____ that survives to this day. His years in office are often referred to as "The Age of Jackson."

The problems created by rapid changes in American society soon drew the attention of countless reformers who tried to improve things. The women's rights movement began in these years. A push for better education led to the spread of free _____ elementary schools in many states. These were all signs of a growing egalitarian spirit in this era. Still, the millions of immigrants arriving in these decades usually faced a tough struggle to get a new start in crowded cities or on the western frontier. Most, like the Irish, came because conditions were _____ in many parts of Europe, and America offered a new start.

By 1860 the map of America looked much as it does today. Many aspects of American life as we know it had become well established. But a huge split had developed between the North, which favored the new industrial system, and the South, which did _____. Then there was the issue of slavery, which many Northerners felt was totally out of place now. They often joined the growing abolition movement, which worked hard to _____ slavery and help escaped slaves reach freedom. But as Abraham Lincoln was elected in 1860, some Southern leaders decided they really didn't want to be part of the changed America that had grown up in the North. The great decades of growth ended in a bloody Civil War between the North and the South.

Use these terms to fill in the blanks: *abolish, books, Gold, leave, machine, not, one, politics, public, seeds, upstream, worse*

CHARTING POPULATION AND IMMIGRATION

In the years from 1800 to 1860, America's population grew dramatically. Complete the graphs on these pages to see just how significant this growth was. What conclusions can you reach from the pattern these two charts show?

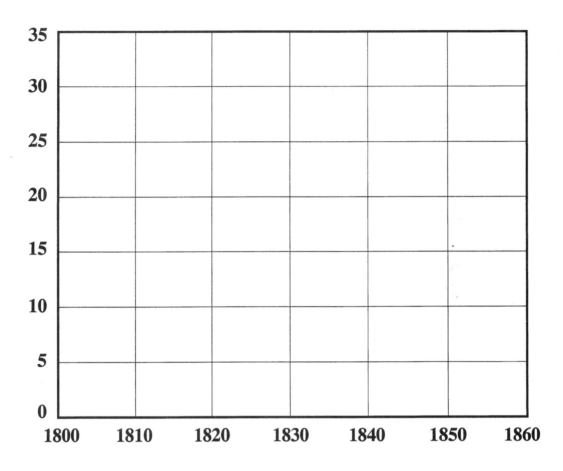

U.S. Population (Millions) 1800 to 1860

Use the table below to find the information to make the line graph above. Place dots on the graph for the data, then connect the dots with lines.

Year	Population (Millions)	Year	Population (Millions)	Year	Population (Millions)	Year	Population (Millions)
1800	5.3	1820	9.6	1840	17.1	1860	31.4
1810	7.2	1830	12.9	1850	23.2		

source: *Historical Statistics of the United States*

Immigration, mostly from northern and western Europe, provided a big part of America's population growth in this era. Notice that immigration figures for the first two decades of the century are not available from the records. This is a common problem historians face: facts and statistics are often incomplete. Start the bar graph with data for the decade 1820 - 1829.

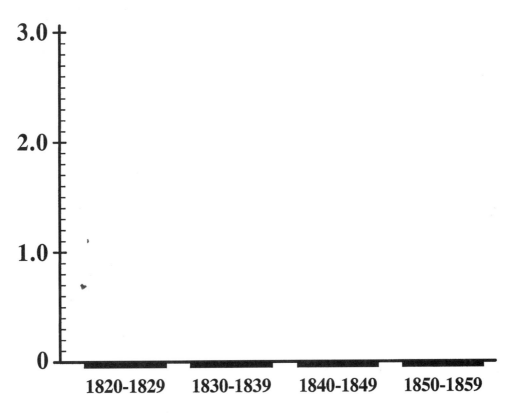

Immigration by Decade (Millions) 1820 - 1859

Use the table below to find the information to make the bar graph above. Draw a vertical bar for each of the decades shown on the graph, with the length corresponding to the number of immigrants arriving in that decade. (Notice that you must convert the numbers in the table to make the graph. 129,000 is equal to .129 million, so the first bar will be very short.)

Decade	Immigrants	Decade	Immigrants
1800 - 1809	(not available)	1830 - 1839	538,000
1810 - 1819	(not available)	1840 - 1849	1,427,000
1820 - 1829	129,000	1850 - 1859	2,815,000

source: *Historical Statistics of the United States*

RED JACKET'S RESPONSE

Red Jacket was a Seneca Indian leader who met in 1805 with other chiefs of the Six Nations to hear an address by a white missionary. His remarks (condensed here) express the Indians' independence of mind as Americans accelerated their spread westward.

Brother, this council fire was kindled by you. Listen to what we have to say. There was a time when our forefathers owned this great island. Their seats extended from the rising to the setting sun. The Great Spirit made it for the use of the Indians. He had created the buffalo, the deer, and other animals for food. He had caused the earth to produce corn for bread. All this He did for His red children because He loved them. If we had some disputes about our hunting-ground they were generally settled without the shedding of much blood.

But an evil day came upon us. Your forefathers crossed the great water and landed on this island. Their numbers were small. They asked for a small seat. We took pity on them, granted their request, and they sat down among us. We gave them corn and meat.

We took them to be friends. They called us brothers. At length their numbers had greatly increased. They wanted more land; they wanted our country. Our eyes were opened. Wars took place. Indians were hired to fight against Indians, and many of our people were destroyed. They also brought strong liquor among us. It was strong and powerful, and has slain thousands.

Brother, our seats were once large and yours small. You have now become a great people, and we have scarcely a place left to spread our blankets. You have got our country, but are not satisfied; you want to force your religion upon us.

You say that you are sent to instruct us how to worship the Great Spirit. How do we know this to be true? We understand that your religion is written in a Book. If it was intended for us, as well as you, why did He not give to our forefathers the knowledge of that Book?

Brother, you say there is but one way to worship and serve the Great Spirit. If there is but one religion, why do you white people differ so much about it?

We also have a religion that was given to our forefathers and has been handed down to us, their children. We worship in that way. It teaches us to be thankful for all the favors we receive, to love each other, and to be united. We never quarrel about religion.

Brother, the Great Spirit has made us all, but He made a great difference between His white and His red children. He has given us different complexions and different customs. To you He has given the arts. To these He has not opened our eyes. Since He has made so great a difference between us in other things, why may we not conclude that He has given us a different religion according to our understanding?

We hope the Great Spirit will protect you on your journey and return you safe to your friends.

Group Discussion: *What are Red Jacket's main complaints about the behavior of white settlers? What arguments does he make to convince the missionary that the Indian religion is just as valid as the religion of the missionary?*

AN IMMIGRANT'S LETTER

Not all immigrants fared as well as this letter, written in 1845, suggests. In many cases, immigrants faced terrible struggles just to survive. But use this letter (condensed here) to get a sense of why so many came to America in this era.

In the following lines I intend, to the best of my ability, to give you a clear idea of the prospects that an emigrant may reasonably hope for here, compared to those he might expect in Norway during a similar period and under normal conditions.

Let us assume that a young, able-bodied man from the country, who has saved up a small sum of thirty or forty dollars, leaves Norway with the intention of emigrating to America. He then presents himself in the Great West with a few dollars in his pocket. His intention and wish must consequently be to get work, the sooner the better, and this he will soon be able to do by consulting those of his countrymen who arrived before him.

Depending on the time of year and other circumstances, his daily wage will be from 60 to 100 cents. Thus his average pay will be 80 cents, out of which he must subtract 30 for good board [food] and clothing, and in this way he has saved 50 cents a day.

If we figure that the number of working days is 250, at the end of the year he will have saved up $120. If he gets permanent employment he will be paid by the current wages here, $10 a month.

It is easily seen that after two years, this young man will have saved up $200, and consequently for $50 he can buy one sixteenth of a section, or forty acres of land.

For the rest of his money he will build houses, buy animals, farming tools and so on. Thus at the end of two years he has become an independent man and is in a position to marry without having to worry about himself or his family.

Now, if this young man had stayed in Norway, he would have been in about the same position as he was in the beginning.

For a laborer who has a wife and children the prospects are about the same. By washing, knitting, and other indoor work, the wife will always be able to make enough to support herself, and if she is good at this sort of work she can make much more. Every year new cities are founded, and these offer fine opportunities for beginning artisans [craftsmen or tradesmen].

We are well pleased with public administration [government] here, for neither taxes nor other burdens are weighing heavily on us. For a piece of land of forty acres a yearly tax of something over $1.00 is paid.

The conduct of officials is, as might be expected in a truly free country, obliging, gentle, and polite to everybody, not the aristocratic, haughty, repelling kind of address that I met with on several occasions in my old native country.

Group Discussion: *What are the main steps an immigrant should follow to find success in America in 1845, according to this letter? What impresses this immigrant most about America and its government?*

CHARTING THE TRANSPORTATION REVOLUTION

In the decades after 1800, the technology of transportation changed in ways that had a big impact on America's development. Complete the display chart below to make it easier to study the impact of what is sometimes called the Transportation Revolution. How would the changes shown here benefit farms and businesses?

	1800	Type of Transportation	**1850**
Land			

Water			

Cost to Transport One Ton (Cents per Mile)

Use the table below to find the information to finish the display chart above. Notice that the table below lists the types of vehicles in order of their historical use, while the chart above organizes the data into the categories of land transportation and water transportation. (Be sure to add the symbol for cents when you write the numbers in the chart.)

Type of Vehicle	Cost to Transport One Ton (Cents per Mile)		
	1800	1825	1850
Wagon	30	15	15
Canal Boat	7	5	1
Steam Boat	(not invented)	1	1/2
Railroad	(not invented)	(not in use)	4

source: North, *Growth and Welfare in the American Past*

The building of canals in the U.S. peaked in the 1840s, then declined. Complete the bar graph below to show how the railroad industry grew in these years. What reasons can you think of to explain why the railroad industry became even more important than canals in promoting the growth of the U.S.?

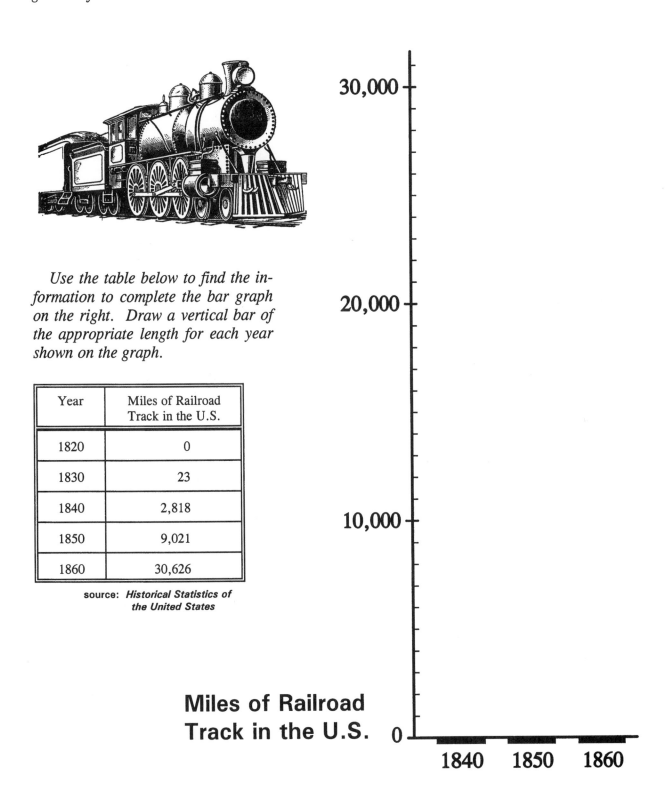

Use the table below to find the information to complete the bar graph on the right. Draw a vertical bar of the appropriate length for each year shown on the graph.

Year	Miles of Railroad Track in the U.S.
1820	0
1830	23
1840	2,818
1850	9,021
1860	30,626

source: *Historical Statistics of the United States*

Miles of Railroad Track in the U.S.

30,000

20,000

10,000

0

1840   1850   1860

GROWING WEST

Daniel Boone, Northwest Ordinances, Louisiana Purchase, Lewis and Clark Expedition,

National Road, Erie Canal, Trail of Tears, Oregon Trail, Texas & The Alamo,

Mexican War/Mexican Cession, California Gold Rush

By the year 1800, thousands of Americans had already moved west over the Appalachian Mountains. Kentucky and Tennessee had already been admitted as states. Early paths into that area, including the Wilderness Road, were marked and opened by Daniel Boone.

Another region that was part of the United States before 1800 was the Old Northwest - the area that today is usually called the Midwest. Congress promoted settlement there by passing the Northwest Ordinances. Those laws set up a survey of the land, so it could be divided for sale in a regular _____ pattern. Slavery was prohibited in the region. In the early 1800s the federal government paid for construction of a famous road into the area. It was called the National Road, and travelers paid a small _____ to use it. After 1825 the Erie Canal carried even more people into the region.

In 1803 President Jefferson approved an incredible land deal with the French leader, Napoleon. It was called the Louisiana Purchase, and roughly doubled the land area of the country for a price of $15 million. Lewis and _____ were the famous explorers of the territory. Their travel journals and maps told of vast lands stretching to the Rockies and the Oregon territory, and described the Indian tribes they met along their path.

Trappers and frontier farmers led the new wave of settlers in the rich land of the Mississippi River Valley. Big improvements in transportation, such as turnpikes, canals, and steamboats, soon helped countless others to "go West." By the 1840s towns and even cities were springing up, and _____ - wheel boats were a common sight going up and down the Mississippi River.

In the East, constant conflicts, mostly caused by settlers who wanted to take Indian land, led Congress to pass the Indian Removal Act in 1830. It encouraged tribes to _____ their land for new territory west of the Mississippi. Some agreed to the exchange. But others were later forced at gunpoint to give up their land and move. The Trail of Tears is the name the Cherokee gave the path they took from Georgia to the Indian Territory in the West.

In the 1830s some fur traders and explorers were going as far as the _____ Mountains. Many were involved in the beaver fur trade with the Indians. Other traders were traveling the Santa Fe Trail into Mexican territory. The travels of all these groups helped increase the _____ of many Americans in the Far West.

Around this time, Texas was attracting many settlers. Mexico, which owned the area, actually invited Americans in. They came, but disagreements over issues like slavery, religion, and style of government soon led each side to resent the other. Friction rose, and the American settlers declared themselves independent in 1836, as the _____ of Texas. A famous battle at a mission in San Antonio called the Alamo gave Texans their battle cry, "Remember the Alamo!" Texas joined the U.S. as a state in 1845.

By the 1840s some Americans were moving even further west by way of the Oregon Trail. The stories of rich farm land north of California drew thousands on the risky trip of 2,000 miles. The trail began in Missouri. Settlers faced a dangerous trip of about five months with their covered _____, much of it across wild territory. America and England both claimed the area, and it was eventually divided between the two.

A branch off the Oregon Trail took travelers to California, which was controlled by Mexico. In the mid-1840s only a few thousand Americans lived there. But many of the Mexican and Spanish people in the region felt little loyalty to the unstable government of Mexico. During one outbreak of political turmoil, the American settlers proclaimed California independent as the Bear Flag Republic. They expected to _____ the U.S. quickly.

Meanwhile, outright war with Mexico had broken out as Texas joined the United States. The fighting began over which river should be the border between Texas and Mexico. But many Americans had their eye on the vast territory west of Texas, and figured that a full-blown war would help get it. American troops marched and soon occupied Mexico City. The war ended in 1848, and the border with Mexico was put at the river known as the _____. Mexico was also forced to give up a vast area including California for a payment of $15 million. Historians call that area the Mexican Cession.

The California Gold Rush of 1849 flooded the Far West with prospectors and soon, settlers and families. America had fulfilled what some called its "Manifest Destiny." But the expansion wasn't painless. Indians lost _____ and ways of life. Settlers faced hardship and death. The spread of slavery in many areas angered abolitionists. But the main pieces of the American map were in place, all destined to play big roles in the years ahead.

Use these terms to fill in the blanks: Clark, exchange, grid, interest, join, land, paddle, Republic, Rio Grande, Rocky, toll, wagons

MAP - LAND AREAS AND EXPANSION TO 1860

Label and color the map to show these:

NEIGHBORING COUNTRIES

Mexico   **Canada**

LAND AREAS AND EXPANSION

Label and color the map to show the areas listed below, and indicate the date each became part of the U.S. The dotted lines will help guide you.

Area of the Original States, the area that grew from the 13 _____ that existed when the American Revolution began. *(1776)*

Old Southwest, part of the land gained by the treaty with England that ended the Revolution. Daniel _____ helped open paths into the region. *(1783)*

Old Northwest, also part of the land gained after the Revolution through the peace treaty with England. Settlement here was encouraged by the Northwest Ordinances, which made it easy for settlers to _____ land in the region. *(1783)*

Florida, which was _____ territory until the U.S. obtained it, partly by force and partly by negotiation. *(1810-1819)*

Louisiana Purchase, a vast area west of the Mississippi River bought for $15 million dollars from _____. President Thomas Jefferson sent Meriwether Lewis and William Clark to explore the region. *(1803)*

Red River Basin, a small area just north of the Louisiana Purchase. It became part of the U.S. in an agreement with England on placement of the border between _____ and America. *(1818)*

Texas Annexation, the large area of the Republic of Texas, which joined the U.S. less than ten years after winning its independence from _____. After it joined, the Mexican War began. *(1845)*

Oregon Country, an area reached by Lewis and _____ in 1805 during their exploration of the Louisiana Purchase. An agreement with England made this territory officially part of the U.S. *(1846)*

Mexican Cession, the land gained partly by force through the Mexican War, and partly with a _____ of $15 million dollars to Mexico after the war. *(1848)*

Gadsden Purchase, a small patch of land bought from Mexico as a possible path for a _____. *(1853)*

Use these terms to fill the blanks: Boone, buy, Canada, Clark, colonies, France, Mexico, payment, railroad, Spanish

---

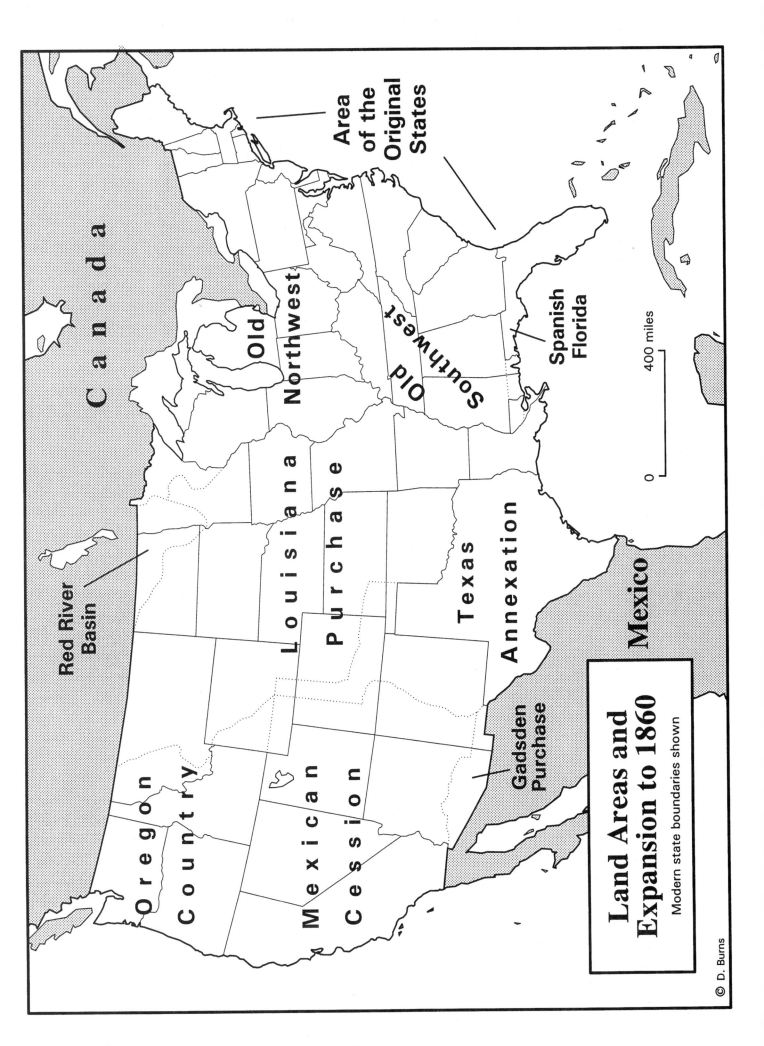

Area
of the
Original
States

Canada

Old
Northwest

Old
Southwest

Spanish
Florida

400 miles

0

Red River
Basin

Louisiana

Purchase

Texas

Annexation

Oregon

Country

Mexican

Cession

Gadsden
Purchase

Mexico

**Land Areas and
Expansion to 1860**

Modern state boundaries shown

© D. Burns

GROWTH TO THE MISSISSIPPI

Finish labeling and drawing the map to show the items listed below.

FAMOUS EARLY ROADS TO THE WEST
Use different colors to show these famous roads to the West in the early 1800s.

Great Valley Road - This old route was a path for frontier farmers headed into _____ and Kentucky. It connected the cities of **Lynchburg, Knoxville,** and **Nashville.**

Wilderness Road - Daniel Boone explored and marked this route that passed through a natural break in the Appalachian Mountains called the _____. The road branched off the **Great Valley Road** and ran to **Harrodsburg** and other towns in Kentucky.

Natchez Trace - It connected _____ with **Natchez** in Mississippi. The word "trace" means it was the remnant of an old Indian path.

Pennsylvania Road - It ran from **Philadelphia** to the fast-growing city of _____ on the Ohio River.

National Road - By connecting **Cumberland** to **Wheeling**, it provided an easy route west to the _____ River. The road was gradually extended to **Columbus, Indianapolis,** and **Vandalia.** (The first section of the National Road is sometimes called the Cumberland Road.)

Chicago Turnpike - The cities of _____ and **Chicago** were linked with this route. Like the National Road and other turnpikes, travelers paid a small fee at a toll house to use the road.

THE MOST FAMOUS CANAL
Show the route of this famous canal in New York State with a blue line. Then label all five of the Great Lakes.

Erie Canal - This canal connected **Albany** and **Buffalo.** By doing so, it opened an easy water route stretching from **New York City** and the _____ Ocean to the vast waterways of the Great Lakes.

Use these terms to fill in the blanks: Atlantic, Cumberland Gap, Detroit, Ohio, Nashville, Pittsburgh, Tennessee

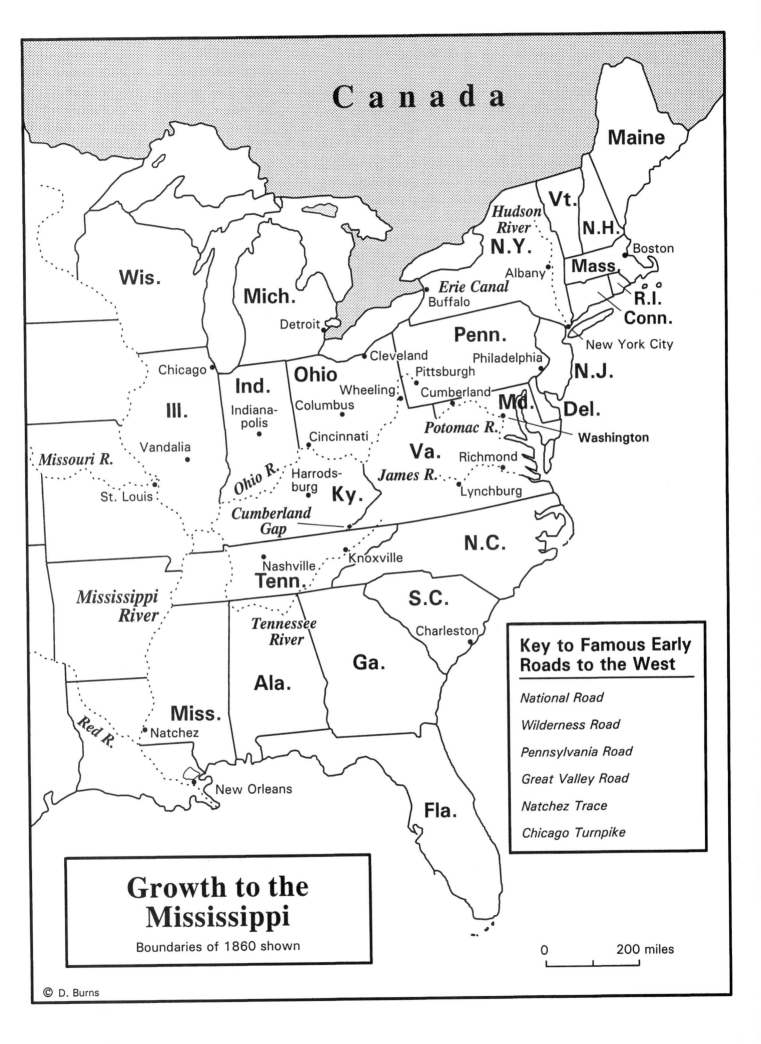

Canada

Maine

Vt.

N.H.

Hudson River

N.Y.

Albany

Erie Canal

Buffalo

Mass.

Boston

R.I.

Conn.

New York City

Wis.

Mich.

Detroit

Penn.

Cleveland

Philadelphia

Pittsburgh

N.J.

Chicago

Ind.

Ohio

Wheeling

Cumberland

Md.

Del.

Ill.

Indiana-polis

Columbus

Cincinnati

Potomac R.

Washington

Vandalia

Missouri R.

Ohio R.

Harrods-burg

Ky.

Va.

Richmond

James R.

Lynchburg

St. Louis

Cumberland Gap

N.C.

Mississippi River

Nashville

Knoxville

Tenn.

S.C.

Tennessee River

Ga.

Charleston

Ala.

Miss.

Red R.

Natchez

New Orleans

Fla.

Key to Famous Early Roads to the West

National Road

Wilderness Road

Pennsylvania Road

Great Valley Road

Natchez Trace

Chicago Turnpike

Growth to the Mississippi

Boundaries of 1860 shown

0   200 miles

© D. Burns

GROWTH TO THE FAR WEST

Finish labeling and drawing the map to show these:

FAMOUS TRAILS AND PATHS TO THE FAR WEST
Use red lines to show these trails, and label each one.

Santa Fe Trail - In the early 1800s this trail connected the American city of **Independence, Missouri** to the Mexican city of **Santa Fe**. Trade goods were often exchanged for Mexican _____ coins, mules, buffalo hides and other products.

Old Spanish Trail - It was a tough route that crossed through the _____ Mountains and took travelers from **Santa Fe** to **Los Angeles** when both cities were part of Mexico.

Oregon Trail - Around 1840, Americans began traveling this route to reach the rich farmland along the **Willamette River** in Oregon country. The five month journey usually started in **Independence, Missouri**. The first half of the route generally followed along the _____ **River.** Then the wagons crossed the Rockies and followed the **Snake River** through what later became Idaho. Finally, they would follow the **Columbia River** to **Oregon City**.

California Trail - This route branched off the **Oregon Trail** and took gold-seekers and others across the Sierra Nevada mountain range to **Sacramento**. As on all western trails, travelers had to get over the mountains by late summer or risk early _____ storms that could trap wagons and people.

Butterfield Overland Mail - This trail swung south to connect the cities of **St. Louis, El Paso, Tucson, Los Angeles**, and _____.

FAMOUS TEXAS RIVERS

Rio Grande - This river forms part of the border between Mexico and the U.S. But when **Texas** joined the U.S. in 1845, Mexico wanted the border at the _____ **River**, a bit further to the north. The dispute over the border helped spark the Mexican War.

GOLD REGION
Color yellow the oval-shaped area just east of Sacramento that was the center of mining activity in the California Gold Rush of 1849.

Use these terms to fill in the blanks: Nueces, Platte, Rocky, San Francisco, silver, snow

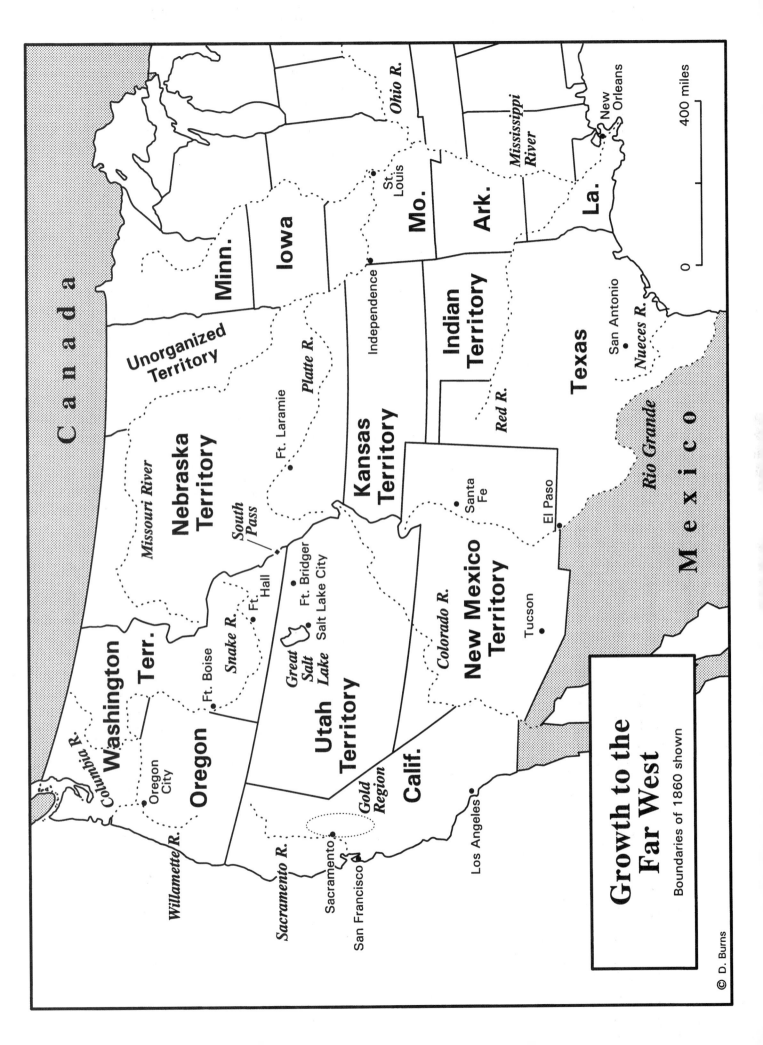

Growth to the Far West

Boundaries of 1860 shown

400 miles

Canada

Mexico

Ohio R.

Mississippi River

New Orleans

La.

Ark.

Mo.

St. Louis

Minn.

Iowa

Unorganized Territory

Independence

Indian Territory

Texas

San Antonio

Nueces R.

Platte R.

Ft. Laramie

Kansas Territory

Red R.

Nebraska Territory

Missouri River

South Pass

Santa Fe

El Paso

Rio Grande

Ft. Bridger

Salt Lake City

Snake R.

Ft. Hall

Ft. Boise

Great Salt Lake

New Mexico Territory

Tucson

Colorado R.

Washington Terr.

Oregon

Oregon City

Columbia R.

Willamette R.

Utah Territory

Calif.

Gold Region

Sacramento R.

Sacramento

San Francisco

Los Angeles

© D. Burns

GROWING CAPITALISM, INDUSTRY, AND CITIES

capitalism/capitalist, factory system, laissez-faire policy, Utopian societies,

socialism/socialist, labor unions

Only a few decades after the American Revolution there was another big upheaval underway in the new nation. It was the start of the Industrial Revolution, which spread to America from England around 1800. Combined with business attitudes and work habits that turned increasingly cash and profit oriented, it became a powerful engine of economic growth and social change.

In early America about 90 percent of the population were farmers. Many grew or made by hand almost everything they needed, or traded with neighbors in the small communities where they lived. Products like shoes and guns were still made by skilled craftsmen and women who worked in a small shop or at _____. Since people were dependent on neighbors in dozens of ways, anyone who put money making and personal profit very far ahead of neighborliness was taking a real risk. Religious leaders often criticized chasing after profit as a _____.

But from the earliest settlement at Jamestown, a profit-making or capitalist spirit had been growing. For example, the big plantations in the South sold tobacco and other products to British merchants for a profit. In the Northern colonies, merchants and ship owners developed a strong pattern of business and trade. These are all examples of capitalism before the growth of factories.

By 1800 there was a growing understanding that the wider community would actually be helped - not hurt - if each person and business simply pursued their own profit. The spread of the idea that the profit motive is morally good, or at least not morally evil, was of enormous importance in America's history. It unleashed the power of individual initiative - and sometimes plain old _____ - as never before.

Starting around 1820 the factory system grew rapidly in the Northern states as merchants sought ways to make greater profits. Factories use the principle of "division of labor." That means a complex job is divided into many small steps that can be done easily by unskilled workers. Factory managers also developed the use of interchangeable parts. That means each part of a product is made to the exact _____ pattern, so the parts can be easily and quickly assembled.

New machines powered by _____ wheels or steam engines made the factory system far more efficient than even the best individual craftsmen. The textile (cloth) industry in the New England states led the way in adopting machine production methods.

Factories produced things the growing population wanted, at lower prices than ever. The factory system created new _____ and opportunities for people who flocked to the growing cities and factory towns. The "get ahead" spirit of capitalism was embraced widely. It was clearly a liberating attitude when compared to older, traditional patterns of work and production. But many complained that the new attitude encouraged a heartless competition for wealth.

The cities of this period revealed an increasingly sharp contrast between business owners and the new factory labor class. Prosperous neighborhoods were easy to find. But workers often lived in harsh conditions that grew even _____ when factories had to lay off their employees for lack of business.

Even in good times many factories were unhealthy places to work. Many employed children. Twelve hour days were common, six days a week. Some critics of the new pattern of factory labor started calling it "wage slavery." Still, very _____ people at that time believed the government should interfere with business practices. The policy of leaving businesses to set their own rules is often called a laissez-faire policy.

Some people denounced the spreading capitalist spirit as a great corrupting force that should be rejected. A small number even bought land and formed their own separate communities, commonly called Utopian societies. With names like "Harmonists" and "Perfectionists," these groups often combined religious and socialist principles. They often believed in common ownership of all property, equal wages for everyone, and an _____ role for women. Most fell apart after a few years. Utopian socialism never spread widely, in part because few Americans could accept the group mentality found in such communities.

A different approach was taken by labor unions and workers' associations that grew in this period. Their goal was to improve working conditions and wages. But they had only limited success in these years, partly because high immigration rates supplied plenty of willing workers. In addition, most business owners fiercely _____ labor unions.

But around 1850 the big question centered on the growing split between the industrialized _____ and the agricultural South. Half the country had begun transforming into a modern capitalist society of wage labor, factories, and farms without slavery. How could the nation remain partly stuck in the past with a vast region still tied to a slave labor system held over from the ancient world? By 1860, the South had an answer: Break the nation in two. It was a solution the North would _____ accept.

Use these terms to fill in the blanks: *equal, few, greed, home, jobs, North, not, opposed, same, sin, water, worse*

CHARTING INVENTIONS AND COTTON

The role of technology grew slowly in early America, but then accelerated as the Industrial Revolution and the factory system spread. Finish this line graph to show figures from the U.S. Patent Office. (A patent gives an inventor an exclusive right to sell his or her invention.) What decades seem to be key periods of change in the history of technology in this period?

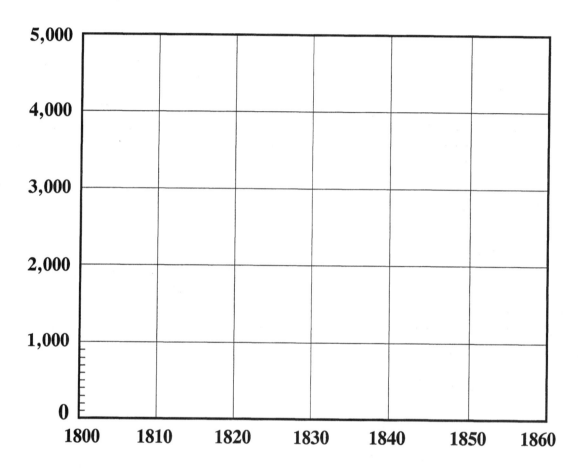

Inventions Patented in the U.S.   1800 - 1860

Use the table below to find the information to make the line graph above. Place dots on the graph for the data, then connect them with lines.

Year	Inventions Patented	Year	Inventions Patented	Year	Inventions Patented	Year	Inventions Patented
1800	41	1820	155	1840	458	1860	4,357
1810	223	1830	544	1850	883		

source: *Historical Statistics of the United States*

The invention of the cotton gin helped expand the cotton crop dramatically after 1800. Finish this bar graph to see how cotton grew to become "King Cotton." How did the cotton crop tend to pull the North and South together, and in what ways did it tend to push them apart?

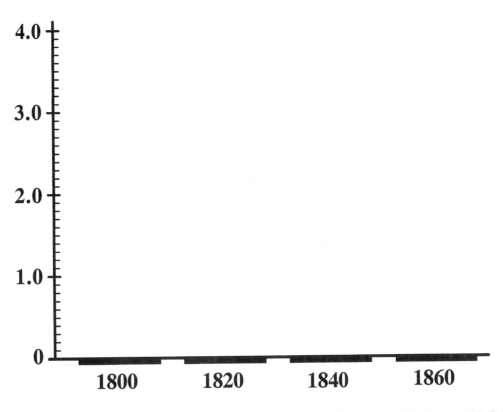

Cotton Production (Millions of Bales) 1800 - 1860

Use the table below to find the information to make the bar graph above. Draw a vertical bar for each year shown, with the length corresponding to the production of cotton in that year. (Remember that 73,000 is less than one-tenth of one million, so the first bar will be very short. The second bar will also be fairly short, since 335,000 is equal to .335 million.)

Year	Cotton Production (Bales of Cotton)	Year	Cotton Production (Bales of Cotton)
1800	73,000	1840	1,348,000
1820	335,000	1860	3,841,000

source: *Historical Statistics of the United States*

A GROWING CITY AND ITS PEOPLE

While early settlers in the new territories usually established farms, growing cities soon followed. Gustaf Unonius immigrated from Sweden in 1841, and began a small farm in Wisconsin. Later, he became a minister, moved to Chicago, and witnessed much of the growth of the region. In this condensed account, he describes some of what he saw. It begins with his first short visit to the city in the 1840s.

I remained two weeks in Chicago, the Garden City, as it was called, but at that time anything but a garden. The surroundings resembled a trash can more than anything else. The entire area on which that "wonder of the western world" was to grow up might best be likened to a vast mud puddle. The principal site of the city is low and swampy, almost at the same level as Lake Michigan, and most of the buildings were at that time built close to the lakeshore or by the river flowing right through the city.

During the rainy season, and sometimes far into the summer, the streets were impassable for driving [wagons] as well as for walking. To be sure, they were provided with board sidewalks, but getting from one side of the street to the other entailed decided difficulties.

Twelve years have passed, and what a change in its appearance as well as in its population, which is now 120,000! The formerly low, swampy streets have been raised several feet and paved with planks or stone. The river has been dredged and widened, its shores have been supported with piles, evened off, raised well above the water level, and are now occupied by loading piers or used as foundations for gigantic warehouses or factories.

It is now a city in which private and public buildings have been erected that compare favorably both in size and style with the most splendid structures in the capitals of Europe. In a single summer, in 1855, 2,700 new homes were built, many of which would be a source of pride to any city.

The web of railroads which Chicago has spun around itself during the last ten years is the thing that more than anything else has contributed to its wealth and progress. Thereby the city has communication with the

rich copper districts and other mining regions around Lake Superior, with Canada, with all the Atlantic states, with the rich grain producing lands beyond the Mississippi, and with the cotton states around the Gulf of Mexico.

Next to traffic in grain the lumber business is the most important in Chicago. From the pine woods of Michigan and the northern sections of the lake of that name, masses of boards and other lumber are shipped annually to Chicago, whereupon they are transhipped by railroad to the interior of the country and to the southern states. Along the shores of the Chicago River there is nothing to be seen for a distance of six miles but lumberyard after lumberyard.

In addition, Chicago has great locomotive works, foundries, and all kinds of machine shops employing thousands of workmen. Among factories, McCormick's establishment for the manufacture of agricultural machinery deserves mention.

Add to this the fact that Chicago has more than fifty churches, twenty-five newspaper presses, about a dozen banks, and a countless number of stores and hotels. All of these things will give the reader an idea of how the city has grown from practically nothing during the last twenty years.

While living in Chicago in the 1850s, Unonius also witnessed the hardships faced by its people. As a minister, he often was called upon for help when epidemics of deadly diseases such as cholera and typhus swept through the city.

The cholera spread further and further, and raged with great violence among the poorer population. In great haste a temporary hospital was nailed together in an empty block. But that hospital was completely inadequate to the need. The Swedish immigrants who arrived in greater numbers than ever before were attacked by the disease and succumbed to it [died] in masses.

And how could it be otherwise? Packed together in immigrant ships during the long ocean journey, unaccustomed to idleness, often eating spoiled and unwholesome food, living in filth and dirt, they were predisposed to the disease even before arriving in Chicago. Lodged in miserable hovels [shacks], often hungry, it was natural that in most cases medical treatment proved unavailing [unsuccessful].

The misery of those poor people cannot be described. More than half of those who remained in Chicago succumbed. Among those who stood hale and hearty at my side in the cemetery, filling the grave of a relative or friend, I could always be certain that someone, before another day was gone, would be provided with a resting place of the same kind.

The greatest problem was taking care of the children whose parents had died, and many of whom had been attacked by the diseases. To be sure, there was in the city a place for orphaned children, but when children left behind at the death of their parents were taken to the orphanage they carried the infection with them. The directors decided that they could not be admitted until they

had been in the city several weeks and might be considered perfectly healthy.

I asked some members of the church to come to the rectory [church residence] which at that time was occupied by me alone. We moved all the furniture from the first floor to the attic. Some of the women were sent out  into the city with a hastily written appeal in which I told of what had happened and asked assistance for those in need.

Before evening I had more than twenty fatherless and motherless children in the house. But I also received beds and bedclothes for them to sleep in, money to buy the food for them, suitable food and drink prepared for their immediate needs, medical aid for the sick, and fine, noble people to watch at their bedsides. For several weeks these children enjoyed shelter and care which I cannot imagine how they would have secured otherwise.

Where else but in America could a thing like that have been done? I dare not say nowhere, but I doubt that in any other country aid could have come so speedily, so willingly, and been so freely given as on that occasion. When such memories from my sojourn [travel] in that country arise before my mind's eye, I love and honor its people. In spite of their faults - and what people, what individual, is without faults? - they have proved that their hearts possess as great treasure as the ground on which they tread.

Group Discussion: *What were the main factors that contributed to the rapid growth of Chicago in this era? What impressed Unonius most about Americans when an epidemic of cholera hit Chicago?*

GROWING REFORM AND RELIGION

Second Great Awakening, Dorothea Dix, Horace Mann, Shakers, Mormons, temperance,

Seneca Falls Convention, abolition movement, Harriet Tubman, Know-Nothings

One remarkable fact about America today is that whenever a social problem comes to light, an organization of individual citizens springs up to try to solve it. This pattern, of individuals organizing to help other people in need, really blossomed in the early 1800s. One reason was that the number of people in need was growing as the population rose. Expanding cities, the factory system, and immigration were quickly changing American society in ways that created opportunities, but also problems.

Another factor in this reform movement was a revival of religious belief and feeling called the Second Great Awakening. The reform activity that grew at the time was deeply rooted in Christian and _____ religious traditions. These traditions put a high value on the individual, regardless of his or her circumstances, and teach that there is an obligation to help those who are in need.

One group sorely in need of help in the early 1800s was the mentally ill. In the absence of any effective therapy, the insane were often considered and treated the same as common criminals. Dorothea Dix took up their cause, and worked tirelessly to convince public officials to build state-supported hospitals for the mentally ill. Other reformers pushed for the construction of special schools for the deaf and the _____, some of which survive to this day.

Schools were seen as a key to solving many of the problems of the day. A democracy, people felt, needed educated citizens. Decent schools would also give children of the working class a better chance to move _____ the economic ladder of success. Horace Mann and other reformers pushed for improved public schools, better training for teachers, and free public education at the elementary level.

A few Americans thought the best approach to reform was to buy some land, and simply set up a new society. These "Utopian" communities, like Brook Farm in Massachusetts, often adopted elaborate _____ aimed at creating social equality. Many blended religious and socialist ideas, and held their land in common ownership. Most fell apart within a few years, although a few, like the religious communities of the Shakers, lasted longer.

One religious group that set up a separate society and prospered was the Church of Jesus Christ of Latter Day Saints, commonly called the Mormons. This group was established near Rochester, New York, in 1830 by Joseph Smith. But they were chased out of one settlement after another for their beliefs, which included _____, or having more than one wife. They fled to the desert of Utah, and founded _____ Lake City. Eventually the Mormons gave up polygamy, in order for Utah to be accepted by Congress as a new state. But they maintain to this day the strong community sense that helped keep them together in the toughest years of the mid-1800s.

Most reformers didn't want to withdraw from American society, however, they just wanted to make things better. Alcohol and drunkenness were at the top of many reformers' lists of big problems to be solved. The temperance movement was the result. By 1860 the movement had convinced more than a dozen states to pass laws prohibiting or restricting the sale of liquor. Women were the driving force behind this effort, because they often suffered the most when their _____ drank up a paycheck, or even became physically abusive.

Women were often involved in reform activities because social traditions and laws at the time kept them out of so many other fields. Women could not vote, and divorce, property, and inheritance laws treated the sexes unequally. At a famous convention held in 1848 in Seneca Falls, New York, one group of women declared their intention to fight for full _____ in society. It was an uphill battle. Most men - and probably most women - felt that separate roles helped create stronger families. In the changing society of the time, the role seen for women - the _____ - was counted as vitally important. It brought her great respect, but also tended to cut off other possibilities.

Certainly the greatest of all reform movements was the drive to end slavery. The abolition movement grew in the North rapidly after 1831, when William Lloyd Garrison began publishing a newspaper called *The Liberator*.

A more dangerous role was taken up by the people who formed a secret network of routes and safe houses called the Underground Railroad. This network helped thousands of slaves escape to the free states of the North. Harriet Tubman, an escaped slave, became famous as a "conductor" who risked _____ going back again and again to the South to help others escape.

Neither religion nor the reform movement made everyone, or even most people, into perfect citizens. Crime, poverty, and ignorance were only too widespread. Free blacks faced prejudice in the _____ as well as the South. Most churches, especially in the South, refused to confront the evil of slavery. Prejudice against immigrants of the Catholic faith, especially the Irish fleeing the potato famine, was _____. This sort of hostility gave rise to a secret society, commonly called the Know - Nothings, which favored restricting the rate of immigration. Yet amid the many conflicts of these years, the reform movements showed that individual citizens could organize and work effectively to make needed changes in American life.

Use these terms to fill in the blanks: blind, common, death, equality, homemaker, husbands, Jewish, North, polygamy, rules, Salt, up

A CALL FOR FACTORY REFORM

Conditions in early factories began to attract the attention of reformers by the 1830s. The factories that grew in Lowell, Massachusetts, drew particular attention because the textile mills there generally relied on young women to operate the machinery. This report (condensed here) describes the working conditions.

We have lately visited the cities of Lowell and Manchester, and have had an opportunity of examining the factory system more closely than before.

In Lowell live between seven and eight thousand young women, who are generally daughters of farmers of the different States of New England. The operatives [workers] work thirteen hours a day in the summer time, and from daylight to dark in the winter. At half past four in the morning the factory bell rings, and at five the girls must be in the mills.

At seven the girls are allowed thirty minutes for breakfast, and at noon thirty more for dinner, except during the first quarter of the year, when the time is extended to forty-five minutes. But within this time they must hurry to their boarding-houses and return to the factory. A meal eaten under such circumstances must be quite unfavorable to digestion and health, as any medical man will inform us. At seven o'clock in the evening the factory bell sounds the close of the day's work.

Thus thirteen hours per day of close attention and monotonous labor are exacted from the young women in these manufactories. So fatigued are numbers of the girls that they go to bed soon after their evening meal.

Enter with us into the large rooms, when the looms are at work. The largest that we saw is four hundred feet long, and about seventy broad. There are five hundred looms. The din [noise] and clatter struck us as something frightful and infernal.

The girls attend upon an average of three looms; many attend four, but this requires a very active person, and the most unremitting care. Attention to two is as much as should be demanded of an operative.

The atmosphere of such a room cannot of course be pure; on the contrary it is charged with cotton filaments and dust, which, we  were told, are very injurious to the lungs. Although the day was warm, the windows were down. We asked the reason, and a young woman answered, that "when the wind blew, the threads did not work so well."

After we had been in the room for fifteen or twenty minutes, we found ourselves in quite a perspiration, caused by a certain moisture in the air, as well as by the heat.

The young women sleep upon an average six in a room; three beds to a room. There is no privacy; it is almost impossible to read or write alone, as the parlor is so full. So live and work the young women of our country in the boarding-houses and manufactories, which the rich and influential of our land have built for them.

1. Highlight three sentences that describe the conditions that you would consider the worst if you were working in this factory.

Group Discussion: *What were conditions like for workers in early textile factories in Massachusetts? How do you think the factory owners might have responded to this report?*

DOROTHEA DIX PLEADS FOR THE MENTALLY ILL

Perhaps the most famous of the early 19th century reformers was Dorothea Dix. Born in Maine, she ran a school and published several children's books. Later, she began fighting to improve conditions for the mentally ill. This selection is condensed from her report to the Massachusetts state legislature in 1843.

Gentlemen - I come to place before the Legislature of Massachusetts the condition of the miserable, the desolate, the outcast.

I come as the advocate [defender] of helpless, forgotten, insane, and idiotic men and women; of beings sunk to a condition from which the most unconcerned would start [cringe] with real horror; of beings wretched in our prisons, and more wretched in our almshouses [houses for the poor].

I proceed, gentlemen, briefly to call your attention to the present state of insane persons confined within this Commonwealth [State], in cages, closets, cellars, stalls, pens! Chained, naked, beaten with rods, and lashed into obedience.

It is defective legislation which perpetuates [allows to continue] and multiplies these abuses. I offer the following extracts from my Note-book and Journal:

Springfield. In the jail, one lunatic woman, furiously mad, improperly situated, both in regard to the prisoners, the keepers, and herself.

In the almshouse [poorhouse] of the same town is a woman apparently only needing judicious care, and some well-chosen employment, to make it unnecessary to confine her in solitude, in a dreary, unfurnished room. Her appeals for employment and companionship are most touching, but the mistress replied she had no time to attend her.

Lincoln. A woman in a cage. Medford.

One idiotic subject chained, one in a close stall for seventeen years. Pepperell. One often doubly chained, hand and foot, another violent; several peaceable now.

Brookfield, one man caged, comfortable.

Granville. One often closely confined; now losing the use of his limbs from want of exercise. Lenox. Two in jail, against whose unfit condition the jailer there protests.

Besides the above, I have seen many who, part of the year, are chained or caged. I encountered during the last three months many poor creatures wandering recklessly and unprotected through the country.

Men of Massachusetts, I beg, I implore, I demand pity and protection for these of my suffering, outraged sex. Become the benefactors of your race, the just guardians of the solemn rights you hold in trust.

Gentlemen, I commit to you this sacred cause. Your action upon this subject will affect the present and future condition of hundreds and thousands. In this legislation, as in all things, may you exercise that "wisdom which is the breath and power of God."

1. Highlight three sentences that you think would have made the biggest impression on the state officials who heard this report.

Group Discussion: *What were conditions like for the mentally ill and insane people seen by Dorothea Dix? What did she do to get convincing evidence? Who does she think has the main obligation to do something about the situation?*

GROWING APART: NORTH AND SOUTH

tariff, states' rights, nullification, secede/secession, Missouri Compromise, *The Liberator*,

Underground Railroad, Frederick Douglass, Fugitive Slave Law, *Uncle Tom's Cabin*,

Dred Scott Decision, Bleeding Kansas, John Brown's raid

As America expanded rapidly after 1800 it also developed a split personality. The Industrial Revolution was changing America dramatically, but these changes were mainly concentrated in the North. The South remained a region of farms, with few factories. While most Northern states eliminated slavery, the South kept the system of bound labor. Decade by decade the spilt widened.

Conflict between the two sections began long before the Civil War. One good place to start is with the tariffs passed by Congress in the 1810s and 1820s. (A tariff is a tax on imported goods.) Higher tariffs, Congress decided, would protect the growth and profits of American manufacturers. The North got most of the benefit of this policy, since that's where most of the country's early factories were located. But Southerners were angered, since high tariffs raised the _____ of imported products. Some South Carolina leaders even argued that the principle of "states' rights" gave states the power of "nullification" - the right to ignore the federal tariff law within their own borders.

The dispute between the two regions got so nasty that in 1832 South Carolina threatened to pull out of the United States, or secede, over the tariff issue. Fortunately, President Andrew Jackson helped work out a compromise. But already some leaders in the South were seeing their political and economic interests as _____ from the North's. They were already starting to talk about a right to leave the Union.

Soon another sore point between the regions was growing. The slavery issue had been sleeping since the Missouri Compromise of 1820. That agreement in Congress set up a deal in which new territories came in as states two at a time: one without slavery and one with slavery allowed. That kept a safe _____ balance. But in 1831 William Lloyd Garrison began publishing a newspaper in Boston called *The Liberator*, dedicated to ending all slavery. Thousands of people began joining the great cause of abolition, and the issue of slavery slept no more.

Slavery became even more strongly a North *vs.* South issue, even though three-quarters of Southerners did _____ own slaves, and Northern states generally did not permit free blacks full rights as citizens.

The Underground Railroad, which helped escaped slaves find their way north, directly involved the _____. Slave owners were angered when many Northerners refused to obey a federal law that required the return of fugitive slaves. Frederick Douglass, himself an escaped slave, started another abolitionist newspaper called *The North Star*. Douglass and other escaped slaves brought the reality of slavery alive to Northerners with speeches and appearances at public rallies.

In 1852 a novel about slavery by Harriet Beecher Stowe, _____, became an instant best-seller and inflamed the passions of millions of people on both sides of the slavery issue.

Soon enough, passion turned to gunfire. In 1854 a law called the Kansas-Nebraska Act ended the Missouri Compromise. The new law said the territories could simply take a _____ on whether to allow slavery. The error of this approach became obvious in Kansas. Both sides armed themselves with guns and went at it in fighting that was almost a preview of the Civil War. The conflict is often called "Bleeding Kansas."

Events continued to drive wedges between the regions. In 1857 the Dred Scott decision of the U.S. Supreme Court declared that slavery legally could exist in _____ territory. Many people in the North were outraged, especially because a majority of the justices who approved the decision were Southerners.

Two years later a white abolitionist named John Brown led his supporters on a raid on the federal government's arsenal and gun factory at _____, Virginia. He hoped to start a widespread slave rebellion, but none occurred. He was captured, put on trial, convicted, and _____. Even so, Southerners were angered because he became a hero or martyr in the eyes of many people in the North who opposed to slavery. Slave owners in the South saw the incident as dangerous treason. They had not forgotten the bloody revolt by slaves many years earlier in Virginia called the Nat Turner Rebellion.

This was the climate as Abraham Lincoln ran in the presidential election of 1860. In his campaign, Lincoln said he opposed allowing slavery in any _____ territories, but he did not call for outright abolition of slavery. Still, many Southern leaders were convinced that the North, and Lincoln, would _____ them sooner or later. The four-way presidential race gave Lincoln and the Republican Party victory with votes from states in the North and West. Six weeks after the election, South Carolina seceded from the Union. Half a dozen other Deep South states quickly followed. Within a matter of months the Confederacy grew to include 11 states, and the Civil War began.

Use these terms to fill in the blanks: abolitionists, any, cost, different, hanged, Harpers Ferry, new, not, political, ruin, Uncle Tom's Cabin, vote

CHARTING STATISTICS OF SLAVERY

The decades before the Civil War saw the spread of slavery into new territories and states as the nation grew. At the same time, the number of free blacks also grew, both in the North and South. Complete the bar graph below to show some of the key statistics about the growing population of African-Americans.

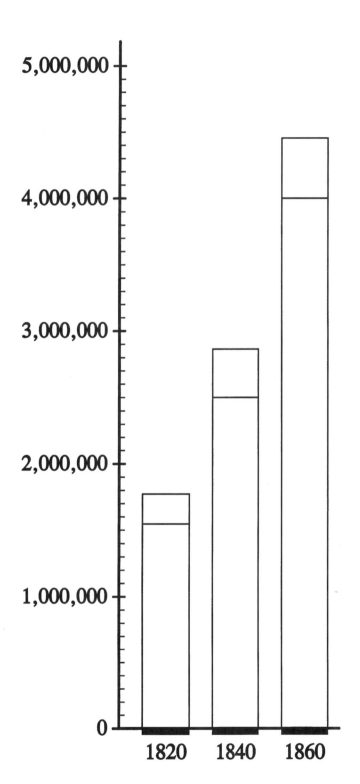

Use the table shown below to help you finish labeling the bar graph on the left. Label each segment of the graph bars with the correct percentage figure. (Be sure to add the "%" sign.)

Then choose two colors for the color key, and lightly shade the segments of the bars with the appropriate colors.

Year	Black Population of U.S.	
	Percent Slave	Percent Free
1820	87	13
1840	87	13
1860	89	11

source: *Historical Statistics of the United States.*

Black Population in the U.S. 1820-1860

Slave [   ]   Free [   ]

Complete the chart below to show the pattern of slave ownership by whites in the South just before the Civil War. There are 100 small circles in the graph, so each circle represents one percent of the white population of the South. (A very small number of free blacks living in the South also owned slaves, a fact that often surprises people today.)

Use the table below to find the information to complete the chart on the right. First choose three colors for the color key. Start at the top of the graph, and color the correct number of circles to represent whites who owned 10 or more slaves.

Next, color the correct number of circles to represent those owning 1 to 9 slaves. Color the rest of the circles to represent whites who owned no slaves at all.

Number of Slaves Owned (1860)	Percent of Southern Whites in Category
10 or more	7
1 - 9	17
None	76

source: *Historical Statistics of the United States*

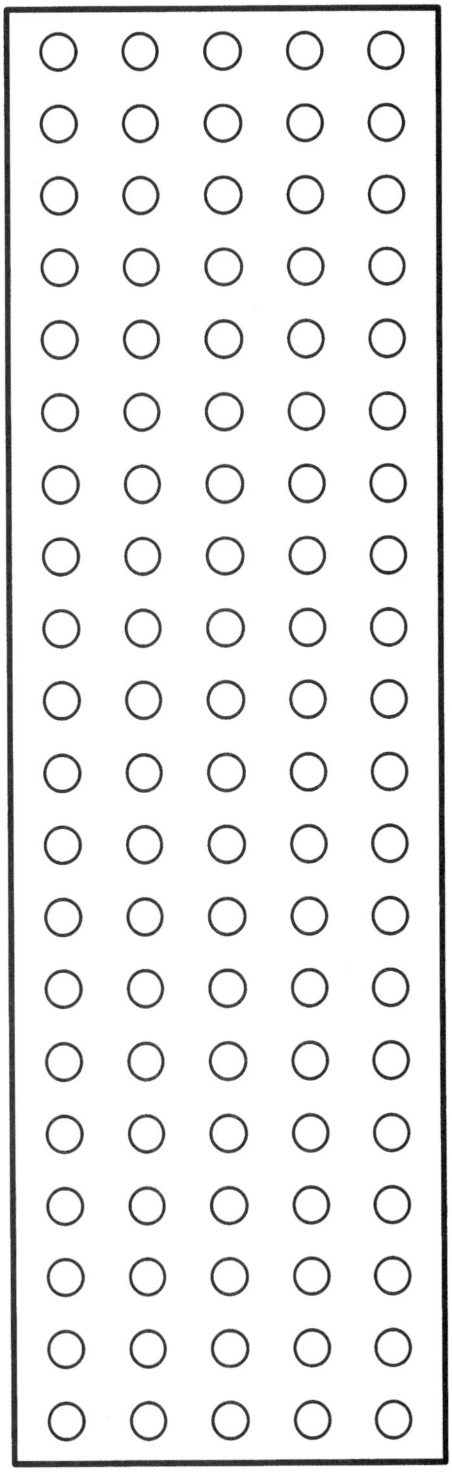

Slave Ownership by Southern Whites in 1860

(1 circle = 1% of white population)

Own 10 or more slaves [   ]
Own 1 - 9 slaves [   ]
Own no slaves [   ]

FREDERICK DOUGLASS SPEAKS FOR THE SLAVES

Frederick Douglass delivered the famous speech condensed here in 1852, when the citizens of Rochester, New York invited him to speak at a Fourth of July celebration. His address was titled, "The Meaning of the Fourth of July for the Negro."

Fellow citizens: Pardon me, and allow me to ask, why am I called upon to speak here today? What have I or those I represent to do with your national independence? Are the great principles of political freedom and of natural justice, embodied in that Declaration of Independence, extended to us?

Would to God, both for your sakes and ours, that an affirmative answer could be truthfully returned to these questions. Then would my task be light, and my burden easy and delightful.

But such is not the state of the case. I am not included within the pale of this glorious anniversary!

The rich inheritance of justice, liberty, prosperity, and independence bequeathed by your fathers is shared by you, not by me. This Fourth of July is yours, not mine. You may rejoice, I must mourn.

Fellow citizens, above your national, tumultuous joy, I hear the wail of millions!

My subject, then, fellow citizens, is "American Slavery." I shall see this day and its popular characteristics from the slave's point of view. Standing here, identified with the American bondman, making his wrongs mine, I do not hesitate to declare, with all my soul, that the character and conduct of this nation never looked blacker to me than on this Fourth of July.

Standing with God and the crushed and bleeding slave on this occasion, I will, in the name of humanity, which is outraged, in the name of liberty, which is fettered, in the name of the Constitution and the Bible, which are disregarded and trampled upon, dare to call in question and to denounce everything that serves to perpetuate slavery - the great sin and shame of America!

Oh! had I the ability, and could I reach the nation's ear, I would today pour out a fiery stream of biting ridicule, blasting reproach, withering sarcasm, and stern rebuke. For it is not light that is needed, but fire; it is not the gentle shower, but thunder. We need the storm, the whirlwind, and the earthquake.

The feeling of the nation must be quickened; the conscience of the nation must

be roused; the hypocrisy of the nation must be exposed; and its crimes against God and man must be denounced.

What to the American slave is your Fourth of July? I answer, a day that reveals to him more than all other days of the year, the gross injustice and cruelty to which he is the constant victim.

To him your celebration is a sham; your boasted liberty an unholy license; your national greatness, swelling vanity.

Your sounds of rejoicing are empty and heartless, your shouts of liberty and equality, hollow mockery; your prayers and hymns, your sermons and thanksgivings, with all your religious parade and solemnity, are to him mere bombast, fraud, deception, impiety, and hypocrisy - a thin veil to cover up crimes which would disgrace a nation of savages.

Group Discussion: *What message about the Fourth of July does Douglass have for the people of Rochester? What does he mean when he says "the hypocrisy of the nation must be exposed"?*

ABRAHAM LINCOLN AGAINST SLAVERY

In the 1850s Abraham Lincoln, then a lawyer in Illinois, began speaking out on the issue of slavery. He did not call for its immediate abolition in states where it already existed. He did, however, stand against allowing it to spread any further. These are condensed selections.

Before proceeding, let me say that I think I have no prejudice against the Southern people. They are just what we would be in their situation. If slavery did not now exist among them, they would not introduce it. If it did now exist among us, we should not instantly give it up.

Doubtless there are individuals on both sides who would not hold slaves under any circumstances, and others who would gladly introduce slavery anew if it were out of existence. We know that some Southern men do free their slaves, go North and become tip-top Abolitionists, while some Northern ones go South and become most cruel slave masters.

When Southern people tell us they are no more responsible for the origin of slavery than we are, I acknowledge the fact. When it is said that the institution exists and that it is very difficult to get rid of it in any satisfactory way, I can understand and appreciate the saying.

I surely will not blame them for not doing what I should not know how to do myself. If all earthly power were given to me, I should not know what to do as to the existing institution. *(1854)*

A house divided against itself cannot stand. I believe this government cannot endure permanently half slave and half free. I do not expect the Union to be dissolved - I do not expect the house to fall - but I do expect it will cease to be divided. It will become all one thing, or all the other.

Either the opponents of slavery will arrest the further spread of it, and place it where the public mind shall rest in the belief that it is in the course of ultimate extinction; or its advocates will push it forward, till it shall become alike lawful in all the States, old as well as new - North as well as South. *(1858)*

In a famous series of debates in 1858 with Senator Stephen Douglas, Lincoln summed up his view of the slavery issue:

That is the issue that will continue in this country when these poor tongues of Judge Douglas and myself shall be silent. It is the eternal struggle between these two principles - right and wrong - throughout the world.

They are the two principles that have stood face to face from the beginning of time, and will ever continue to struggle. The one is the common right of humanity, and the other the divine right of kings.

It is the same principle in whatever shape it develops itself. It is the same spirit that says, "You toil and work and earn bread, and I'll eat it." No matter in what shape it comes, whether from the mouth of a king who seeks to bestride the people of his own nation and live by the fruit of their labor, or from one race of men as an apology for enslaving another race, it is the same tyrannical principle. *(1858)*

Group Discussion: *Why does Lincoln feel he cannot blame the Southern states for not immediately ending slavery? What was his fear about the future of the nation? What was his position on the morality of slavery?*

5 | Civil War and Reconstruction: 1860 - 1877

"My paramount object in this struggle is to save the Union, and is not either to save or to destroy slavery."

"All we ask is to be let alone."

"On the first day of January in the Year of Our Lord, one thousand eight hundred and sixty three, all persons held as slaves within any state, or designated part of a state, the people whereof shall then be in rebellion against the United States shall be then, thenceforward, and forever free."

"...We here highly resolve that these dead shall not have died in vain; that this nation, under God, shall have a new birth of freedom; and that government of the people, by the people, for the people, shall not perish from the earth."

Study Checklist

When you have completed this section, working with the Internet support site at *www.fasttrackteaching.com* or other resources, you should be able to:

 Identify and explain the context of the **Famous Quotes** shown on the Section Title Page.

 Identify and explain the importance of the **Famous Names and Terms** listed on the topic summary pages in this section.

 Identify on a map and explain the importance of the **Famous Places** shown on the maps in this section.

 Explain the general sequence of events in this period and tell from memory the **Famous Years**:

- Abraham Lincoln was elected president (**1860**).
- The Civil War began (**1861**).
- The Civil War ended (**1865**).
- The Reconstruction period ended (**1877**).

Take a Practice Test!

 (A)   (B)   (C)   (D)

A multiple-choice practice test for this section can be found on the Internet support site at:

www.fasttrackteaching.com

Textbook Page References:

 Discuss or write briefly on such questions and topics as these:

1. What were the reasons the South had in 1861 for deciding that it didn't want to be part of the United States any more?

2. What advantages and disadvantages did each side have in the Civil War? What strategies did the North use during the war to weaken and eventually defeat the South?

3. Describe how President Lincoln's view of the slavery question changed during the Civil War. Explain why he decided to make ending slavery a main goal of the Civil War.

4. Explain why Lincoln's Emancipation Proclamation did not immediately end slavery in the U.S., and why the 13th Amendment was needed to accomplish that goal.

5. Why did the Radical Republicans in Congress want to take such dramatic steps to reconstruct the South? How successful were they in helping the freed slaves? Why did they consider the 14th Amendment so important?

6. How did the end of the Civil War and the Reconstruction Era change the social and economic patterns of life for whites and blacks in the South?

Timeline 1860 - 1877

Find when these events occurred, fill in the blanks, and place them on the main timeline. The thin timeline shows the presidents of this period.

Lincoln elected - This election convinced some of the Southern states to _____ .

South Carolina secedes - Within two months, the _____ was born.

C.S.A. formed - Jefferson _____ was president of the Confederate States of America.

Fort Sumter shelled - This event _____ the fighting of the Civil War.

Bull Run - This was the first big Civil War battle, near _____, Virginia.

Monitor* fights *Virginia - Neither of these _____-covered ships could defeat the other.

Antietam - This bloody battle in Maryland was a victory for the _____ .

Emancipation Proclamation - It marked the beginning of the end of _____ .

Gettysburg - This famous battle in Pennsylvania was the _____ point of the war.

Sherman's March - It _____ large areas in Georgia and the Carolinas.

Lee surrenders - He surrendered after retreating from the city of _____ .

Lincoln assassinated - He was fatally shot at Ford's _____, in Washington, DC.

13th Amendment ratified - This amendment _____ all slavery in the U.S.

Reconstruction Acts - These set up a system of _____ occupation of the South.

Pres. Johnson impeached - He was saved from conviction by _____ vote in the Senate.

14th Amendment ratified - This amendment made blacks _____ of the U.S.

15th Amendment ratified - This amendment gave _____ men the right to vote.

Amnesty Act passed - It gave back the right to _____ to most former Confederates.

Last federal troops withdrawn - This marks the end of _____ .

Use these terms to fill in the blanks: black, citizens, Confederacy, Davis, destroyed, ended, iron, Manassas, North, military, one, Reconstruction, Richmond, slavery, secede, started, Theater, turning, vote

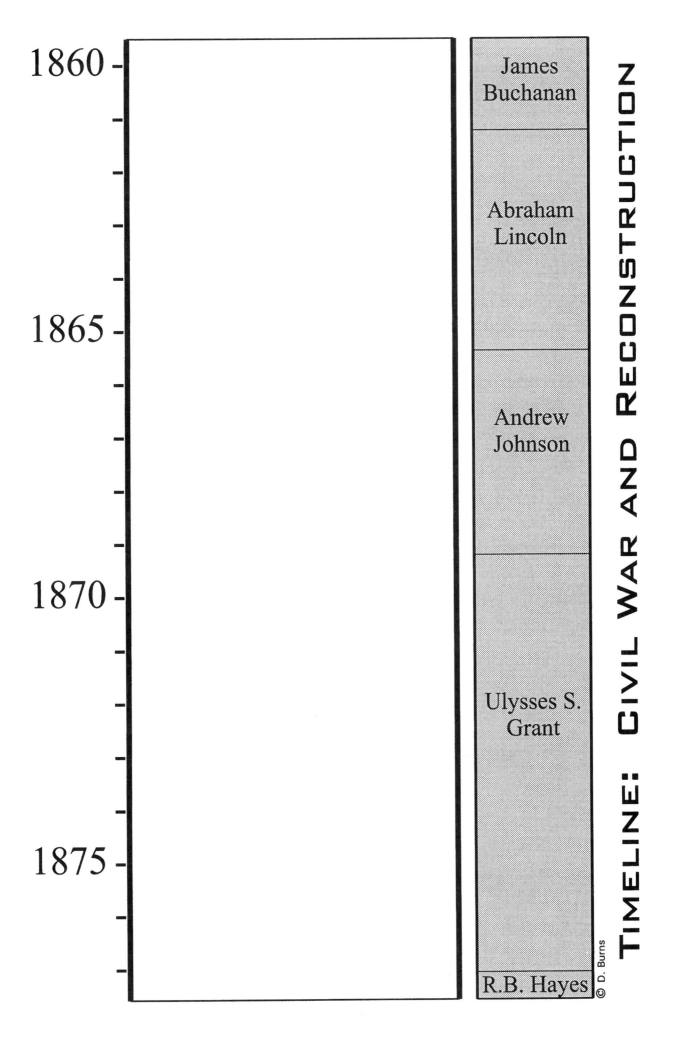

1860 –

1865 –

1870 –

1875 –

James
Buchanan

Abraham
Lincoln

Andrew
Johnson

Ulysses S.
Grant

R.B. Hayes

© D. Burns

TIMELINE: CIVIL WAR AND RECONSTRUCTION

THE CIVIL WAR

Abraham Lincoln, Jefferson Davis, Fort Sumter, Bull Run, blockade, ironclads, Shiloh,

Robert E. Lee, Ulysses S. Grant, Emancipation Proclamation, Antietam, Gettysburg,

Copperheads, Sherman's March, Appomattox Court House, John Wilkes Booth

By 1860, the year Abraham Lincoln was elected president, the North and the South had become two vastly different regions. The North was changing into an industrial society, with factories, growing cities, and wage labor. The South, however, remained a region of farms, with _____ labor a key part of the economy. On many issues, especially policies toward industry, tariffs, and slavery, the two sections of the country had grown increasingly hostile toward each other.

South Carolina had threatened to secede (leave the nation) before. The election of Lincoln was the final straw. His political support came almost entirely from voters in the _____ half of the country. He was not even on the ballot in most states in the South. Only six weeks after the election, South Carolina declared itself out of the Union. It was soon followed by six other Southern states. Together, these states organized into the Confederate States of America.

The new country, headed by its president, Jefferson Davis, felt perfectly justified in this action. The United States, the Confederacy argued, was created as a voluntary union that a state could _____ at any time. Many Confederate leaders believed they were following the principles of self-government that were at the heart of American beliefs.

The war began in 1861 when South Carolina soldiers fired upon U.S. troops who refused to leave Fort Sumter, a Federal fort on a small island in the harbor of Charleston. Lincoln called for volunteers for the Union army. The undecided states (like _____, just south of Washington, D.C.) quickly took one side or the other.

As fighting began, the purpose of the war was to stop the 11 Confederate states from seceding. Although Lincoln had long spoken against slavery, he did not make ending slavery a purpose of the war when it began. Several slave states, in fact, like Maryland and Kentucky, stayed _____ the Union.

The South was at a big disadvantage from the beginning.
The North had over two times the population, most of the factories, and many more miles of railroads. The South, however, was fighting to defend its own territory, and it had very talented military leaders like General Robert E. Lee. Early in the war, these gave the South big victories. But over time, the North's advantages were overwhelming. The North's naval blockade of the Southern coast was not completely effective, but it did worsen the shortages of _____ materials needed by the Confederates.

Both sides figured it would be a quick war when it began. Northern troops marched boldly toward the city of Richmond the first year of the war, but were turned back in the Battle of Bull Run, at Manassas, Virginia.

Further west, Union soldiers had better luck in their strategy to win control of the Mississippi River. A famous battle at Shiloh, Tennessee, was a first step. It also showed both sides how bloody and _____ the war would be. Women on both sides began efforts to improve the terrible medical conditions faced by wounded soldiers.

Southern attempts to strike into the North failed. The first attempt was stopped at Antietam, in Maryland, the second year of the war. The South lost an even more famous battle later at _____, Pennsylvania, the third year of the war.

By 1862 Lincoln was convinced that ending slavery should be declared a specific goal of the war. Such a step would also help keep England from siding with the South. The president issued the Emancipation Proclamation in 1862, to take effect in January 1863. But victory in the war was long in coming and often appeared uncertain. "Copperheads" who wanted to negotiate peace with the South spoke out _____ the war and the president. A draft law to get more soldiers actually led to riots in the streets of New York City.

Lincoln faced a tough re-election campaign in 1864. But he was helped by big military victories such as the taking of Atlanta, Georgia, by the Union army. Soon, General William Tecumseh Sherman was laying waste to vast areas of the South as he marched his army on a mission of destruction through Georgia and the Carolinas. The Northern strategy to _____ the South at the Mississippi, blockade it by sea, and invade it by land, was now clearly succeeding.

In April 1865 the capital of the Confederacy, _____, Virginia, finally fell. General Lee and his army retreated from the city with the Union army in hot pursuit. But within a week, Lee surrendered to General Ulysses S. Grant in a small town called Appomattox Court House. Grant treated the defeated Confederate army generously, and sent supplies of food to the nearly starving soldiers. A few days later, a fanatic named John Wilkes _____ shot and killed President Lincoln. Now the one man who might have re-united the country smoothly was dead. Instead, the re-unification was bitter and chaotic.

Use these terms to fill in the blanks: against, Booth, deadly, divide, Gettysburg, in, leave, northern, Richmond, slave, Virginia, war

CHARTING MANPOWER AND RESOURCES

The Civil War forced Southern states to confront the stark fact that in both manpower and resources, the Confederacy was at a big disadvantage. To compare the two sections of the country at the start of the conflict, finish the bar graphs below.

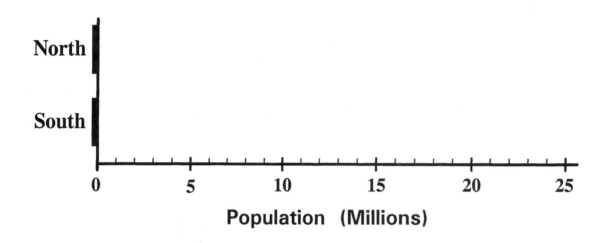

Population (Millions)

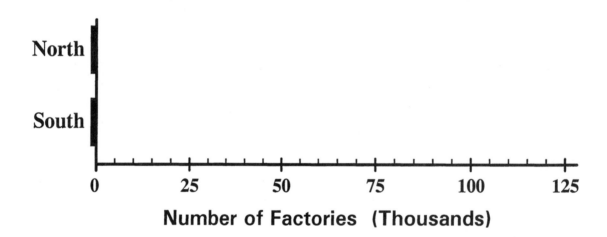

Number of Factories (Thousands)

Use the table below to find the information to complete the bar graphs above. Draw a bar for each region, with the length corresponding to the statistics shown in the table.

	Population (Millions)	Factories (Thousands)
North	22	110
South	9	18

Finish the chart below to compare some of the key statistics for each side of the Civil War. What facts about medical knowledge at the time would explain the patterns shown here?

Civil War Military Manpower and Death Rates

<u>Color Key</u>:   Died from Disease [   ]   Died from Wounds [   ]   Survived [   ]

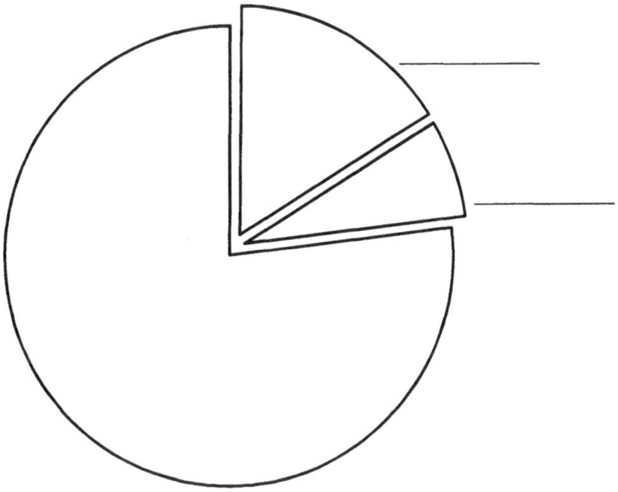

The North

Total Forces: _____

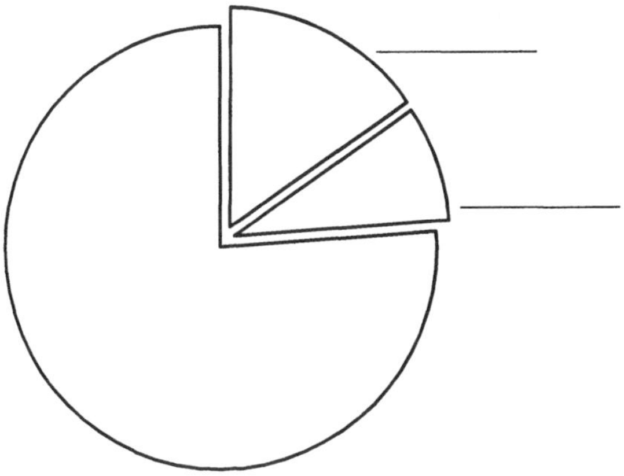

The South

Total Forces: _____

Use the table below to find the total military forces for each side, then fill in the "Total Forces" lines in the chart above. Next, find the <u>percent</u> of each side's forces that died from wounds, and the <u>percent</u> that died from disease. Place the figures (with a % sign) beside the correct segments of the pie graphs. Finally, pick a color for each category in the key, and shade the segments with the appropriate colors.

	Total Military Forces	Died From Wounds	Death Rate From Wounds (Percent of Total Forces)	Died From Disease	Death Rate From Disease (Percent of Total Forces)
North	1,556,678	110,070	7	249,458	16
South	1,082,119	94,000	8.7	164,000	15.2

source: **Nash,** *The American People*

MAP - THE CIVIL WAR'S FAMOUS PLACES

Finish labeling and drawing the map to show these:

Union States *(Shade these states light yellow.)*

Confederate States *(Shade these states light green.)*

Washington, capital of the states that remained the U.S.A.,
　　　　which was also called the _____ or simply the North.

Richmond, capital of the _____ States of America, or C.S.A.

Charleston, where the _____ shots of the war were fired against **Ft. Sumter** in 1861.

Blockade Line, along which the Union placed _____ to stop Southern trade.

Manassas, where the first Union attack was stopped at the Battle of Bull _____.

Norfolk, where the South rebuilt a captured Union ship called the _____ as an
　　　　ironclad ship. It was renamed the *Virginia*, and fought the Union ironclad *Monitor*
　　　　in a famous battle near Norfolk in 1862. Neither ship could defeat the other.

Shiloh, where everyone learned how _____ the war would be.

New Orleans, taken by the Union in a drive to control the _____ River.

Antietam, where the _____ was turned back in one of the last big battles of 1862.

Gettysburg, where the South, under General Lee, was turned back again in 18_____.

Vicksburg, where the North finally won complete _____ of the Mississippi River.

Atlanta, which fell to the North in 18_____, helping Lincoln's re-election campaign.

Sherman's March, which went from _____ to Savannah, then turned north.

Savannah, an important Confederate port on the _____ Ocean.

Appomattox Court House, where Gen. Lee finally _____ in April, 1865.

---

*Use these terms to fill in the blanks: 63, 64, Atlanta, Atlantic, Confederate, control, deadly, first,
Merrimac, Mississippi, Run, South, surrendered, Union, warships*

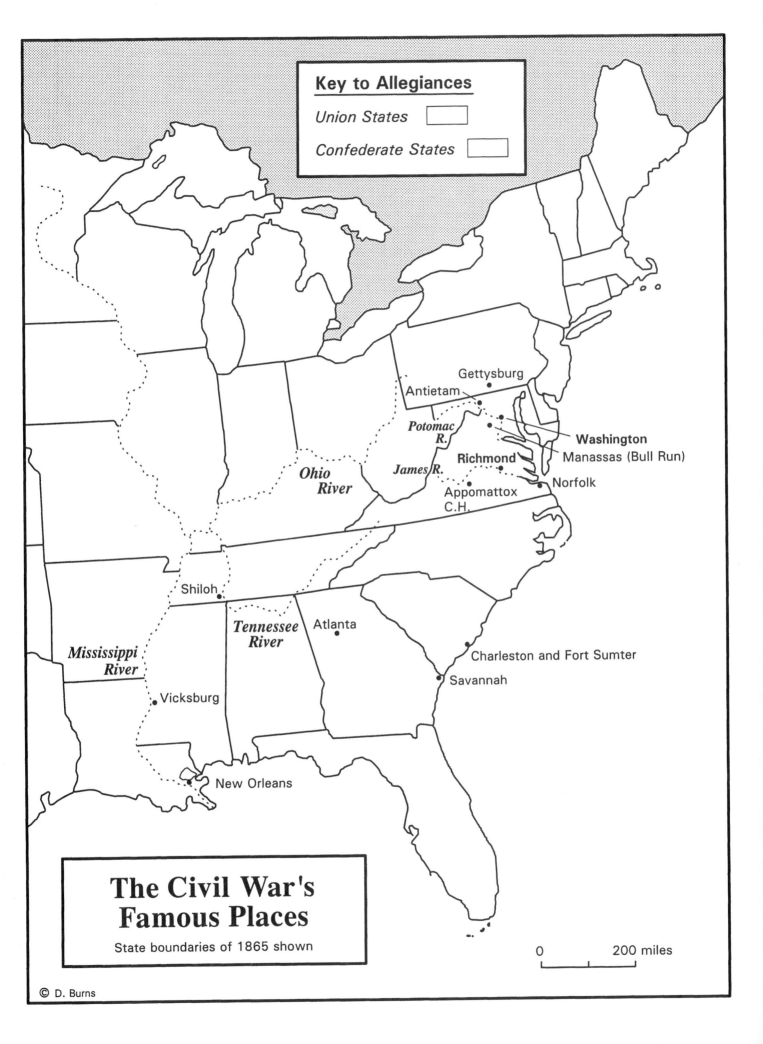

Key to Allegiances

Union States ☐

Confederate States ☐

Gettysburg

Antietam

Potomac R.

Washington

James R.

Richmond

Manassas (Bull Run)

Norfolk

Appomattox C.H.

Ohio River

Shiloh

Tennessee River

Atlanta

Charleston and Fort Sumter

Savannah

Mississippi River

Vicksburg

New Orleans

The Civil War's Famous Places

State boundaries of 1865 shown

0   200 miles

© D. Burns

LINCOLN'S GETTYSBURG ADDRESS

Lincoln gave this brief speech at the dedication of the Gettysburg battlefield in November 1863. It was almost six months after Union troops there turned back a Confederate attack. At first, the words drew little notice. But soon the speech was being widely quoted, and even today it is famous for its simple but powerful words.

Four score and seven years ago our fathers brought forth on this continent a new nation, conceived in liberty, and dedicated to the proposition that all men are created equal.

Now we are engaged in a great civil war, testing whether that nation, or any nation so conceived and so dedicated, can long endure. We are met on a great battlefield of that war. We have come to dedicate a portion of that field as a final resting place for those who here gave their lives that that nation might live. It is altogether fitting and proper that we should do this.

But in a larger sense, we cannot dedicate - we cannot consecrate - we cannot hallow - this ground. The brave men, living and dead, who struggled here, have consecrated it far above our poor power to add or detract.

The world will little note nor long remember what we say here, but it can never forget what they did here. It is for us, the living, rather, to be dedicated here to the unfinished work which they who fought here have thus far so nobly advanced.

It is rather for us to be here dedicated to the great task remaining before us - that from these honored dead we take increased devotion to that cause for which they gave their last full measure of devotion; that we here highly resolve that these dead shall not have died in vain; that this nation, under God, shall have a new birth of freedom; and that government of the people, by the people, for the people, shall not perish from the earth.

1. *Just above the first few words, write the number of years the United States had existed at the time Lincoln gave this speech. ("Score" is an old-fashioned word that means 20.)*

2. *Highlight the two key ideas or principles Lincoln says the nation was based on when it was formed in 1776.*

3. *Lincoln tells the audience that the Civil War is a kind of test for the American nation. Highlight the phrase that tells what the war was testing.*

4. *As his speech ends, Lincoln urges his listeners to dedicate themselves to the "unfinished work" of the battle. Highlight the phrases that tell what he wants his listeners to do.*

THE FREED SLAVES TELL THEIR STORIES

These selections are from interviews with former slaves conducted many years after the Civil War, and were written down phonetically to show speech patterns:

De freedom man come to our place an' read a paper what de Pres'dent had writ what said we was now free, an' he talk to us 'bout freedom and tole us not to work no more, 'less we get paid for it.

When he had finished an' gone, old Buck Adams' wife, old Mary Adams, come out an spoke to us. I rec'lec what she said jes as well as if I jes hear her say it.

She say, "Ten years from today, I'll have you all back 'gain." Yes, sir. "Ten years from today, I'll have you all back 'gain."

Dat ten years been over a mighty long time, an' she ain' got us back yet, an' she is dead an' gone.

-- *William Matthews*

When freedom come, Marster [the master] tell us all to come to front of de house. He am standin on de porch. He 'splains 'bout freedom and says, "You is now free and can go whar you pleases."

Den, he tells us he have larned us not to steal and to be good, and we-uns should 'member dat, and if we-uns gets into trouble, to come to him and he will help us.

He sho' do dat, too, cause de freed slaves goes to him lots of times, and he always helps. Marster says dat he needs help on de place, and sich dat stays, he'd pay em for de work. Lots of dem stayed, but some left.

-- *Betty Bormer*

I remember well how the roads was full of folks walking and walking along, when the slaves were freed.

Didn't know where they was going. Just going to see about something else, somewhere else. Meet a body in the road and they ask, "Where you going?" "Don't know." "What you going to do?" "Don't know."

Then sometimes we would meet a white man, and he would say, "How you like to come work on my farm?" And we say, "I don't know."

And then maybe he say, "If you come work for me on my farm, when the crops is in, I give you five bushels of corn, five gallons of molasses, some ham meat, and all your clothes and vittles [food] while you works for me."

"All right! That's what I do."

And then, something begins to work up here and I begins to think and to know things. And I knowed then I could make a living for my own self, and I never had to be a slave no more.

-- *Robert Falls*

Group Discussion:

1. What attitudes toward the end of slavery did the plantation owners show, based on the first two selections?

2. How does the account in the third selection show that freed slaves and landowners were starting to develop a new economic relationship?

RECONSTRUCTION AND BEYOND

Freedmen's Bureau, Black Codes, Andrew Johnson, Radical Republicans,

Reconstruction Acts, 13th, 14th, & 15th Amendments, impeachment, carpetbagger,

Ku Klux Klan, sharecropping, segregation, Booker T. Washington

Although the Civil War began to "save the Union," it led to changes so vast that it is sometimes called "The Second American Revolution." Four million slaves were now _____, and had to find a new place in a changed South. Millions of former Confederates had to be brought back into the once again United States. The dozen years after the war in which these changes occurred is called the Reconstruction era.

Lincoln wanted the South brought back with as little pain as possible. Even before the war ended, Lincoln set up a new federal government agency called the Freedmen's Bureau to help the former slaves get on their feet. Thousands of _____ were set up to teach basic skills and give other help.

The surrender brought many reactions. Some whites adapted, and even offered to help freed slaves get a new start. Many others swore slavery would return. Some blacks stayed where they had worked before the war, while others could not wait to leave an oppressive master. But the South's economy was totally _____ by the war. Many farms and cities were in ruins. Slavery was ended by the 13th Amendment, but the freed slaves owned no _____ or tools. Southern whites feared what might happen with wandering groups of unemployed blacks, and passed laws called Black Codes. These generally put curfews and travel restrictions on blacks, and prevented them from enjoying full rights as citizens. (In fact, few Northern states at this time gave blacks equal rights as citizens either.)

Lincoln's successor in 1865 was President Andrew Johnson. He issued a pardon covering most of the former rebels, but showed little interest in the plight of the freed slaves. Members of Congress called the Radical Republicans, however, wanted to shatter forever the old social and economic patterns of life in the South. Many wanted the land of the big plantations broken up and _____ among the former slaves. This land reform plan didn't go forward, but other important proposals did.

By 1867 the Radical Republicans in the Congress had enough votes to call the shots on Reconstruction. They passed several laws called the Reconstruction Acts. These set up a military occupation of the Southern states. Whites who had fought for the South were now told they could _____ vote, but freed slaves could. Southern states were also told that they would not be allowed back in the Union until they approved the 14th Amendment, guaranteeing full citizenship to blacks. (The 15th Amendment established voting rights for black men as a national law several years later.)

President Johnson opposed many measures favored by the Radicals, and in 1868 they attempted to remove him. He was charged with misconduct, or impeached, for firing a government official. In reality, the Radicals just wanted any excuse to get rid of him. After his trial before the Senate, the Radicals fell _____ vote short of the total they needed to convict him. Johnson remained, although his political career was badly damaged. Ulysses S. Grant, a famous Union general in the Civil War, won the 1868 election.

Southern whites, already angry about losing the war, felt they were being made "punching bags" by Northerners. Conditions were _____ enough without more disruptions caused by the new Reconstruction laws, they felt. They especially resented the Northerners known as carpetbaggers who came South to make a fast buck. In some cases these Northerners used black voters to get themselves elected to public offices in the South, and worked up crooked schemes of various kinds. White Southerners also resented the fact that blacks were being _____ to various offices, when many whites were still denied the right to vote and hold office because they had fought for the Confederacy.

In reaction, some whites formed secret societies like the Ku Klux Klan to regain their political and social dominance. These groups used threats, beatings, and even murder to frighten blacks away from voting. In 1872 the Amnesty Act restored voting rights to most former Confederate soldiers. Over the next few decades blacks were _____ out of the political process altogether.

Economically, the South's plantation system was destroyed by the war and the end of slavery. Very quickly, however, a new pattern of farm labor called sharecropping grew up in many areas. But it often left the sharecropper, white or black, with little or no profit after paying the landowner his share of the crop. (Typically one-half the harvest.) More hopefully, the war helped end the dependence of the South on a few cash crops, and led to the _____ of industry in some areas. Even so, the region lagged behind the rest of the nation economically for almost a century.

The Reconstruction era ended in 1877, when the last federal troops were withdrawn from the South. But the challenges raised by the Civil War were not entirely worked out. Blacks were increasingly segregated (separated) from whites, and rarely given equal opportunities. This separation would become more rigid with "_____ Crow" laws as the decades went by. It would be many generations before the bitterness of the Civil War faded, and the Civil Rights movement brought Southern whites and blacks together again as equals.

Use these terms to fill in the blanks: bad, destroyed, divided, elected, free, growth, Jim, land, not, one, pushed, schools

VOICES OF RECONSTRUCTION

The task of reconstructing the South was one that divided opinions almost as sharply as the Civil War itself. These condensed excerpts from historical documents and a famous speech highlight the hopes and fears that existed after the war.

Freedmen's Bureau Circular Number 1

This "circular" or notice was printed and distributed by the Freedmen's Bureau in North Carolina in July 1865.

A great social revolution is going on. The united wisdom of all classes will be required to guide it to a successful issue [outcome].

Circular No. 1

Freedmen's Bureau

July 1865

The Negro has become free, but he has not become an object of indifference. His interests and those of the white man are the same. He cannot with safety be treated with neglect, or scorn, or cruelty. He is human, and is entitled to all the rights of a man.

Withhold from the Freedmen fair wages for their labor, deny them a right to a fair hearing before courts of justice, discourage their efforts to accumulate property, and to acquire learning, and you will drive from this state its real wealth - its productive labor.

On the other hand, give to the Freedmen that which is just and equal, give them all the facilities possible for improvement and education, and you will secure in the State its best supporters and its truest friends.

I invite the cooperation of Freedmen also. Without your help this Bureau can do but little for you. Your freedom imposes upon you new duties. Some of you have families; it is your duty to support them. Some of you have aged parents and relatives, to whom liberty has come too late; it is your duty to minister to their comfort.

Some of you will meet with helpless orphans; it is your duty to supply to them, as far as you can, the places of their lost parents. It is your duty, in common to all men, to obey the laws of the land, to live honestly and uprightly.

The Freedmen's Fear

This assessment of the situation of the freed slaves is from an official statement of the Convention of the Colored People of Virginia. It is dated August 1865. The document carries the title, "An Address to the Loyal Citizens and Congress of the United States."

Well, the war is over, the rebellion is "put down," and we are *declared* free! The president has, in his efforts at the reconstruction of the civil government of the States, left us entirely at the mercy of these subjugated but unconverted rebels, in *everything* save the privilege of bringing us, our wives and little ones, to the auction block.

We *know* these men - know them *well* - and we assure you that, with the majority of them, loyalty is only "lip deep," and that their professions of loyalty are used as a cover to the cherished design of getting restored to their former relations with the Federal Government, and then, by all sorts of "unfriendly legislation," to render the freedom you have given us more intolerable than the slavery they intended for us.

We warn you that our only safety is in keeping them under Governors of the *military persuasion* until you have so amended the Federal Constitution that it will prohibit the States from making any distinction between citizens on account of race or color.

The White Planter's View

A newspaper editor from Louisiana gave this view of matters in 1866 during testimony to a Congressional committee.

I think if the whole regulation of the Negroes, or freedmen, were left to the people of the communities in which they live, it will be administered for the best interest of the Negroes as well as of the white men.

I think there is a friendly feeling on the part of the planters towards the freedmen. They are not held at all responsible for anything that has happened.

In talking with a number of planters, I remember some of them telling me they were succeeding very well with their freedmen, having got a preacher to preach to them and a teacher to teach them, believing it was for the interest of the planter to make the Negro feel reconciled; for, to lose his services as a laborer for even a few months would be very disastrous.

The sentiment prevailing is, that it is for the interest of the employer to teach the Negro, to educate his children, to provide a preacher for him, and to attend to his physical wants. Leave the people to themselves, and they will manage very well.

The "Atlanta Compromise"

The decades after the Reconstruction era saw a rigid pattern of segregation grow in the South. Booker T. Washington urged a strategy that emphasized economic progress for blacks, rather than a push for social equality. He believed that segregation would fall away by itself as blacks became a bigger force in the economy. In a speech in Atlanta in 1895, the famous educator explained his strategy.

No race can prosper until it learns that there is as much dignity in tilling a field as in writing a poem. Nor should we permit our grievances to over-shadow our opportunities. In all things that are purely social, we can be as separate as the fingers, yet one as the hand in all things essential to mutual progress.

There is no defense or security for any of us except in the highest intelligence and development of all. If anywhere there are efforts tending to curtail [hold back] the fullest growth of the Negro, let these efforts be turned to encouraging him.

We shall constitute one-third and more of the ignorance and crime of the South, or one-third of its intelligence and progress. Nearly sixteen millions of hands will aid you in pulling the load upward, or they will pull, against you, the load downward.

The wisest among my race understand that the agitation of questions of social equality is the extremest folly, and that progress in the enjoyment of all the privileges that will come to us must be the result of severe and constant struggle rather than artificial forcing.

It is important and right that all privileges of the law be ours, but it is vastly more important that we be prepared for the exercise of those privileges. The opportunity to earn a dollar in a factory just now is worth infinitely more than the opportunity to spend a dollar in an opera house.

Group Discussion: *Summarize the main points made in each selection. What do they reveal about the challenges that faced the South - and the nation - in the decades after the Civil War?*

6 | The Gilded Age: 1865 - 1900

*"From where the sun now stands,
I will fight no more forever."*

"In God we trusted. In Kansas we busted."

*"Give me your tired, your poor,
Your huddled masses yearning to
        breathe free,
The wretched refuse of your
        teaming shore.
Send these, the homeless,
        tempest-tost to me,
I lift my lamp beside the golden door."*

*"So long as all the increased wealth which
modern progress brings goes but to build up
great fortunes, to increase luxury and make
sharper the contrast between the House of
Have and the House of Want, progress is not
real and cannot be permanent."*

Study Checklist

When you have completed this section, working with the Internet support site at www.fasttrackteaching.com or other resources, you should be able to:

 Identify and explain the context of the **Famous Quotes** shown on the Section Title Page.

 Identify and explain the importance of the **Famous Names and Terms** listed on the topic summary pages in this section.

 Identify on a map and explain the importance of the **Famous Places** shown on the maps in this section.

 Explain the general sequence of events in this period and tell from memory the **Famous Years:**

- The first transcontinental railroad was completed (**1869**).
- The telephone was invented (**1876**).
- The Spanish-American War began (**1898**).

Take a Practice Test!

 (A) (B) (C) (D)

A multiple-choice practice test for this section can be found on the Internet support site at:

www.fasttrackteaching.com

Textbook Page References:

 Discuss or write briefly on such questions and topics as these:

1. Why might it be said that the railroad created the cowboy era, and barbed wire ended it?

2. What were the consequences of westward growth for Native Americans in this era? What was the goal of the Dawes Act, and why did most Indians object to it?

3. How does the growth of business in this era show both the positive and negative consequences of "raw" or unregulated capitalism? How did labor unions try to deal with the growth of big business?

4. In what ways did immigrants to America in these years get what they hoped for, and in what ways were they likely disappointed? How did the sources of immigration change in this period?

5. What signs were visible by the late 1800s that showed many Americans were trying to solve the problems that grew up in the Gilded Age?

6. Describe the changes of this era that would have impressed a city resident in 1900 who was old enough to remember what life in America was like in 1865.

Timeline 1865 - 1900

Find when these events occurred, fill in the blanks, and place them on the main timeline. The thin timeline shows the presidents of this period.

Civil War ends - The economy of the _____ was left in ruins.

Typewriter invented - It soon opened a whole new career to _____.

Transcontinental R.R. opens - Irish and _____ immigrants did much of the back-breaking work on this famous railroad.

Boss Tweed exposed - His crooked ways in New York politics finally sent him to _____.

Susan B. Anthony's illegal vote - She fought for woman _____.

Carnegie's steel company begins - He made millions, then _____ much of it away.

Telephone invented - It was invented by Alexander Graham _____.

Light bulb invented - It was just one of Thomas _____'s many inventions.

Standard Oil trust started - It aimed to get _____ control of the oil industry.

A. F. of L. forms - The American Federation of Labor became the leading organization of workers in the U.S., and was led by Samuel _____.

Dawes Act - It tried to "_____" the Indians, but failed.

Kodak camera invented - It made photography easy for _____.

Sherman Antitrust Act - This law passed by Congress was an attempt to control the growing power of big business, but it proved to be _____ very effective.

Populist Party begins - Many _____ and workers liked this reform-minded party.

Ellis Island opens - It was the gateway for millions of _____.

Plessy v. Ferguson - This famous Supreme Court case allowed _____ to continue, by accepting the concept of "separate but equal" facilities for whites and blacks.

Spanish-American War - It won _____ and the Philippines for the U.S.

Use these terms to fill in the blanks: Americanize, Bell, Chinese, Edison, everyone, farmers, gave, Gompers, immigrants, jail, not, Puerto Rico, segregation, South, suffrage, total, women

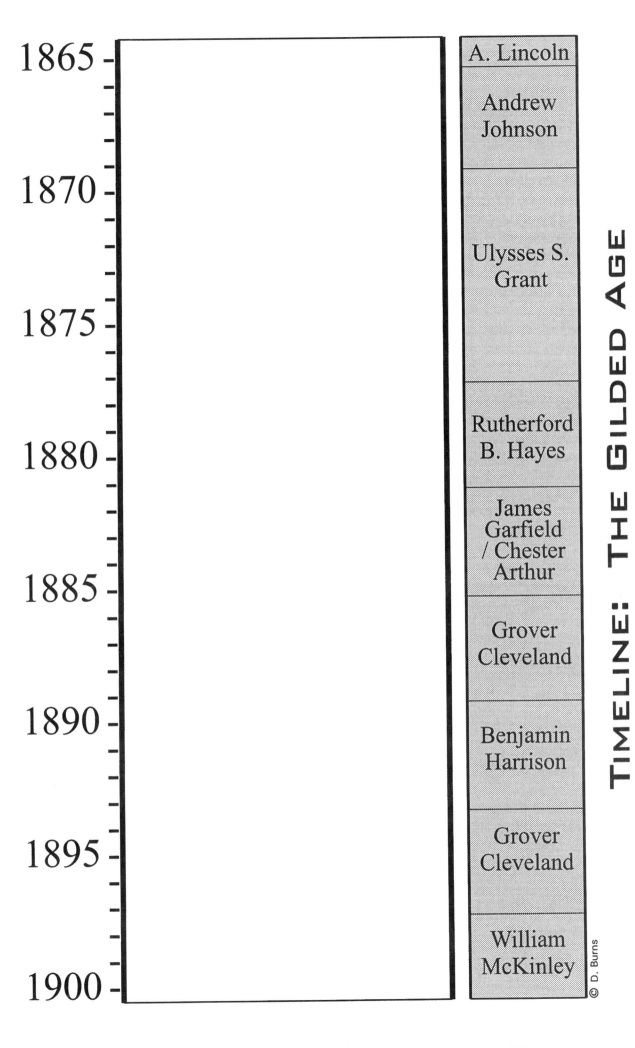

1865

1870

1875

1880

1885

1890

1895

1900

A. Lincoln

Andrew Johnson

Ulysses S. Grant

Rutherford B. Hayes

James Garfield / Chester Arthur

Grover Cleveland

Benjamin Harrison

Grover Cleveland

William McKinley

TIMELINE: THE GILDED AGE

THE GILDED AGE

Andrew Carnegie, John D. Rockefeller, trusts, Thomas Edison, tenement, political machine,

graft, Boss Tweed, Sherman Antitrust Act, American Federation of Labor,

Homestead Act, Dawes Act, Ellis Island, Spanish-American War, Susan B. Anthony

The Civil War left the South devastated, but it gave a big boost to the North and the West. In the Gilded Age business and industry grew to a size and power that rivaled the government itself. Men like Andrew Carnegie (in the steel business) and John D. Rockefeller (in the oil business) were at the head of this trend. The companies they created, and others like them, made great advances in technology and efficiency. But some, like the Standard Oil trust, organized whole industries in ways designed to restrict or _____ competition.

Cities continued growing rapidly. By 1900 many had electric trolley systems and large downtown department stores. The first steel framed "skyscrapers" were being built in Chicago. New inventions like the telephone and Thomas Edison's electric light bulb were developed. Books, magazines, and newspapers spread much more widely. Sports like _____, boxing, and bicycling captured the interest of millions.

Gilded Age cities held sharp contrasts. Rich business owners built extravagant mansions, but the lower classes lived in overcrowded tenement buildings. Big-city "political machines" gave some small help to the poor in return for their _____ at election time. But those who ran the political machines often grew wealthy through various forms of graft and even outright theft. New York City's Boss Tweed is often ranked as the best example of such crooks.

A few new laws tried to deal with problems that appeared in the Gilded Age. The Sherman Antitrust Act was passed by Congress to try to control the trusts. New York City passed laws to improve tenement buildings. But the "get ahead, go ahead" attitude toward business made such laws hard to _____. There was a related attitude of "rugged individualism": determination and hard work would get you ahead, so if you stayed poor, it was your own fault. Labor unions objected to that view of poverty. They blamed poverty mainly on employers' greed, and organized strikes for better pay and working conditions. The American Federation of Labor, a nation-wide union led by Samuel Gompers, was formed in these years.

This era is also remembered for the Wild West. Railroads were spreading after the Civil War, and the first transcontinental railroad was completed in 1869. But it was another set of tracks reaching into Kansas that solved a big problem for ranchers in Texas. Now, cowboys could round up Texas Longhorns and move them up the Chisholm Trail to the rail line at Abilene, Kansas. From there, railroads carried the cattle for sale in cities like St. Louis and Chicago. New trails and new "cow towns" like _____ City were soon growing.

Mining and lumbering also drew many people to the West. But farmland was the biggest draw of all. The Homestead Act passed by Congress gave 160 acres in the West to anyone who would settle there and farm the land. Many tried and gave up. Others, however, stayed and slowly claimed the countryside with the help of the new _____ wire fences.

As more people moved west, Indians already living there were forced to move to reservations. Settlers feared attacks by the Indians. Indians resented the constant _____ by dishonest government agents.

Indians fought the plan to restrict them to reservations. The vast numbers of settlers and soldiers, and the destruction of the wild _____ herds, soon overwhelmed them. One of the most famous incidents in the Indian Wars was Custer's Last Stand. But that Indian victory in what is now Montana was the exception to the pattern. Eventually Congress developed a plan to dissolve the tribes and "Americanize" the Indians. This policy was put forth in the Dawes Act (1887), but it failed miserably. Most Indians did not wish to lose their tribal identity, and _____ the efforts to make them do so.

Immigrants were another part of the Gilded Age story. After 1880 many more were arriving from Eastern and Southern European countries. They found opportunity, but sometimes also resentment from the native-born, who feared the cultural changes the newcomers might bring. Still, _____ Island became famous as the first stop for millions of new Americans.

By 1900 America had grown well beyond its shores with the addition of Alaska and Hawaii. It fought to help Cuba free itself from Spain in the Spanish-American War. With victory in that conflict, the U.S. took control of Puerto Rico and the _____ from Spain.

At home, inventors were tinkering with early automobiles. Women, led by Susan B. Anthony, were pushing hard for the right to vote. Women like Jane Addams also led the attack on social problems, often focusing their efforts on city slums. Journalists - both men and women - were exposing the problems of the era in newspapers and magazines. A new movement called Populism was organizing farmers and workers into the National People's (or Populist) Party. It didn't last long, but it promoted many reforms that later became law, such as the _____ hour work day and the secret ballot. The century ended with the hopeful expectation that America's growing pains, while very real, would be cured.

Use these terms to fill the blanks: barbed, baseball, buffalo, cheating, Dodge, eight, eliminate, Ellis, enforce, Philippines, resisted, votes

MAP - RAILROADS, COWBOYS, AND INDIANS

Finish labeling and drawing the map to show these:

THE FIRST TRANSCONTINENTAL RAILROAD
Use red for all railroad lines. Label both of these lines that together formed the first transcontinental railroad.

Union Pacific R.R. - This company started in the city of **Omaha** and laid track westward across the Great Plains. For each mile of track laid, the federal government gave land and loans to the companies. The land was later sold to farmers to help finance the construction.

Central Pacific R.R. - This company laid track eastward from the city of **Sacramento**, and faced the more difficult work of putting track across the Sierra Nevada mountain range. Federal loans were higher for track laid in the mountains or driven through them with tunnels.

Promontory Point - This is the spot where the two lines met and were joined with a golden spike in 1869. By the end of the century, there were four other transcontinental railroad lines in operation.

CATTLE TRAILS, RAILROADS, AND RELATED PLACES
Use red to show the rail lines listed below, but do not label them on the map. Use green to show each of the famous cattle trails.

Missouri Pacific R.R., connecting **St. Louis** and **Kansas City**.

Kansas Pacific R.R., connecting **Kansas City, Topeka, Abilene,** and **Denver**.

Atchison, Topeka, and Santa Fe R.R., connecting **Atchison, Topeka, Dodge City, Pueblo,** and **Santa Fe**.

Original range of Texas Longhorn *(Shade this area in southern Texas light green.)*

Chisholm Trail   **Western Trail**   **Goodnight-Loving Trail**

INDIAN TERRITORY AND BATTLE / MASSACRE SITES

Little Bighorn   **Wounded Knee**

Indian Territory *(Shade this area light yellow.)*

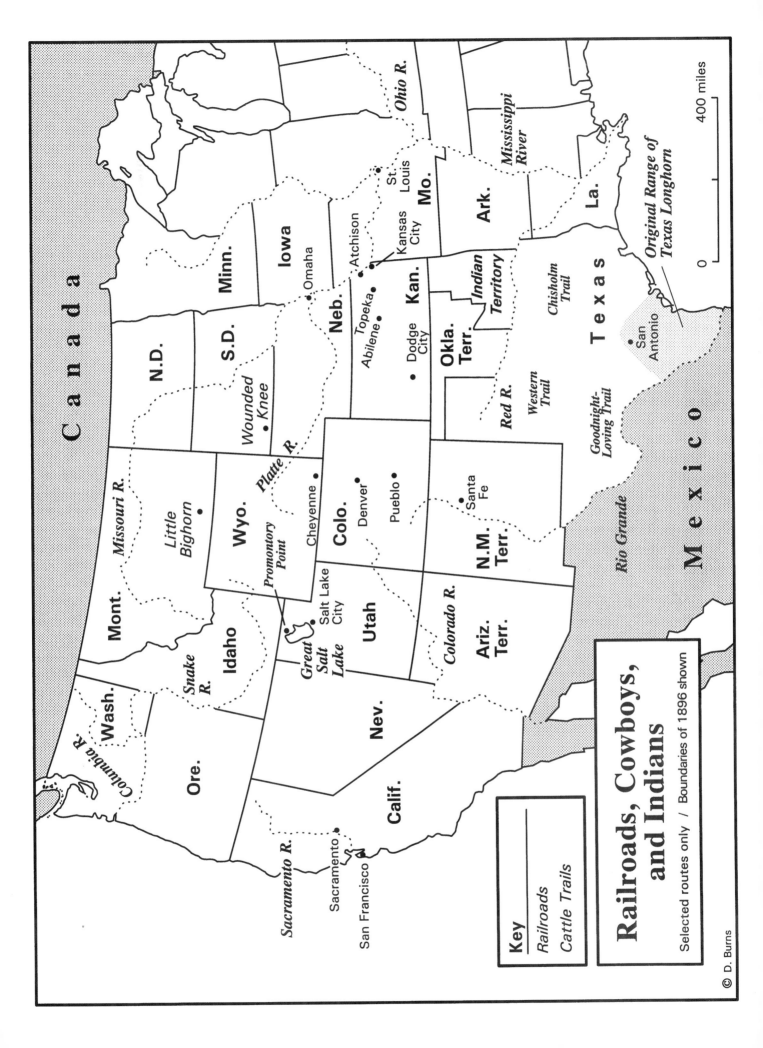

Railroads, Cowboys, and Indians

Selected routes only / Boundaries of 1896 shown

Key
Railroads
Cattle Trails

© D. Burns

Canada

Mexico

Ohio R.

Mississippi River

La.

Ark.

Mo.

St. Louis

Kansas City

Atchison

Omaha

Iowa

Minn.

N.D.

S.D.

Neb.

Kan.

Topeka

Abilene

Dodge City

Okla. Terr.

Indian Territory

Texas

Original Range of Texas Longhorn

San Antonio

Chisholm Trail

Western Trail

Goodnight-Loving Trail

Red R.

Wounded Knee

Platte R.

Wyo.

Cheyenne

Colo.

Denver

Pueblo

Santa Fe

N.M. Terr.

Ariz. Terr.

Rio Grande

Mont.

Missouri R.

Little Bighorn

Promontory Point

Salt Lake City

Great Salt Lake

Utah

Colorado R.

Idaho

Snake R.

Wash.

Columbia R.

Ore.

Nev.

Calif.

Sacramento R.

Sacramento

San Francisco

400 miles

0

MAP - AMERICA GROWS OVERSEAS

Finish labeling the maps, using red to show the areas acquired by the U.S. from 1865 to 1903. The locations have been highlighted on the large map for clarity.

GAINED BY PURCHASE

Alaska, purchased from _____ in 1867. The deal was much criticized at the time as a waste of money, but Alaska has proven to be a very valuable addition to the U.S.

GAINED BY ANNEXATION

Hawaii, which joined the U.S. five years after American settlers and businessmen living there worked up a scheme to overthrow the Hawaiian _____ and her government in 1893. (Annexation is the term used when a government absorbs or adds new territory.)

GAINED AS A RESULT OF THE SPANISH-AMERICAN WAR (1898)

Cuba, which was controlled after the war by the U.S. for several years until a new government was formed. America still has control of some Cuban land for a naval base at _____ Bay.

Puerto Rico, an island that is still part of the U.S., but _____ a state.

The Philippines, where the Filipinos wanted independence, and fought the U.S. (unsuccessfully) to get it. Independence came only after World War _____.

Guam, which is still part of the U.S., and important as an American _____ base in the Pacific.

SMALL ISLANDS OBTAINED MAINLY FOR USE AS SHIPPING OR TRADING STOPS

Midway (1867)   **Wake** (1899)   **Samoa** (1900)

LAND OBTAINED BY THE UNITED STATES TO BUILD THE PANAMA CANAL

Panama Canal Zone, on the Isthmus of Panama. When Colombia stalled the sale of the small strip of land America needed for the canal, Theodore Roosevelt sent a

naval force to support a _____ by the Panamanians, who wanted the canal. The year was 1903. (Before the rebellion, Panama was part of Colombia.)

Use these terms to fill in the blanks: Guantanamo, military, not, queen, rebellion, Russia, Two

---

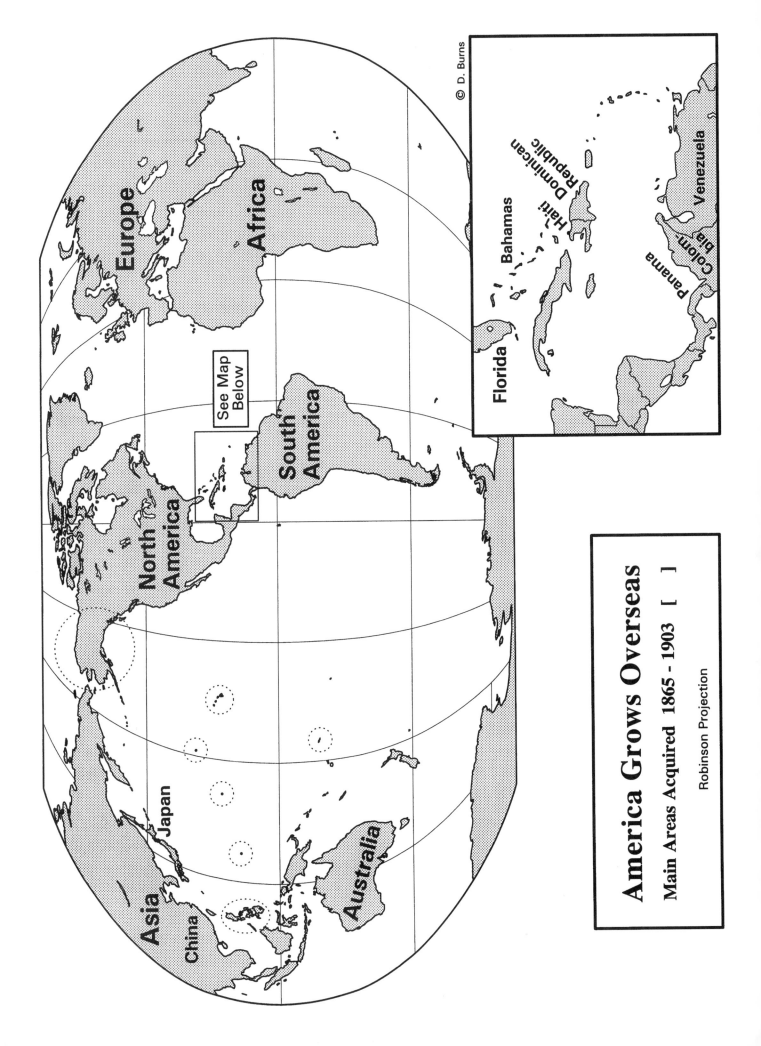

© D. Burns

Florida
Bahamas
Haiti
Dominican
Republic
Colombia
Panama
Venezuela

See Map
Below

Europe
Africa
Asia
China
Japan
North
America
South
America
Australia

America Grows Overseas

Main Areas Acquired 1865 - 1903 [   ]

Robinson Projection

BIG INDUSTRY AND LABOR UNIONS

These selections highlight some of the issues in the debates about big industry and labor unions in the Gilded Age.

Carnegie Defends the Millionaires

These excerpts are condensed from a famous article by Andrew Carnegie titled "Wealth." Its message later became known as "The Gospel of Wealth."

The conditions of human life have not only been changed, but revolutionized, within the past few hundred years. The contrast between the palace of the millionaire and the cottage of the laborer with us today measures the change which has come with civilization. This change, however, is not to be deplored, but welcomed as highly beneficial.

The "good old times" were not good old times.

Formerly articles were manufactured at the domestic hearth [in the home] or in small shops which formed part of the household. But the inevitable result of such a mode of manufacture was crude articles at high prices.

Today the world obtains commodities of excellent quality at prices which even the generation preceding this would have deemed incredibly low. The poor enjoy what the rich could not before afford. What were luxuries have become the necessaries of life.

The price we pay for this change is great. We assemble thousands of operatives [workers] in the factory and in the mine, of whom the employer can know little or nothing. Under the law of competition, the employer is forced into the strictest economies, among which are the rates paid to laborers, and often there is friction between employer and the employed, between capital and labor, between rich and poor.

The price which society pays for the law of competition is great. But the advantages of this law are greater still, for it is to this law that we owe our wonderful material development, which brings improved conditions.

While the law of competition may be sometimes hard for the individual, it is best for the race, because it insures the survival of the fittest. We accept and welcome, therefore, great inequality of living conditions and the concentration of business in the hands of a few. The law of competition between these is not only beneficial, but essential for the future progress of the race.

Ida Tarbell Criticizes Business Practices

Journalist Ida Tarbell exposed the way John D. Rockefeller organized the Standard Oil Company to control the oil refining industry. She showed that often, business in the Gilded Age involved practices that were far from fair competition.

These condensed excerpts are from the conclusion of her famous report on the Standard Oil Company.

Every great campaign against rival interests which the Standard Oil Company has carried on has been inaugurated [started], not to save its life, but to build up and sustain a monopoly in the oil industry.

Very often people who admit the facts, who are willing to see that Mr. Rockefeller has employed force and fraud to secure his ends, justify him by declaring, "It's business." That is, "it's business" has come to be a legitimate excuse for hard dealing, sly tricks, special privileges. It is a common enough thing to hear men arguing that the ordinary laws of morality do not apply in business.

Now, if the Standard Oil Company were the only concern in the country guilty of the practices which have given it monopolistic power, this story would never have been written. Were it alone in these methods, public scorn would long ago have made short work of the Standard Oil Company. But it is simply the most conspicuous type of what can be done by these practices.

One of the most depressing features of the ethical side of the matter is that instead of such methods arousing contempt they are more or less openly admired.

Samuel Gompers Defends Labor Unions

Samuel Gompers rose to fame as president of the American Federation of Labor. These lines are condensed from an 1894 letter to a judge who was critical of the strategy of collective action (such as strikes) by workers.

You know, or ought to know, that the introduction of machinery is turning into idleness [unemployment] thousands faster than new industries are founded. The laborer is a man, he is made warm by the same sun and made cold - yes, colder - by the same winter as you. He has a heart and brain, and feels and knows the human and paternal instinct for those depending on him as keenly as you.

What shall the workers do? Sit idly by and see the vast resources of nature and the human mind be utilized and monopolized for the benefit of the comparative few?

No. The laborers must learn to think and act, and soon, too, that only by the power of organization and common action can their manhood be maintained, their rights to work be recognized, and liberty and rights secured.

I am not one of those who regards the entire past as a failure. I recognize the progress made and the improved conditions of which nearly the entire civilized world are the beneficiaries.

I ask you to explain, however, how it is that thousands of able-bodied, willing, earnest men and women are suffering the pangs of hunger? We may boast of our wealth and civilization, but to the hungry man and woman and child our progress is a hollow mockery, our civilization a sham, and our "national wealth" a chimera [fantasy].

You recognize that the industrial forces set in motion by steam and electricity have materially changed the structure of our civili-zation. You evidently have observed the growth of corporate wealth and influence.

You recognize that wealth, in order to become more highly productive, is concentrated into fewer hands, and yet you sing the old siren song that the workingman should depend entirely upon his own "individual effort."

If, as you say, the success of commercial society depends on the full play of competition, why do not you turn your attention and your attacks against the trusts and corporations?

In conclusion, let me assure you that labor will organize, and despite relentless antagonism, achieve for humanity a nobler manhood, a more beautiful womanhood, and a happier childhood.

Group Discussion: *Summarize briefly each writer's main points. On what point do Andrew Carnegie and Samuel Gompers agree? In what ways do their views differ?*

CHARTING ECONOMIC TRENDS

The Gilded Age is often remembered for its extremes of wealth and poverty, as well as the sometimes violent conflicts between labor unions and business owners. Complete the line graphs on these pages to see a more complete picture of the era, which included many positive trends. What conclusions about the Gilded Age can you draw from these four graphs?

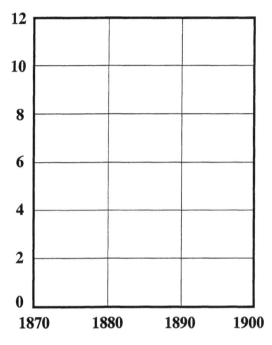

**Production of Raw Steel
(Millions of Tons)
1870 to 1900**

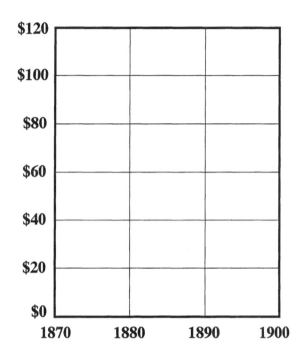

**Price of Steel Rails
(Dollars per Gross Ton)
1870 to 1900**

Use the table below to find the information to make the line graphs above. A gross ton is slightly heavier than the U.S. standard ton of 2,000 pounds.

Year	Raw Steel Production (Millions of Tons)	Steel Rail Prices (Dollars per Gross Ton)
1870	.1	107
1880	1.4	68
1890	4.8	32
1900	11.2	32

source: *Historical Statistics of the United States*

The two graphs below show trends in job creation and wages received by workers. The wage figures are adjusted for changes in the purchasing power of the dollar. Historians call these adjusted figures "real wages," since they reflect what a paycheck actually could buy when compared to paychecks many years earlier or later.

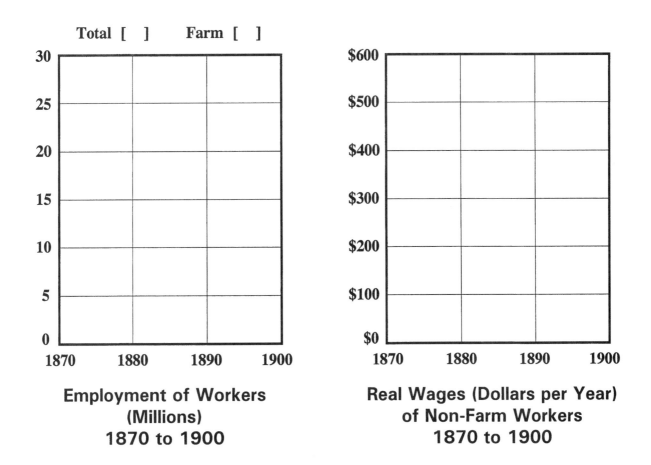

Total [ ]   Farm [ ]

**Employment of Workers
(Millions)
1870 to 1900**

**Real Wages (Dollars per Year)
of Non-Farm Workers
1870 to 1900**

Use the table below to find the information to make the line graphs above. Use two different colors to show total employment and farm employment on the same graph.

Year	Total Workers (Millions)	Farm Workers (Millions)	Real Wages (Dollars per Year) of Non-Farm Workers
1870	12.9	6.8	375
1880	17.4	8.6	395
1890	23.3	9.9	519
1900	29	10.9	573

source: *Historical Statistics of the United States*

JANE ADDAMS WORKS FOR BETTER CITIES

Jane Addams opened Hull House as a kind of community center in one of Chicago's working class neighborhoods in 1889. This "settlement house" was staffed by Addams and other volunteers who acted as neighborhood organizers and social workers. These are condensed selections from her famous books and articles.

The social organism has broken down through large districts of our great cities. Many of the people living there are very poor, the majority of them without leisure or energy for anything but the gain of subsistence [the bare necessities]. They move from one wretched lodging to another. They live for the moment side by side, many of them without knowledge of each other, without fellowship, without local tradition or public spirit, without social organization of any kind.

Practically nothing is done to remedy this. The people who might do it, who have the social tact and training, the large houses, and the traditions and custom of hospitality, live in other parts of the city. The club-houses, libraries, and galleries are also blocks away.

We find the working men organized into armies of producers [in factories] because men of business ability have found it in their interests thus to organize them. But these working men are not organized socially. Their ideas and resources are cramped. They have no share in the traditions and social energy which make for progress. Too often their only place of meeting is a saloon, their only host a bartender. Men of ability and refinement, of social power and university cultivation, stay away from them.

Personally, I believe the men who lose most are those who stay away.

It is constantly said that because the masses have never had social advantages they do not want them, that they are heavy and dull. This divides the city into rich and poor; into the favored, who express their sense of social obligation by gifts of money, and into the unfavored, who express it by clamoring for a "share" - both of them actuated [motivated] by a vague sense of justice.

It is inevitable that those who feel most keenly this insincerity should be our young people. I think it is hard for us to realize how seriously many of them are taking to the notion of human brotherhood, how eagerly they long to give expression to the democratic ideal.

They hear constantly of the great social maladjustment, but no way is provided for them to change it. Our young people feel the need of putting theory into action, and respond quickly to the Settlement house form of activity [as volunteer staffers].

Jane Addams criticized the system of "boss" politics found in many big cities. In some city neighborhoods, she noted, votes were bought at election time for "drinks or dollars." After the election, however, the real needs of poor neighborhoods were mostly ignored by the political system.

The policy of the public authorities of never taking an initiative, and always waiting to be urged to do their duty, is fatal in a neighborhood where there is no initiative among the citizens. The idea underlying our self-government breaks down in such a neighborhood.

The streets are inexpressibly dirty, the

number of schools inadequate, factory legislation unenforced, the street-lighting bad, the paving miserable and altogether lacking in the alleys and smaller streets, and the horse stables defy all laws of sanitation.

Hundreds of houses are unconnected with the street sewer. The older and richer inhabitants seem anxious to move away as rapidly as they can afford it. They make room for the newly arrived immigrants who are densely ignorant of civic duties.

Addams and the volunteers at Hull House put pressure on city officials to improve garbage collection and other services vital to life in any neighborhood. She also took time to observe the lives around her.

To one who has lived for years in a crowded quarter where men, women and children constantly jostle each other and press upon every inch of space in shop, tenement and street, nothing is more impressive than the strength, the continuity, the varied and powerful manifestations of family affection.

Every tenement house contains women who for years spend their hurried days in preparing food and clothing and pass their sleepless nights in tending and nursing their needy children. Every shop is crowded with workingmen who year after year spend all of their wages upon the nurture and education of their children, reserving for themselves but the shabbiest clothing and a crowded place at the family table.

The wonderful devotion to the child seems at times, in the midst of our stupid social and industrial arrangements, all that keeps society human. This devotion to the child is the inevitable conclusion [result] of the devotion of man to woman.

It is, or course, this tremendous force which makes possible the family, that bond which holds society together and blends the experience of generations into a continuous story.

Addams argued that city governments would have to take a larger, more active role to meet the social needs of the citizens. Cities, she said, should promote recreation, cultural life, and better schools. She hoped that the energy and idealism of young people would light the way to a brighter future for America's cities.

Nothing is more certain than that each generation longs for a reassurance as to the value and charm of life, and is secretly afraid lest it lose its sense of the youth of the earth.

One generation after another has depended upon its young to equip it with gaiety and enthusiasm, to persuade it that living is a pleasure.

The spontaneous joy, the clamor for pleasure, the desire of the young people to appear finer and better and altogether more lovely than they really are, the idealization not only of each other but of the whole earth which they regard but as a theater for their noble exploits, the unworldly ambitions, the romantic hopes - What might they not do to make our sordid [ugly] cities more beautiful and more companionable?

Group Discussion: *What social problems did Jane Adams see in Chicago in the 1890s? What impressed her about the families she met around Hull House? Why did she think young people could be a key part of the effort to improve cities?*

JACOB RIIS EXPOSES CHILD LABOR

*Jacob Riis was one of the first journalists to photograph and write about the condition of the poor living in New York City. In books like **How the Other Half Lives**, and in newspaper stories, he exposed the hard life of children working in factories, sweatshops and mines. This is an excerpt from one of his articles.*

Of Susie's hundred little companions in the alley - playmates they could scarcely be called - some made artificial flowers, some paper boxes, while the boys earned money at "shinin'" [shining shoes] or selling newspapers. The smaller girls "minded the baby," so leaving the mother free to work. Most of them did something toward earning the family living, young as they were.

The occupations that claim children's labor in and out of the shop are almost as numberless as the youngsters that swarm in tenement neighborhoods. The poorer the tenements the more of them always.

In an evening school class of nineteen boys and girls which I polled once, I found twelve boys who "shined," five who sold papers, one of thirteen years who by day worked in a printing office, and one of twelve who worked in a wood-yard.

Of the girls, one was thirteen and worked in a paper box factory, two of twelve made paper lanterns, one twelve-year-old girl sewed coats in a sweat-shop.

The four smallest girls were ten years old, and of them one worked for a sweater [sweatshop owner] and "finished twenty-five coats yesterday," she said with pride. She looked quite able to do a woman's work. The three others minded the baby at home; one of them found time to help her mother sew coats when baby slept.

The trouble is not so much that the children have to work early as with the sort of work they have to do. It is, all of it, of a kind that leaves them, grown to man and womanhood, just where it found them, knowing no more, and therefore less, than when they began. The years that should have prepared them for life's work are gone in hopeless and profitless drudgery.

The general result was well put by a tireless worker in the cause of improving the condition of the poor, who said to me, "They are down on the scrub level; there you find them and have to put them to such use as you can. They don't know anything else, and that is what makes it so hard to find work for them. Even when they go into a shop to sew, they come out mere machines, able to do only one thing, which is a small part of the whole they do not grasp. And thus, without the slightest training for the responsibilities of life, they marry and transmit their incapacity to another generation that is so much worse to start off with."

She spoke of the girls, but what she said fitted the boys just as well.

1. Highlight each mention of a specific age of a child (or group of children) in this report by Jacob Riis.

Group Discussion: *What kind of work did children in the poor tenement neighborhoods do? What were the typical ages of those Riis talked to for this report? Factory owners at that time sometimes argued that children were getting an education by working. How would Riis probably respond to such an argument?*

WHY WOMEN SHOULD VOTE

Susan B. Anthony was among the most active organizers for women's voting rights. These arguments (condensed here) are from a speech she gave after being arrested in Rochester, New York. Her crime: voting in the presidential election of 1872. (Women finally won "the franchise" - full voting rights nationwide - in 1920.)

It was we, the people; not we, the white male citizens; nor yet we, the male citizens; but we, the whole people, who formed this Union. And we formed it, not to give the blessings of liberty, but to secure them; not to the half of ourselves and the half of our posterity [descendants], but to the whole people - women as well as men.

It is a downright mockery to talk to women of their enjoyment of the blessings of liberty while they are denied the use of the only means of securing them provided by this government - the ballot.

For any state to make sex a qualification that must ever result in the disfranchisement [loss of voting rights] of one entire half of the people is therefore a violation of the supreme law of the land.

By it the blessings of liberty are forever withheld from women and their female posterity. To them this government is not a democracy. It is not a republic. It is an odious [repulsive] aristocracy; a hateful oligarchy [rule by the few] of sex; the most hateful aristocracy ever established on the face of the globe.

Another famous advocate for women's rights was Amelia Bloomer. She was the first woman in America to own and edit a newspaper for women. These lines are condensed from an 1895 essay.

There is no positive rule by which to fix woman's sphere, except that of capacity. It is to be found, I should say, wherever duty or interest may call her, whether to the kitchen, the parlor, the nursery, the workshop or the public assembly.

It is objected that it would be immodest and "unbecoming a lady" for women to go to the ballot-box to vote, or to the halls of the capitol to legislate.

A few years ago it was thought very unladylike and improper for women to study medicine, and when Elizabeth Blackwell forced her way into the Geneva, New York, medical college people were amazed at the presumption. But she graduated with high honors, went to Europe to perfect her studies, and now stands high in her chosen profession.

Now there are several colleges for the medical education of women, and women physicians without number. And so of many other departments of trade, profession and labor that within my recollection were not thought proper for woman, simply because she had not entered them.

Women are debarred [prevented] from voting and legislating, and therefore it is unfashionable for them to do either; but let their right to do so be once established, and all objections of that kind will vanish away.

Group Discussion: *What is the basic argument each woman makes to justify voting rights for women? Which woman do you think makes the most effective argument? Why?*

7 | Becoming a World Leader: 1900 - 1950

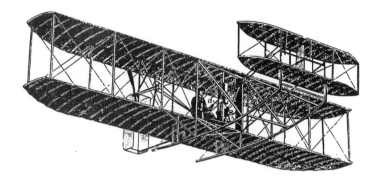

"Speak softly and carry a big stick."

"And we won't come back 'till it's over over there!"

"Brother, Can You Spare a Dime?"

"I pledge you, I pledge myself, to a New Deal for the American people."

"Yesterday, December 7, 1941 - a date which will live in infamy - the United States of America was suddenly and deliberately attacked by naval and air forces of the Empire of Japan."

Study Checklist

When you have completed this section, working with the Internet support site at *www.fasttrackteaching.com* or other resources, you should be able to:

 Identify and explain the context of the **Famous Quotes** shown on the Section Title Page.

 Identify and explain the importance of the **Famous Names and Terms** listed on the topic summary pages in this section.

 Identify on a map and explain the importance of the **Famous Places** shown on the maps in this section.

 Explain the general sequence of events in this period and tell from memory the **Famous Years**:

- World War One began in Europe (**1914**).
- The stock market crashed (**1929**).
- Franklin D. Roosevelt was elected president (**1932**).
- Pearl Harbor was attacked, bringing the U.S. into World War Two (**1941**).

Take a Practice Test!

 (A) (B) (C) (D)

A multiple-choice practice test for this section can be found on the Internet support site at:

www.fasttrackteaching.com

Textbook Page References:

 Discuss or write briefly on such questions and topics as these:

1. What were the goals of the Progressive movement? What impact did the movement have on American life and laws?

2. What were the main reasons why World War One began? Why was the war so deadly? How did America's response to the war change? What were the main goals of President Woodrow Wilson's Fourteen Points plan?

3. What were the main reasons the U.S. stock market rapidly grew, then crashed, in the late 1920s?

4. Explain the main steps FDR took to try to end the Great Depression. Were his policies successful? How did his policies change the role of the federal government in the lives of the American people?

5. An American leader during World War Two said Hitler and the Axis powers were not just after new territory, but were fighting "a counter-revolution against our ideas and ideals." In what ways was the war really about ideas and ideals?

6. How did America respond to the threat of the Soviet Union and communism in the years just after World War Two?

Timeline 1900 - 1950

Find when these events occurred, fill in the blanks, and place them on the main timeline. The thin timeline shows the presidents of this period.

First airplane flies - It was invented by Wilbur and Orville _____.

Panama Canal work begins - It was _____ Roosevelt's big project.

Pure Food and Drug Act - It was a victory for the _____ movement.

Model T Ford introduced - Henry Ford also pushed for higher _____ for workers.

World War I begins - One terrible feature of this war was deadly _____ gas.

U.S. enters WW I - The war had already been underway for about _____ years.

WW I ends - Germany signed an _____ agreement to stop the killing.

Prohibition begins - It didn't stop abuse of _____, and ended in 1933.

Women get voting rights - It was the 19ᵗʰ Amendment to the _____.

Stock market crash - The worst day was called "Black _____."

FDR elected - He promised voters what he called a "_____ Deal."

New Deal programs begin - Many, like the CCC, were aimed at creating new _____.

Social Security Act - It still provides many Americans' _____ money.

World War Two begins - Hitler's attack on _____ started the war in Europe.

Hitler takes France - The attack was lightning fast warfare, called _____.

Pearl Harbor attacked - FDR called it "a day that will live in _____."

Germany surrenders - The date was called "_____ Day," for victory in Europe.

Japan surrenders - It surrendered after being hit with two _____ bombs.

NATO formed - The countries of Western Europe were now worried about _____.

Use these terms to fill in the blanks: alcohol, armistice, atomic, blitzkrieg, Constitution, infamy, jobs, New, poison, Poland, Progressive, retirement, Russia, Theodore, three, Tuesday, VE, wages, Wright

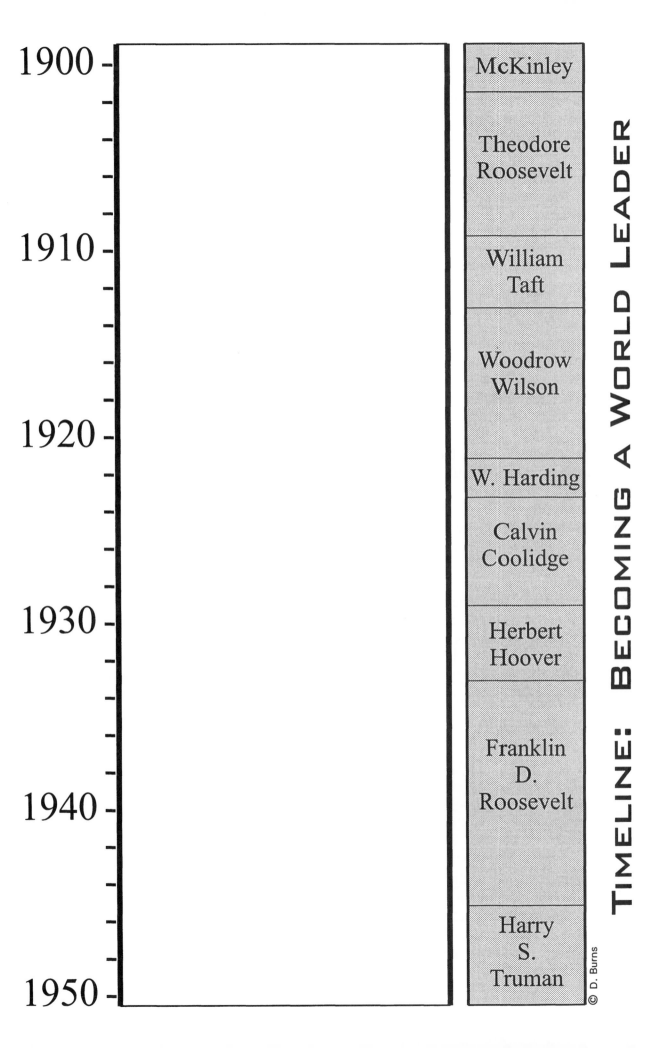

1900 —
—
—
1910 —
—
—
—
1920 —
—
—
—
1930 —
—
—
—
1940 —
—
—
—
1950 —

McKinley

Theodore
Roosevelt

William
Taft

Woodrow
Wilson

W. Harding

Calvin
Coolidge

Herbert
Hoover

Franklin
D.
Roosevelt

Harry
S.
Truman

© D. Burns

TIMELINE: BECOMING A WORLD LEADER

DECADE: 1900s   The Progressive Era

Theodore Roosevelt, imperialism, Panama Canal, Progressive movement,

conservation, muckrakers, *The Jungle,* Pure Food and Drug Act, trust busting,

Wilbur and Orville Wright, Model T, Mother Jones, NAACP

As 1900 rolled around, America was becoming a world power. In the Spanish American War (1898) our country helped liberate Cuba from Spain, and took control of Puerto Rico and the Philippines. The term "imperialism" describes the relationship that followed. We kept control of these islands partly to help them, but also to benefit ourselves for trade. Critics called it "un-American." Many other nations around the world were making similar grabs for distant lands in order to build or expand empires.

Theodore Roosevelt became president in 1901. He believed America had a big role to play in the world, and should not avoid it. One good example is the _____ Canal, begun in 1904. Many people there wanted the canal, but some other nations in the region felt America had bullied the project through.

Theodore Roosevelt was also a great supporter of conservation measures designed to protect natural resources for future generations. He pushed for more wildlife sanctuaries, protected large areas of forests, and added a number of new _____ parks.

Many people, including Roosevelt, believed that reforms to help "the average guy" were badly needed because of the changes that had been occurring in America. This attitude was expressed in the Progressive movement. Journalists called muckrakers kept attention on the issues of Progressivism. They took photographs and wrote about problems like _____ labor, sweatshops, and the life of the poor in big cities. They exposed the ways big city bosses still controlled many American cities. They also wrote about unsafe practices in the food industry, and the danger of many medicines. Upton Sinclair's famous book *The Jungle*

is the best known example. It helped win Roosevelt's support for the proposed Pure Food and Drug Act and the Meat Inspection Act, which were passed in 1906.

Roosevelt felt the power of the federal government had to grow to match the power of big business. He became known as the "trust buster" because of his efforts to stop abusive trusts and monopolies. His administration sued in the courts to break up dozens of giant companies controlling oil, beef, sugar, steel, and other products. He also pushed to give the Interstate Commerce Commission more power to regulate businesses that operated across state lines, such as the _____. (Still, businesses faced nothing like the extensive safety and labor regulations that are common today in America.)

One reason the Progressive movement was so successful was that it had broad appeal to middle class city residents, not just the working classes and farmers. It was supported by religious leaders, and even many business leaders. Some feared that if reforms were not made to America's capitalist system, voters might elect socialist candidates. Socialists like Eugene Debs said the _____ should take over the factories and railroads, and operate them for everyone's benefit, instead of for the profit of the owners. (Business owners argued that America's capitalist system was a much better system for creating economic growth, jobs, and opportunity.)

The Progressive movement did not instantly solve all of America's problems. But it proved that the American system of government could respond to modern problems affecting ordinary citizens. (Compare this to Russia, where the Czar's refusal to make any reforms was already leading to violent revolution.) The Progressive movement was not just part of national politics, however. At the local level, reform-minded mayors in many cities worked to improve schools, parks, and water systems. Many state governments were passing laws to restrict child labor, and many set up workmen's compensation systems to help support people _____ on the job.

The main engine of growth and change in America, however, was not the government, but private industry and private individuals. Two bicycle mechanics from Ohio went to the windy dunes of North Carolina to prove they could _____! The automobile, especially the Model T developed by Henry Ford, began changing the look of America in this decade. Ford soon achieved mass production of cars on moving assembly lines. He later pushed the idea of paying workers higher wages to give them a decent life and keep them _____.

Many working class Americans did share some of the growing prosperity of this era. But for many others, work conditions were bad, the hours _____, and pay rates low. Labor unions like the United Mine Workers and labor leaders like Mother Jones continued fighting against excessive work hours and child labor. Black leaders, including W.E.B. Du Bois, organized the _____ to fight racial discrimination. Success for most of these efforts was many years away, and for millions of people, the American Dream seemed distant and impossible to attain. Still, there was widespread confidence that progress for the common man was being made in America. The long lines on Ellis Island proved that millions of _____ from many other countries agreed.

Roosevelt helped his fellow Republican, William Taft, win the White House in the 1908 election, but was not satisfied with the job he did. In 1912 he ran as the candidate of a new political party, the Progressive Party (also called the _____ Party), but the three-way split gave the election to Woodrow Wilson, a Democrat.

Use these terms to fill in the blanks: Bull Moose, child, fly, government, immigrants, injured, long, NAACP, national, Panama, productive, railroads

MOTHER JONES FOR THE MINERS

Mary Harris "Mother" Jones was a fiery Irish immigrant who took up the cause of miners. She helped organize strikes for better conditions and pay, and fought against child labor. In 1903 her efforts took her to Colorado. In this condensed excerpt from her autobiography, she gives her view of what she saw.

The state of Colorado belonged not to a republic but to the Colorado Fuel and Iron Company, the Victor Company and their dependencies [other companies]. The governor was their agent. Whenever the masters of the state told the governor to bark, he yelped for them like a mad hound.

The people of Colorado had voted overwhelmingly for an eight-hour work day. The legislature passed an eight hour law but the courts had declared it unconstitutional. Then when the measure was submitted directly to the people, they voted for it with a 4,000 votes majority. But the next legislature, which was controlled by the mining interests, failed to pass the bill.

The miners saw that they could not get their demands through peaceful legislation. That they must fight. That they must strike. All the metal miners struck first. The strike extended into New Mexico and Utah. It became an ugly war. The metal miners were anxious to have the coal miners join them in their struggle.

The executive board of the United Mine Workers was in session in Indianapolis. The board asked me to go to Colorado, look into conditions there, and make a report.

I went there immediately, first to the office of The Western Federation of Miners where I heard the story of the industrial conflict.

I then got myself an old calico dress, a sunbonnet, some pins and needles, elastic and tape and such sundries, and went down to the southern coal fields of the Colorado Fuel and Iron Company.

As a peddler, I went through the various coal camps, eating in the homes of the miners, staying all night with their families. I found the conditions under which they lived deplorable. They were in practical slavery to the company, which owned their houses, owned all the land, so that even if a miner did own a house he must vacate whenever it pleased the land owners.

They were paid in scrip [paper certificates] instead of money so that they could not go away if dissatisfied. They must buy at company stores and at company prices.

The coal they mined was weighed by an agent of the company and the miners could not have a check weighman to see that full credit was given them. The schools, the churches, the roads belonged to the Company. I felt, after listening to their stories, after witnessing their long patience, that the time was ripe for revolt against such brutal conditions.

Mother Jones' account goes on to tell how miners in part of the state won some improvements through the strike. But in other areas they were defeated by mine owners using violent tactics. Her work helped bring attention to the need for better labor laws to protect workers.

Group Discussion: *What does Mother Jones say was the political situation in Colorado that made it difficult to improve working conditions? What practices did the mine owners use to keep an unfair advantage over workers?*

THE PROGRESSIVE PARTY CALLS FOR CHANGES

The views of many reform-minded Americans around 1910 can be found in the "platform" or official position statement of the Progressive Party. Theodore Roosevelt ran as the Progressive Party's presidential candidate in the 1912 election. He lost that election to Woodrow Wilson, but many of the party's proposals became law over the next few decades. These excerpts are condensed from the party's 1912 platform.

The conscience of the people, in a time of grave national problems, has called into being a new party, born of the nation's sense of justice. We of the Progressive Party here dedicate ourselves to the fulfillment of the duty laid upon us by our fathers to maintain the government of the people, by the people, and for the people.

Political parties exist to secure responsible government and to execute [put into effect] the will of the people.

From these great tasks both of the old parties have turned aside. They have become tools of corrupt interests. Behind the ostensible [visible] government sits enthroned an invisible government owing no allegiance and acknowledging no responsibility to the people.

To destroy this invisible government, to dissolve the unholy alliance between corrupt business and corrupt politics is the first task of the statesmanship of the day.

In particular, the party declares for direct election of United States Senators by the people.

The Progressive Party pledges itself to the task of securing equal suffrage [voting rights] to men and women alike.

We pledge our party to legislation that will compel strict limitation of all campaign contributions and expenditures.

We pledge ourselves to work unceasingly in State and Nation for:

Effective legislation looking to the prevention of industrial accidents, occupational diseases, overwork, and unemployment.

The fixing of minimum safety and health standards for the various occupations.

The prohibition of child labor.

Minimum wage standards for working women, to provide a "living wage" in all industrial occupations.

One day's rest in seven for all wage workers.

The eight hour day in continuous twenty-four hour industries.

The protection of home life against the hazards of sickness, irregular employment and old age through the adoption of a system of social insurance. [*Social insurance was the term used at that time for what today is called Social Security and unemployment insurance.*]

We favor the organization of the workers, men and women [into labor unions], as a means of protecting their interests and of promoting their progress.

Group Discussion: *What did the Progressive Party say was corrupting the American system of government in the early 1900s? What were the party's main proposals to give more political power to the ordinary citizens of the country? What were its main proposals to improve conditions for American workers?*

CHARTING 20ᵗʰ CENTURY VITAL STATISTICS

"Vital statistics" is the term for the basic figures about life, health, and death in a nation or community. Finish these line graphs to chart the data. Do the graphs support the argument that the Progressive Era was a period of improving conditions for the average American?

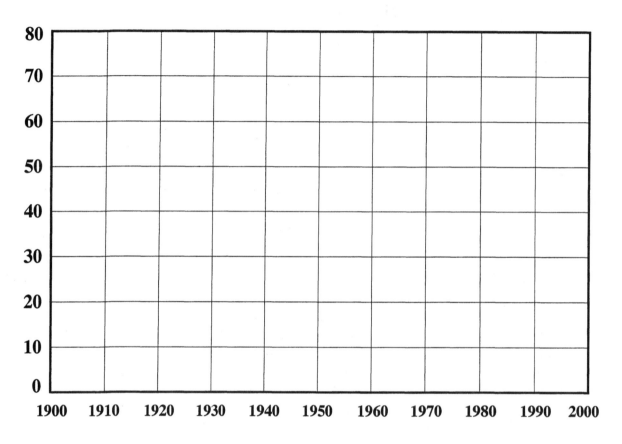

Life Expectancy at Birth (Years) 1900 to 2000

Use the table below to find the information to make the line graph above.

Year	Life Expectancy	Year	Life Expectancy	Year	Life Expectancy	Year	Life Expectancy)
1900	47.3	1930	59.7	1960	69.7	1990	75.4
1910	50.0	1940	62.9	1970	70.8	2000	76.9
1920	54.1	1950	68.2	1980	73.7		

sources: *Historical Statistics of the United States* and *Statistical Abstract of the United States*

The infant mortality rate is especially valuable for showing health conditions in a society. It tells the number of children out of each 1,000 live births who die before reaching their first birthday. What factors do you think contributed most to the pattern shown on these graphs?

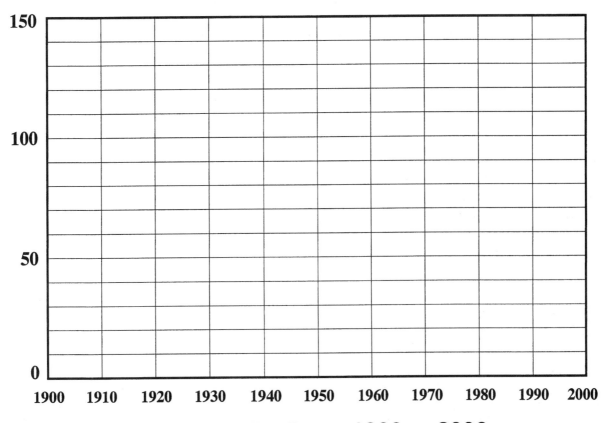

Infant Mortality Rate 1900 to 2000
(Deaths Within 1st Year per 1,000 Live Births)

Use the table below to find the information to make the line graph above.

Year	Infant Mortality Rate	Year	Infant Mortality Rate	Year	Infant Mortality Rate	Year	Infant Mortality Rate
1900	141.4 *	1930	64.6	1960	26.0	1990	9.2
1910	116.7 *	1940	47.0	1970	20.0	2000	6.9
1920	85.8	1950	29.2	1980	12.6		

* figure available for Massachusetts only

sources: *Historical Statistics of the United States* and *Statistical Abstract of the United States*

DECADE: 1910s WORLD WAR ONE

Woodrow Wilson, Federal Trade Commission, Clayton Act, Federal Reserve System,

income tax, Central Powers, Allied Powers, isolationism, *Lusitania*,

Espionage Act/Sedition Act, communism, League of Nations, reparations

This decade opened with the optimistic spirit set by the Progressive movement the previous decade. But people might well have taken the sinking of the unsinkable *Titanic*, a floating symbol of modern industrial progress, as a warning to beware.

In 1912 Woodrow Wilson was elected president. He agreed with the Progressives on many issues of the day. For example, he pushed for creation of the Federal Trade Commission. It had the power to investigate crooked dealings by businesses and take action against them. A new law called the Clayton Act was a strong legal weapon against businesses that tried to form monopolies. It also set up the first solid legal protection for labor unions. Public anger over a fire that killed more than a hundred women and girls at the Triangle Shirtwaist Company in New York City (1911) helped create public support for new laws designed to protect _____.

The nation's money and banking system was greatly improved with the creation of the Federal Reserve System. Also in this decade, a federal income tax system was created by Congress. That helped the working class by shifting a larger share of the nation's tax burden to people with _____ incomes.

World War One broke out in Europe in 1914. It was caused by a number of factors. Most of the countries of Europe were competing with each other for power. They had entered into various alliances with each other for self-protection. The big nations were all armed to the teeth. Many military leaders, especially in Germany, were eager for any kind of a fight that might help them _____ their territory.

The spark to ignite the war flashed when a Serbian assassinated the heir to the throne of Austria-Hungary. The complicated web of treaties and alliances in Europe led one country after another to gear up for war. Germany moved first, marching across Belgium to attack France. Germany became head of the Central Powers. This group also included Austria-Hungary, Bulgaria, and Turkey (at that time, part of the Ottoman Empire.)

On the other side were the Allied Powers: England, France, Russia, and Italy. Many Americans wanted to stay out of the fight. This attitude is usually called _____. But submarine attacks on ships like the *Lusitania* by German U - Boats angered many, and helped sway public opinion. America entered the war in 1917 on the Allied side.

Suddenly, anti-German feelings exploded nationwide. As the war fever grew, Congress passed the Espionage Act and the Sedition Act to stop critics of the war from agitating against the American involvement. There were objections that the laws violated the right of free _____ guaranteed by the Constitution, but hundreds of Americans were arrested and jailed none the less. Socialists and radical labor leaders were often singled out as targets, since many of them criticized the war as a creation of big businesses interested only in profits.

Submarines, machine guns, tanks, _____ gas, trench warfare, and airplanes made this war especially brutal. The incredible death and destruction shook the traditional social order of Europe. It also broke the confidence that reason and technology would bring only progress for mankind. People later said this war was "the end of innocence" for the human race.

The most extreme example of the breakup of the old order came in Russia. The Bolsheviks, a communist group, seized power in the chaotic conditions there during the war. The communists killed the _____ and his family, and ended the absolute rule of the old aristocratic class. Socialists everywhere cheered the Revolution and its leader, Lenin. They hoped communism (a form of socialism) would point the way to a great future for mankind without impoverished working classes and warfare. Few guessed how quickly the new Communist Party government would become an oppressive and brutal _____.

America sent about two million troops to the war. By the end of 1918, Germany asked for an armistice (a cease-fire) to end the fighting. The peace treaty was negotiated at Versailles, outside Paris. President Wilson came with his Fourteen Points plan, which he felt would create a stable peace. It was designed to settle boundary disputes, and eliminate some of the problems that had led to the war in the first place. For example, it called for an end to _____ treaties. It also called for a general reduction in each nation's armaments.

The 14th Point in the plan called for creation of a League of Nations to settle future international disputes before they became wars. But Americans, by now sick of the troubles of Europe, would not support the idea. The U.S. Senate voted to _____ the treaty, and prevented America from joining the League of Nations.

In a move that proved a big mistake, the Allies demanded that Germany accept total _____ for causing the war, and make a "pay back" through reparations payments. The payments and debt made it difficult for Germany to get back to a normal economy after the war. The poverty that resulted, and resentment over the peace treaty, helped thugs like Nazi leader Adolf Hitler rise to power. The stage was set for another _____ War just twenty years later.

Copyright 1998 D. Burns

Use these terms to fill in the blanks: Czar, dictatorship, expand, higher, isolationism, poison, reject, responsibility, secret, speech, workers, World

Becoming a World Leader   7 - 12

FORD'S PROGRESSIVE WAGE PLAN

The Ford Motor Company was the first of the industrial giants to take up the challenge of improving the lives of factory workers. Henry Ford, at the urging of his business partner, James Couzens, outlined their new plan in a famous 1914 announcement from the company's headquarters in Detroit. These are condensed excerpts.

The Ford Motor Company, the greatest and most successful automobile manufacturing company in the world, will, on January 12, inaugurate the greatest revolution in the matter of rewards for its workers ever known in the industrial world.

At one stroke it will reduce the hours of labor from nine to eight, and add to every man's pay a share of the profits of the house. The smallest amount to be received by any man 22 years old and upwards will be $5.00 per day. The lowest wage is now $2.34 per day of nine hours.

This will apply to every man of 22 years of age or upward without regard to the nature of his employment. In order that the young man, from 18 to 22 years of age, may be entitled to a share in the profits, he must show himself sober, saving, steady, industrious, and must satisfy the superintendent and staff that his money will not be wasted in riotous living.

"The commonest laborer, who sweeps the floor, shall receive his $5.00 per day," said Henry Ford.

"It is our belief," said James Couzens, "that social justice begins at home. We want to help those who have helped us to produce this great institution and who are helping to maintain it to share our prosperity."

"If we are obliged," said Mr. Ford, "to lay off men for want of sufficient work at any season, we propose to plan our year's work so that the lay-off shall be in the harvest time, not in the winter.

"No man will be discharged [fired] if we can help it, except for unfaithfulness or inefficiency. No foreman in the company  has the power to discharge a man. He may send them out of his department if they do not make good. The man is then repeatedly tried in other work until we find the job he is suited for."

"We shall still pay," Mr. Couzens said, "we are quite sure, good, handsome dividends [profits] to our stockholders, and will set aside reasonable amounts for additions and improvements. And after that it is our hope to be able to do still better by our employees. We want them to be in reality partners in our enterprise.

"Believing as we do, that a division of our earnings between capital [owners] and labor [workers] is unequal, we have sought a plan of relief suitable to our business. We think that one concern [business] can make a start and create an example for others. And that is our chief object.

"The public need have no fear that this action of ours will result in any increase in prices of our products. On the contrary we hope to keep up with our past record of reducing prices each year."

Group Discussion: *How does Ford's wage plan show the influence of Progressive Era ideas about social justice and workers? Why was the new policy probably a good business decision for Ford, as well as a good step from a social point of view?*

CHARTING AUTOMOBILE USE

During the decades of the 1910s and 1920s, the automobile become a big part of American life. Its success, and the growth of related industries, helped create new jobs and prosperity. On this page, create a bar graph to show the number of automobiles registered in this period. What advantages did automobiles have over horses that made them desirable to city residents?

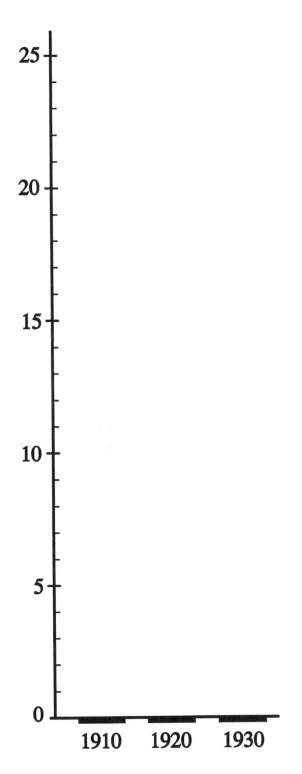

Use the table shown below to find the information to finish the bar graph on the left. Draw a vertical bar for each year shown, with the length corresponding to the number of automobiles registered in the U.S. in that year.

Year	Automobiles Registered in the U.S.
1910	458,000
1920	8,132,000
1930	23,035,000

source: *Historical Statistics of the United States.*

Passenger Autos Registered (Millions) 1910 - 1930

MAP - WORLD WAR ONE: WHO'S WHO

Finish labeling and coloring the map to show the items listed below. The dotted lines will help guide you in showing some of the information.

Central Powers in 1917

Allied Powers in 1917

Neutral Countries in 1917

The Western Front of 1915 - 1917

GEOGRAPHICAL FEATURES

Atlantic Ocean, where the sinking of the _____ and other ships by German U-Boats helped swing public opinion in the U.S. against Germany.

Mediterranean Sea   **Suez Canal**   **Black Sea**   **Caspian Sea**

NATIONAL CAPITALS AND OTHER FAMOUS CITIES

Sarajevo, the city in Austria-Hungary where the assassination of an Austrian _____ by Serbian nationalists sparked the war.

London, the capital of Great Britain and the _____ -wide British Empire, which included Egypt and other parts of Africa, as well as India.

Paris, the capital of France, whose empire included chunks of Africa and _____.

Berlin, the capital of Germany, eager to _____ up in the empire game.

Petrograd, also known as St. Petersburg, the capital of the _____ Empire when the war began. Not long after the communist revolution of 1917, **Moscow** became the new capital. In 1924 Petrograd was renamed Leningrad.

Rome, the capital of _____, whose empire included Libya in North Africa.

Constantinople, also called _____, the capital of the Ottoman Empire. After the war, this empire was broken up into Turkey and several other countries in the Middle East.

Use these terms to fill the blanks: archduke, Asia, catch, Istanbul, Italy, Lusitania, Russian, world

Iceland

Great
Britain

Norway

Sweden

Petrograd

Moscow

Denmark

Russia

Nether-
lands

Berlin

London

Germany

Belg.

Lux.

Paris

Western
Front

Austria-
Hungary

Switz.

France

Italy

Sarajevo

Romania

Portugal

Spain

Rome

Montenegro

Serbia

Albania

Bulgaria

Constantinople (Istanbul)

Greece

Turkey
The Ottoman Empire

Morocco

Algeria

Tunisia

Suez
Canal

(Neutral
Area)

Libya

Egypt

© D. Burns

World War One:
Who's Who

Alliances in 1917

Pre-war national boundaries shown

0   600 miles

Key to Alliances in 1917

Central Powers

Allied Powers

Neutral Nations

DECADE: 1920s   THE ROARING TWENTIES

Prohibition, woman suffrage, flappers, Amelia Earhart, Margaret Sanger,

Scopes trial, Great Migration, Harlem Renaissance, Duke Ellington,

Ku Klux Klan revival, Charles Lindbergh, Babe Ruth, Stock Market Crash

World War I devastated Europe, but America thrived in the decade after the surrender of Germany. For a great many Americans, the future seemed bright. Cities and wealth were growing. Airplanes in the sky, _____ broadcasting, and Hollywood films in the theaters were just some of the signs that a new age had indeed arrived.

The "new woman" got the right to vote in 1920. Social expectations still divided jobs into some proper for women, and some not. But women were increasingly found in business offices, and Amelia Earhart showed that women were ready to break traditional barriers. The flapper became one symbol of the times, with short bobbed hair and a new style of clothing her _____ probably didn't approve of.

Not everyone was happy with the arrival of new ideas, new styles, and other changes in American life. Margaret Sanger, a nurse and social reformer, was actually jailed in New York City for her campaign to make birth control information more available. The sensational trial of teacher John Scopes drew even wider attention. He broke a state law in Tennessee that prohibited the teaching of evolution in public schools. The case revealed a deep split between people with traditional _____ beliefs and those who embraced different views.

People with religious and traditional views were certainly the main force behind another famous aspect of the decade. In 1920 America outlawed alcohol. But all during the time of Prohibition, bootleggers kept an illegal supply going. Gangsters like Al Capone were soon prospering. Speakeasies were clubs where alcohol was served in spite of the laws, thanks to payoffs to _____. A bottle of booze became, for some young people, a sign of being sophisticated. Many people became convinced that the new law actually made alcohol more destructive to society than it was when it was legal. Prohibition was repealed 13 years later the same way it began, with a constitutional amendment.

Black Americans in the South began moving North in great numbers during World War One. This trend, called the Great Migration, continued in the 1920s. They went to take jobs in factories in cities like Chicago and Detroit. A new music called _____ spread with them. Like immigrants from overseas, the new arrivals often landed in the worst areas of the cities. New York City's large black neighborhood, Harlem, became a center of African-American literature, music, dance, and painting. But shocking cases of lynchings of blacks and the reappearance of the Ku Klux Klan demonstrated the sad state of race relations nationwide. A spirit of intolerance often extended to immigrants as well, especially those involved in labor disputes and radical reform movements.

The automobile, now being produced by the millions on assembly lines, became a key force shaping American social and economic life in the 1920s. By the middle of the decade, the average family owned a car. Roads were steadily improved, and scores of businesses related to automobiles and tourism began growing rapidly.

In this decade, silent movies were replaced by the new "talkies" out of Hollywood as new sound film technology developed. Sports figures like baseball's Babe Ruth and daring aviators like _____ also captured the public imagination. The age of the celebrity had begun.

The high life of the rich could be followed by the envious reader in daily newspapers. But writers like F. Scott Fitzgerald criticized the times in books like *The Great Gatsby*. Americans, he suggested, were fast losing their character and _____ in a never-ending chase after status, wealth, and glamour.

In 1929 the Roaring Twenties came crashing down. Business had been growing, and stock market prices had been rising for years. Many investors, eager to jump on the wagon, were even borrowing money to buy stocks. As prices rose, more buyers wanted a piece of the action. Prices continued to shoot up beyond any reasonable value.

In fact, the economy was not as good as it seemed. Farmers, using tractors and reapers, were producing plenty of food. But they were growing _____ than they could sell, and prices were slumping. Factories were turning out plenty of things to buy. But the nation's consumers, as a whole, did not have enough income to _____ all that the nation's factories could produce. Most working class people, for example, were still poorly paid and had little purchasing power. There were other troublesome economic signs as well.

High tariffs passed by Congress in these years hurt international _____. European countries, still trying to recover from World War I, had very little money to buy American products. In addition, many American banks had _____ money recklessly.

Suddenly the bubble burst, as a growing number of people decided to get their money out of the stock market. Soon there were more sellers than buyers, and prices slipped. Once the fall started, everyone wanted out. The market _____ as fearful stock owners ried to sell at any price. Many people saw a lifetime of saving (and even borrowed money) wiped out in days. It was a dark ending to a decade in which everything had seemed possible.

Use these terms to fill in the blanks: buy, Charles Lindbergh, crashed, jazz, loaned, mother, more, police, radio, religious, trade, values

TALK OF THE TWENTIES

As you read the passages below and study the images from magazines of that era, tell how each reflects or illustrates some aspect of the decade of the 1920s.

"America's present need is not heroics, but healing; not nostrums, but normalcy, not revolution, but restoration; not surgery but serenity."
- Presidential candidate Warren G. Harding, 1920

My candle burns at both ends;
It will not last the night;
But, ah, my foes, and, oh, my friends -
It gives a lovely light
- Poet Edna St. Vincent Millay

"The business of America is business."
- President Calvin Coolidge, 1925

Bryan: I believe that everything in the Bible should be accepted as it is given there.
Darrow: But when you read that Jonah swallowed the whale - or that the whale swallowed Jonah - do you literally interpret it?
Bryan: Yes, sir. If the Bible says so.
- Attorney Clarence Darrow questioning William Jennings Bryan in the Scopes Trial, 1925

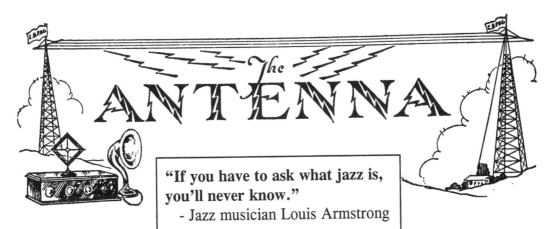

The ANTENNA

"If you have to ask what jazz is, you'll never know."
- Jazz musician Louis Armstrong

"The business of evading Prohibition and making mock of it has ceased to wear any aspects of crime and has become a sort of national sport."
- Newspaperman H.L. Mencken

I swear to the Lord
I still can't see
Why Democracy means
Everybody but me.
- African American Poet
Langston Hughes

"The restlessness approached hysteria. The parties were bigger. The pace was faster, the shows were broader, the buildings were higher, the morals were looser and the liquor was cheaper. But all these benefits did not really minister to much delight. Young people wore out early - they were hard and languid at twenty-one."
- Writer F. Scott Fitzgerald

CHARTING THE CRASH OF 1929

During the decade of the 1920s, the rapid growth of American business was reflected in rising stock values. Before completing the line graph on the next page, review this page to be sure you understand the terms and concepts involved.

Acme Products Corporation

(It needs to get money to start or expand a business, and seeks investors.)

Stock Certificate   1 Share
Acme Products, Inc.

(These are given to investors as proof of their investment. As part owners, the investors receive a share of the company's profits.)

Investors

(These are people who have saved money and want to invest in a corporation by purchasing stock.)

Investors make money from stocks in two ways:

 If the company makes profits, these are divided among the investors. The stockholders receive the **dividends** in a check sent to them.

 Investors can sell their stock certificates to someone else. If the company is very successful, other people will pay a higher price to purchase the stock from a current shareholder.

 Sometimes, as in the 1920s, a condition called a **"bubble"** occurs. A bubble is a rapid rise in stock prices far above what actual business conditions can justify. Investors keep buying stocks at high prices because they don't want to miss out on the chance to sell later at even higher prices. But eventually the bubble bursts and stock prices crash.

Complete the line graph below to show stock prices from the 1920s and early 1930s. To help investors keep track of the stock market, calculations are done to create daily "index" figures. One well known index figure is the Standard and Poor's Index of Common Stocks.

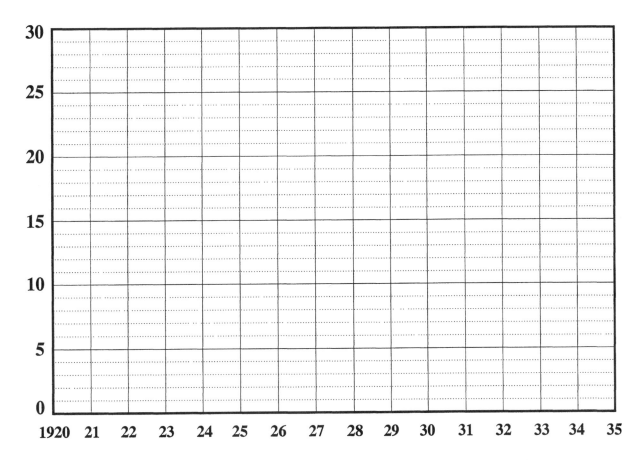

Standard and Poor's Index of Common Stocks
1920 to 1935

Use the table below to find the information to make the line graph above.

Year	S&P Index	Year	S&P Index	Year	S&P Index	Year	S&P Index
1920	7.9	1924	9.05	1928	19.95	1932	6.93
1921	6.86	1925	11.15	1929	26.02	1933	8.96
1922	8.41	1926	12.59	1930	21.03	1934	9.84
1923	8.57	1927	15.34	1931	13.66	1935	10.60

source: *Historical Statistics of the United States*

DECADE: 1930s   THE GREAT DEPRESSION

depression, Herbert Hoover, bank run, Franklin Delano Roosevelt, The New Deal,

Social Security, Dust Bowl, Adolf Hitler, Nazi, Benito Mussolini, fascism, appeasement

The Stock Market Crash in 1929 was not the only cause of the Great Depression. Mechanization of farms and factories had been throwing people out of work. Improved production led farms and factories to produce more than consumers as a group could afford to buy. A depression easily starts when farms and factories can't sell what they produce. Soon, there are layoffs and falling prices, but as people _____ their jobs, they buy even less.

The Great Depression was a terrible blow to American pride. In every big city, tens of thousands of people were _____, while many factories sat idle. Many people waited in relief lines for a bowl of soup, while grain elevators overflowed. Thousands of banks failed, and many people's life savings were wiped out. The American economic system, capitalism, seemed to have hit a dead end. As if things weren't bad enough already, a drought struck and turned Oklahoma and many neighboring states into a "Dust _____." The plight of farmers there was portrayed in a famous book (and movie) titled *The Grapes of Wrath*.

By 1932 about one quarter of the nation's workers had no job. President Herbert Hoover tried bailing out banks and industries with federal loans. But he wanted to avoid involving the federal government in direct help for individual citizens. That, he feared, would represent a dangerous _____ in American ideas about the proper role of the government.

Franklin Delano Roosevelt promised in the 1932 elections to give a "New Deal" to Americans. Once elected, he was willing to try anything that might help, starting with federal relief money for desperate families. He launched the Civilian Conservation Corps to give _____ to unemployed young men, mostly working in parks or on soil conservation projects. The Public Works Administration put people to work building bridges, hospitals, and airports. Roosevelt hoped such projects, and their huge payrolls, would get money circulating and boost the economy. (This approach is often called "pump-priming.")

One of Roosevelt's first steps, however, was to close all banks briefly until they proved they were financially stable. Better banking regulations were created to protect deposits and stop the financial panics that were causing bank runs.

Roosevelt tried to deal with the basic causes of the depression as well. The Agriculture Adjustment Act paid farmers to leave some land idle, so the price of farm products would go back _____ enough to give farmers a reasonable profit. The National Recovery Administration created a program that brought together manufacturers to agree on reasonable production levels, prices, working hours, and wages. (Some anti-trust laws had to be suspended to permit these agreements.) The goal was to break up the pattern of over-production by industry that resulted in low profits, low wages, and layoffs of workers.

Later New Deal programs included the Social _____ Act, which created pensions for retired workers as well as payments to support widowed spouses and their children. Another important reform was the Fair Labor Standards Act, which set up the first national minimum wage.

Critics said FDR's policies were "socialistic," and gave far too much power to the federal government. Two New Deal programs were, in fact, declared unconstitutional by the Supreme Court. And while he helped restore confidence in the economy, the depression did _____ quickly end. It took World War Two to accomplish that. The New Deal did, however, greatly expand both the size of the federal government and the roles it played in American life. These years mark the start in America of what is usually called a "welfare state," that is, a country in which the _____ takes on a major responsibility for planning and promoting the welfare of citizens.

Fortunately, the vast majority of Americans avoided extreme ideas of the sort that led to dictatorships in some European countries. Russia had Stalin as a communist dictator in these years. Germany and Italy both developed fascism, a brutal system that glorifies war and aggression. It helped that America's economy was not a complete disaster, in spite of the depression. Many people and businesses actually did well in this period. Labor unions, helped by a new federal labor law, fought for and won a bigger place in mines, steel mills, and auto plants. It was a great decade for Hollywood, and films like _____ expressed the hope that a brighter future would arrive, with American values still intact.

By the time FDR was re-elected in 1936, serious trouble was brewing around the world. Hitler and his Nazi party had risen to power in _____. The dictator Benito Mussolini ruled Italy. Other European leaders followed a policy of appeasement, rather than making a stand against the rising tide of the fascist dictators. In 1937 Japan invaded China.

Americans watched, but most were reluctant to do anything that might involve the country in another _____. Congress even passed several Neutrality Acts to try to keep from being dragged into the conflicts. Then, in 1939, Germany invaded Poland, and World War Two began. The president had once warned, "This generation of Americans has a rendezvous with Destiny." Now, the shape of Destiny was becoming visible.

Use these terms to fill in the blanks: Bowl, change, Germany, government, jobs, lose, not, Security, The Wizard of Oz, unemployed, up, war

---

FDR ATTACKS THE DEPRESSION

As Franklin D. Roosevelt took office in 1933, he declared again his plan to give the federal government a large and central role in attacking the Great Depression. These are condensed excerpts from two of his most famous speeches as president.

First Inaugural Address - 1933

This is the time to speak the truth, the whole truth, frankly and boldly. Nor need we shrink from honestly facing conditions in our country today. This great nation will endure as it has endured, will revive and will prosper.

So first of all let me assert my firm belief that the only thing we have to fear is fear itself - nameless, unreasoning, unjustified terror which paralyzes needed efforts to convert retreat into advance.

In every dark hour of our national life a leadership of frankness and vigor has met with that support of the people themselves which is essential to victory.

In such a spirit on my part and on yours we face our common difficulties. The withered leaves of industrial enterprise lie on every side; farmers find no markets for their produce; the savings of many years in thousands of families are gone.

More important, a host of unemployed citizens face the grim problem of existence, and an equally great number toil with little return [work for low wages].

This nation asks for action, and action now. Our greatest primary task is to put people to work. It can be accomplished in part by direct recruiting by the government itself, treating the task as we would treat the emergency of war, but at the same time, through this employment, accomplishing greatly needed projects.

This task can be helped by definite efforts to raise the values of agricultural products, and with this, the power to purchase the output of our cities.

It can be helped by preventing the tragedy of the growing loss, through foreclosure, of our small homes and our farms.

It can be helped by unifying relief [welfare] activities which are often scattered, uneconomical, and unequal.

Finally, we require two safeguards against a return of the evils of the old order. There must be a strict supervision of all banking and credits and investments.

We do not distrust the future of essential democracy. The people of the United States have not failed. In their need they have registered a mandate that they want direct, vigorous action.

They have asked for discipline and direction under leadership. They have made me the present instrument of their wishes. In the spirit of the gift, I take it.

The New Deal programs developed by FDR and Congress created jobs for a great many unemployed people. Other measures were also adopted to improve the economy.

As he began his second term in 1937, FDR outlined an even more ambitious goal for the federal government.

Second Inaugural Address - 1937

Nearly all of us recognize that as the intricacies of human relationships increase, so power to govern them must also increase - power to stop evil; power to do good.

True, we have come far from the days of stagnation and despair. Vitality has been preserved. Courage and confidence have been restored. Mental and moral horizons have been extended.

I see a great nation, upon a great continent, blessed with a great wealth of natural resources. Its 130 million people are at peace among themselves; they are making their country a good neighbor among the nations.

But here is the challenge to our democracy: In this nation I see tens of millions of its citizens - a substantial part of its whole population - who at this very moment are denied the greater part of what the very lowest standards of living of today call the necessities of life.

I see millions of families trying to live on incomes so meager that the pall [threat] of family disaster hangs over them day by day.

I see millions whose daily lives in city and on farm continue under conditions labeled indecent by a so-called polite society a century ago.

I see millions denied education, recreation, and the opportunity to better their lot and the lot of their children.

I see one third of a nation ill-housed, ill-clad, and ill-nourished.

It is not in despair that I paint you that picture. I paint it for you in hope - because the nation, seeing and understanding the injustice in it, proposes to paint it out.

We are determined to make every American citizen the subject of his country's

interest and concern; and we will never regard any faithful, law-abiding group within our borders as superfluous [unwanted].

The test of our progress is not whether we add more to the abundance of those who have too much; it is whether we provide enough for those who have too little.

Today we reconsecrate our country to long-cherished ideals in a suddenly changed civilization. In every land there are always at work forces that drive men apart and forces that draw men together. In our personal ambitions we are individualists. But in our seeking for economic and political progress as a nation, we all go up, or else we all go down, as one people.

In taking again the oath of office as President of the United States, I assume the solemn obligation of leading the American people forward along the road over which they have chosen to advance.

Group Discussion:

1. In the first speech, what does FDR say is the primary task the federal government must do as the first step in fighting the depression? What other measures does he say are also needed to boost the economy?

2. In the second speech, what goals does FDR set for the American government? How does he explain or justify the need for expanding the role of government in American life?

CHARTING THE NEW DEAL AND UNEMPLOYMENT

FDR's New Deal programs had three main purposes:
- **Relief** *for the needy with government money and jobs.*
- **Recovery** *of the economic health of industry and farms.*
- **Reform** *of the problems that had helped create the depression.*

Try to classify the programs listed below into one of those three categories. If you decide a program falls into two of the categories, list both. Use your own judgement, but be ready to explain and defend your decisions.

New Deal Program	What It Did	Category
Federal Emergency Relief Administration	Sent millions of dollars to states to use in direct relief payments and food for the unemployed.	
Civilian Conservation Corps (CCC)	Created jobs for over two million young unmarried men in conservation work and parks.	
Agriculture Adjustment Act (AAA)	Paid farmers to reduce the amount of crops they planted, in order to cut excess production.	
Federal Deposit Insurance Corporation (FDIC)	Protected people's bank deposits, thus eliminating the problem of "bank runs" that were a serious problem in the early 1930s.	
National Recovery Administration (NRA)	Set up voluntary agreements among businesses to cut excess production. The agreements covered production, prices, wages, and hours of work.	
Tennessee Valley Authority (TVA)	Built hydroelectric power plants and flood control dams in seven states in the Tennessee River region.	
Securities and Exchange Commission (SEC)	Created to supervise the stock market and protect investors from dishonest practices.	
Public Works Administration (PWA) and the Works Progress Administration (WPA)	Created jobs for millions of unemployed people constructing roads, hospitals, post offices, parks, and many other projects. The WPA also included a program that hired out-of-work artists, photographers, actors, and writers for a wide range of artistic and educational projects.	
National Labor Relations Act	Gave labor unions the right to organize and represent workers in collective bargaining.	
Social Security Act	Created a federal system of old-age pensions and assistance for orphans and the disabled. It also created an unemployment insurance system.	
Fair Labor Standards Act	Set up the first national minimum wage law and abolished child labor.	

After you complete the line graph on this page, study the pattern and the dates of the elections won by Franklin D. Roosevelt. (He won the presidential elections of 1932, 1936, 1940, and 1944.) How does the pattern help explain FDR's political success?

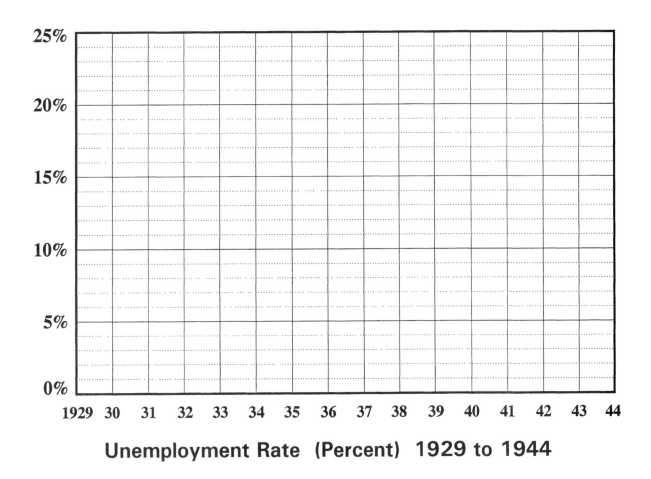

Unemployment Rate (Percent) 1929 to 1944

Use the table below to find the information to make the line graph above.

Year	Unemployed (Percent)	Year	Unemployed (Percent)	Year	Unemployed (Percent)	Year	Unemployed (Percent)
1929	3.2	1933	24.9	1937	14.3	1941	9.9
1930	8.7	1934	21.7	1938	19.0	1942	4.7
1931	15.9	1935	20.1	1939	17.2	1943	1.9
1932	23.6	1936	16.9	1940	14.6	1944	1.2

source: *Historical Statistics of the United States*

DECADE: 1940s   WORLD WAR TWO

Axis, Allies, Battle of Britain, Winston Churchill, Lend-Lease, Pearl Harbor,

rationing, Rosie the Riveter, D-Day, Holocaust, Harry S. Truman, Manhattan Project,

Cold War, containment, Red scare, United Nations, Marshall Plan, NATO

By 1940 Germany, Italy, and Japan - the Axis powers - had already attacked neighboring countries. In June of that year, France fell to the German "blitzkrieg" method of lightning fast attack. Hitler next turned waves of German airplanes against England in the Battle of Britain. Prime Minister Winston Churchill rallied British spirits with his stirring declarations that England would _____ surrender. President Franklin Roosevelt watched the aggression of the Axis powers with alarm, but most Americans were not yet ready to join the fight. He did, however, push Congress to approve the Lend-Lease program, which sent desperately needed weapons and supplies to England and Russia.

When Japan attacked the U.S. naval base at _____, Hawaii, in December 1941, America entered the war. Getting supplies to the other Allies was now critical. Long convoys of ships continued crossing the Atlantic, always under danger of German U-boat attacks. In a move that would later be heavily criticized, Japanese-Americans on the West Coast were removed and confined to internment camps as possible security risks.

Roosevelt knew that victory would depend on out-producing the enemy. Thousands of factories were converted to make _____. A system of rationing with coupons was started to conserve oil, food, and other products, and make sure everyone got a fair share of what was available. Scientists and engineers went to work to develop or improve radar, aircraft design, and the super-secret _____ bomb. Women took many jobs held by men before the war, and even joined special military units like the Women's Army Corps.

Germany's grip on Europe was too strong to attack immediately. To buy time, American and British forces first attacked Germans holding North Africa in 1942. Russians held their battle lines against the German invasion with almost unbelievable courage.

The assault on Hitler's empire began with massive troop landings on the shores of Normandy in France on D-Day - June 6, 1944. After liberating France, the American and other Allied soldiers fought on toward Germany. As the Western Allied armies advanced into Germany early in 1945, the true horror of Nazi concentration camps like Dachau was exposed. Russians advancing against Germany from the east through Poland found more _____ of the Holocaust in Nazi death camps like Auschwitz.

Berlin, the German capital, fell to Russian troops in April 1945. Hitler killed himself. (Mussolini was captured by Italian freedom fighters and shot.)

The fight against the Japanese empire in the Pacific began even before Germany fell, in the islands and seas near Australia. Japan's area of control was slowly pushed back in brutal battles closer and closer to Japan itself.

FDR died during the war, in April of 1945. President Harry Truman, a few months later, made the decision to use the newly developed atomic bomb against Japan. They surrendered after _____ and Nagasaki were completely destroyed that August with the deadly weapon. Truman said he made the decision to save both American and Japanese lives, since a conventional assault on Japan could have killed a million people. America occupied Japan and put a democratic constitution into effect.

America also helped Europe get back on its feet with extensive financial help under the Marshall Plan. This help was offered regardless of which side a nation fought on during the war. By the early 1950s most of Western Europe was flourishing again.

Russia had fought alongside the other Allies, but the terrible war losses only hardened that country's view that it would be safest to keep control over the countries of Eastern Europe. Russia forced these nations, including Poland and the eastern part of Germany, to form _____ governments. American leaders hoped to limit the further spread of communism with a policy called "containment." Many European nations, now as fearful of Russia as they had been of Germany, joined with America in a defense alliance called NATO. The new world struggle, called the _____ War, would last until 1990.

Back in America, fear of Russia's intentions created a "Red scare" and led to some controversial laws and accusations against suspected communists. But the years after 1945 were mostly good ones. Returning soldiers came back to a _____ welcome. The G.I. Bill paid their tuition to college or technical school, and helped veterans get loans for buying _____. Factories converted back to making cars and refrigerators instead of tanks and bombs. "Rosie the Riveter" went home, eager to start a family, but aware of new possibilities in herself.

The war against Hitler's racist system helped America declare its ideals more clearly than ever. One result was that people were more willing to confront _____ in our own society. In 1947 Jackie Robinson broke the color line in professional _____. In 1948 President Truman issued an order calling for racial equality in the armed forces. Years of struggles were still ahead in the long fight for the civil rights of African-Americans, but now there could be no turning back.

Use these terms to fill in the blanks: atomic, baseball, Cold, communist, hero's, Hiroshima, homes, never, Pearl Harbor, proof, racism, weapons

FDR AND WORLD WAR TWO

These selections are condensed from two famous speeches by President Franklin D. Roosevelt in the early 1940s.

December 1940: America as the Arsenal of Democracy

Never before since Jamestown and Plymouth Rock has our American civilization been in such danger as now.

The Nazi masters of Germany have made it clear that they intend not only to dominate all life and thought in their own country, but also to enslave the whole of Europe, and then use the resources of Europe to dominate the rest of the world.

Some of our people would like to believe that wars in Europe and in Asia are no concern to us. But if Great Britain goes down, the Axis powers will control the continents of Europe, Asia, Africa, Australia, and the high seas. It is no exaggeration to say that all of us in all the Americas would be living at the point of a gun. Frankly and definitely there is danger ahead - danger against which we must prepare.

The plain facts are that the Nazis have proclaimed, time and again, that all other races are their inferiors and therefore subject to their orders. And most important of all, the vast resources and wealth of this American hemisphere constitute the most tempting loot in all the round world.

The experience of the past two years has proven beyond doubt that no nation can appease [satisfy] the Nazis. We know now that a nation can have peace with the Nazis only at the price of total surrender.

Some tell you that the Axis powers are going to win anyway, that the United States might just as well throw its influence into the scale of a dictated peace and get the best out of it that we can. They call it a "negotiated peace." Nonsense.

Such a dictated peace would be no peace at all. It would only lead to the most gigantic armament race and the most devastating trade wars in all history. And in these contests the Americas would offer the only real resistance to the Axis powers. With all their vaunted [boasted] efficiency, with all their parade of pious purpose in this war, there are still in their background the concentration camp and the servants of God in chains.

The history of recent years proves that the shootings and the chains and the concentration camps are not just the transient [temporary] tools but the very altars of modern dictatorships. They may talk of a "new order" in the world, but what they have in mind is only a revival of the oldest and worst tyranny. In that there is no liberty, no religion, no hope.

The people of Europe who are defending themselves do not ask us to do their fighting. They ask us for the implements of war: the planes, the tanks, the guns, the freighters which will enable them to fight for their liberty and our security. We must get these weapons to them so that we and our children will be saved the agony and suffering of war which others have had to endure.

Group Discussion: *Why does FDR believe the U.S. cannot just ignore the war in Europe? Why can't the U.S. simply negotiate its own peace agreement with the Nazis? What argument does FDR use to win support for the idea of sending American military equipment to Great Britain and the other Allies?*

America responded and Congress approved millions of dollars of aid for the Allies. But the December 7, 1941 attack by the Japanese on Pearl Harbor ended any hope that America could avoid fully joining the fight. A month after the attack, FDR made a report on the war situation.

January 1942: First War Address Before Congress

I am proud to say to you that the spirit of the American people was never higher than it is today. The response of the American people has been instantaneous, and it will be sustained until our security is assured.

Japan's scheme of conquest goes back half a century. It is not merely a policy of seeking living room, but a plan which included the subjugation [overpowering] of all the peoples in the Far East and in the islands of the Pacific.

A similar policy of criminal conquest was adopted by Italy. The Fascists first revealed their imperial designs in 1935. Their goal was the domination of all North Africa, Egypt, part of France and the entire Mediterranean world.

But the dreams of empire of the Japanese and Fascist leaders were modest in comparison with the aspirations of Hitler and his Nazis. Their plans called for the ultimate domination of the whole earth. When Hitler organized his Berlin-Rome-Tokyo alliance, all these plans of conquest became a single plan.

Our own objectives [goals] are clear: the objective of smashing the militarism imposed by warlords upon their enslaved peoples; the objective of liberating the subjugated nations; the objective of establishing and securing freedom of speech, freedom of religion, freedom from want and freedom from fear everywhere in the world.

We know that modern methods of warfare make it a task not only of shooting and fighting, but an even more urgent one of working and producing. The superiority of the Allies in munitions [weapons] and ships must be overwhelming. We must strain every existing armament producing facility to the utmost. We must convert every available plant and tool to war production.

We are fighting today for security and progress and for peace, not only for ourselves, but for all men; not only for one generation, but for all generations.

Our enemies are guided by a brutal cynicism, by unholy contempt for the human race. We are inspired by a faith which goes back through all the years to the first chapter of the Book of Genesis: "God created man in His own image."

We on our side are striving to be true to that divine heritage. We are fighting, as our fathers have fought, to uphold the doctrine that all men are equal in the sight of God. Those on the other side are striving to destroy this deep belief and to create a world in their own image, a world of tyranny and cruelty and serfdom.

This is the conflict that day and night now pervades our lives.

Group Discussion: *What does FDR say the three Axis nations want? What does he say are the objectives of the Americans? What does he say it will take to win the war? How does FDR contrast the different values and beliefs of the Allies and the Axis nations?*

MAP - AXIS AGGRESSION IN EUROPE

Finish labeling and coloring the map to show the items listed below. The dotted lines will help guide you in showing the areas under Axis control.

Germany and Italy in 1937

Axis Controlled Areas in mid-1942

Allied Controlled Areas in mid-1942

Neutral Nations in mid-1942

GEOGRAPHICAL FEATURES:

English Channel	**Atlantic Ocean**	**North Sea**	**Baltic Sea**
Mediterranean Sea	**Suez Canal**	**Black Sea**	**Caspian Sea**

FAMOUS PLACES IN THE STRUGGLE TO FREE EUROPE

Dunkirk, where more than 300,000 British and French soldiers were saved from being captured as **Germany** attacked **France** in 1940. A large fleet of British ships and boats of all kinds crossed the English _____ to rescue them and carry them to safety in England. But most of the soldiers' equipment had to be abandoned.

London, capital of **Great Britain**, which suffered months of deadly attacks from German airplanes after the fall of France in 1940. This air war was called the Battle of _____.

Leningrad, **Stalingrad**, and **Moscow**, all cities in **Russia**. Heroic fighting by Russians and the bitterly cold winter of 1942-43 helped _____ the advance of the German army. (Leningrad and Stalingrad now go by their former names, St. Petersburg and Volgograd.)

Casablanca and **El Alamein**, where the Americans and British began their attack on Hitler's army in North Africa late in 1942. The Allies fought on to **Tunisia**, then up into **Italy** itself in 1943. The capital of Italy, **Rome**, was liberated by the Allies in 1944. By this time, many Italians were turning _____ their fascist dictator, Benito Mussolini.

Normandy Beaches, on the coast of France. This was the landing site for the Allied attack on Hitler's European empire. The date was June 6, 1944, also known as _____. The Allies liberated France and its capital, **Paris**, then fought on into Germany. In April 1945 **Berlin** fell to the armies of Russia advancing from the east through **Poland**. Hitler _____ himself in the last days of fighting. Nazi Germany surrendered unconditionally in May of 1945.

Use these terms to fill in the blanks: against, Britain, Channel, D-Day, shot, stop

---

Iceland

Union of Soviet
Socialist Republics
(includes Russia)

Great
Britain
(U.K.)

Ireland

Norway

Sweden

Finland

Leningrad

Moscow

Denmark

Estonia

Latvia

Lithu-
ania

E.P.*

Stalingrad

London

Dunkirk

Netherlands

Belg.

Lux.

Berlin

Warsaw

Germany

Poland

*Normandy
Beaches*

Paris

Czechoslovakia

Austria

Hungary

Switz.

France

Italy

Romania

Yugoslavia

Portugal

Spain

Rome

Albania

Greece

Bulgaria

Turkey

Iran

Syria

Iraq

Sicily

Lebanon

Casablanca

Morocco

Algeria

Tunisia

Palestine

Trans-
Jordan

Saudi
Arabia

El
Alamein

Libya

Egypt

*Suez
Canal*

* E.P. = East Prussia, a
province of Germany

© D. Burns

Axis Aggression in
Europe

1937 - 1942

1937 national boundaries shown

0   600 miles

Key to Areas of Control

Germany and Italy in 1937

*Axis Controlled Areas
in mid-1942*

*Allied Controlled Areas
in mid-1942*

Neutral Nations in 1942

MAP - THE JAPANESE EMPIRE

Finish labeling and coloring the map to show the items listed below. The dotted lines will help guide you in showing some of the information.

Japan

Areas Under Japanese Control in mid-1942

Farthest Extent of Japanese Control in the Pacific

PACIFIC ISLANDS FAMOUS FOR THEIR PART IN AMERICA'S COUNTER-ATTACK

Pearl Harbor, in the **Hawaiian Islands**, hit by the Japanese in a _____ attack that brought America into World War Two in December 1941. Almost 2,400 people were killed. Once the base was fully restored, it became the launching point for the American counter-attack on the Japanese Empire.

Midway, an American island where a big Japanese attack was turned back and four Japanese _____ carriers sunk in the Battle of Midway in 1942. This battle proved that airplanes were becoming the new weapons of naval warfare. There was no actual ship to ship contact in this key victory for the American navy.

Solomon Islands, where an American

action on **Guadalcanal** late in 1942 won an important _____ as the push toward Japan began.

Philippines, the islands America was driven from early in the war by the Japanese. Gen. Douglas MacArthur pledged, "I shall _____," and he did, in a massive assault late in 1944.

Marshall Islands, Guam, Iwo Jima, and **Okinawa**, all Pacific islands through which the American forces "leapfrogged" closer to Japan during 1944 and 1945. Japan was given a warning to _____. It did not, and American forces dropped atomic bombs on the Japanese cities of Hiroshima and Nagasaki in August 1945 to end the war.

OTHER PLACES INVOLVED IN THE WAR IN THE PACIFIC

Aleutian Islands, American islands which stretch off the coast of **Alaska**. Several of these were _____ by Japan.

Pacific Ocean, the scene of many naval battles during the war involving surface ships, airplanes, and _____.

Use these terms to fill in the blanks: aircraft, occupied, return, submarines, surprise, surrender, victory

---

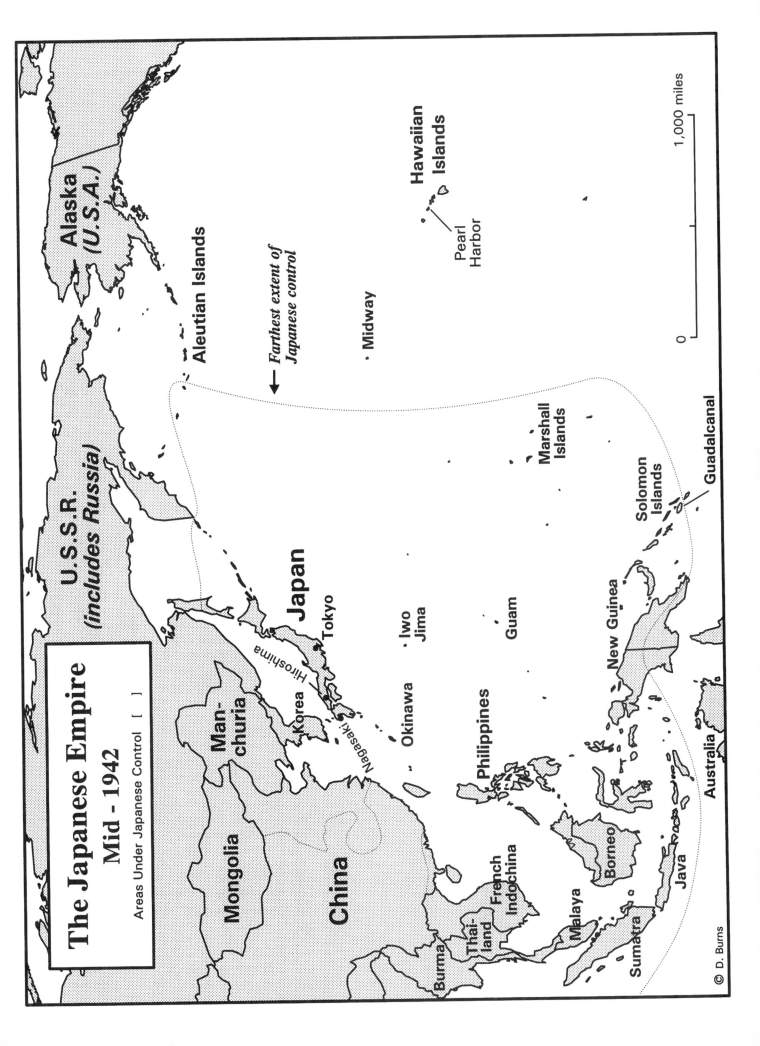

The Japanese Empire
Mid - 1942

Areas Under Japanese Control [ ]

U.S.S.R.
(includes Russia)

Alaska
(U.S.A.)

Aleutian Islands

Farthest extent of Japanese control

Midway

Hawaiian Islands

Pearl Harbor

1,000 miles

0

Mongolia

Man-churia

Korea

Japan

Tokyo

Hiroshima

Nagasaki

Iwo Jima

Okinawa

China

Guam

Marshall Islands

Philippines

Burma

Thai-land

French Indochina

Malaya

Borneo

New Guinea

Solomon Islands

Guadalcanal

Sumatra

Java

Australia

© D. Burns

THE STRUGGLE OF THE COLD WAR BEGINS

Winston Churchill, Prime Minister of England during World War Two, visited America after the war to warn of the new threat posed by the Soviet Union. His 1946 speech, condensed here, is famous for coining the term "the iron curtain."

Winston Churchill's Warning

The United States stands at this time at the pinnacle [peak] of world power. It is a solemn moment for the American democracy. For with this primacy in power is also joined an awe-inspiring accountability to the future.

The awful ruin of Europe, with all its vanished glories, and of large parts of Asia glares us in the eyes. Our supreme task and duty is to guard the homes of the common people from the horrors and miseries of another war. We are all agreed on that.

Nobody knows what Soviet Russia and its Communist international organization intends to do in the immediate future. It is my duty, however, to place before you certain facts about the present position in Europe.

From Stettin in the Baltic to Trieste in the Adriatic, an iron curtain has descended across the Continent.

Behind that line lie all the capitals of the ancient states of Central and Eastern Europe: Warsaw, Berlin, Prague, Vienna, Budapest, Belgrade, Bucharest and Sofia.

All these famous cities and the populations around them lie in what I must call the Soviet sphere, and all are subject, in one form and another, not only to Soviet influence, but to a very high and in some cases increasing measure of control from Moscow.

The Communist parties have been raised to pre-eminence and power far beyond their numbers and are seeking everywhere to obtain totalitarian control. Police governments are prevailing in nearly every case.

In a great number of countries throughout the world, Communist fifth columns [agents and secret supporters] are established, and work in complete unity and absolute obedience to directions they receive from the Communist center.

I do not believe that Soviet Russia desires war. What they desire is the fruits of war and the indefinite expansion of their power and doctrines.

But what we have to consider here today, while time remains, is the permanent prevention of war and the establishment of conditions of freedom and democracy as rapidly as possible in all countries.

Our difficulties and dangers will not be removed by closing our eyes to them. They will not be removed by mere waiting to see what happens, nor will they be removed by a policy of appeasement.

If the Western Democracies stand together in strict adherence to the principles of the United Nations Charter, their influence for furthering those principles will be immense and no one is likely to molest them. If, however, they become divided or falter in their duty, then indeed catastrophe may overwhelm us all.

Group Discussion: *What does Churchill warn is happening in Europe? What does Churchill say Russia and its communist leaders want to accomplish?*

In 1947 President Harry S. Truman urged the U.S. to take an active stand on the side of any nation that asked for help resisting communist take-over attempts. His speech before Congress, condensed here, declared "The Truman Doctrine."

The Truman Doctrine

One of the primary objectives of the foreign policy of the United States is the creation of conditions in which we and other nations will be able to work out a way of life free from coercion [force]. This was a fundamental issue in the war with Germany and Japan.

Our victory was won over countries which sought to impose their will, and their way of life, upon other nations.

To ensure the peaceful development of  nations, free from coercion, the United States has taken a leading part in establishing the United Nations. The United Nations is designed to make possible lasting freedom and independence for all its members.

We shall not realize our objectives, however, unless we are willing to help free peoples to maintain their free institutions and their national integrity against aggressive movements that seek to impose upon them totalitarian regimes [governments].

This is no more than a frank recognition that totalitarian regimes imposed on free peoples, by direct or indirect aggression, undermine the foundations of international peace and hence the security of the United States.

At the present moment in world history nearly every nation must choose between alternative ways of life.

One way of life is based upon the will of the majority, and is distinguished by free institutions, representative government, free elections, guarantees of individual liberty, freedom of speech and religion, and freedom from political oppression.

The second way of life is based upon the will of a minority forcibly imposed upon the majority. It relies upon terror and oppression, a controlled press and radio, fixed elections, and the suppression of personal freedoms.

I believe that it must be the policy of the United States to support free peoples who are resisting attempted subjugation [take-over] by armed minorities or by outside pressures.

I believe that we must assist free peoples  to work out their own destinies in their own way.

The seeds of totalitarian regimes are nurtured by misery and want. They spread and grow in the evil soil of poverty and strife. They reach their full growth when the hope of a people for a better life has died. We must keep that hope alive.

The free peoples of the world look to us for support in maintaining their freedoms. If we falter in our leadership, we may endanger the peace of the world - and we shall surely endanger the welfare of our own nation.

Group Discussion: *Why does President Truman believe it is important for the U.S. to help other nations that are threatened by communism? What conditions does he say promote the growth of communism and other totalitarian government systems?*

8 Modern America: 1950 - Present

"I have a dream that one day this nation will rise up and live out the true meaning of its creed: 'We hold these truths to be self-evident, that all men are created equal.'"

"Make Love, Not War!"

"That's one small step for man, one giant leap for mankind."

"Mr. Gorbachev, tear down this wall!"

"Let's roll!"

Study Checklist

When you have completed this section, working with the Internet support site at
www.fasttrackteaching.com *or other resources, you should be able to:*

 Identify and explain the context of the **Famous Quotes** shown on the Section Title Page.

 Identify and explain the importance of the **Famous Names and Terms** listed on the topic summary pages in this section.

 Identify on a map and explain the importance of the **Famous Places** shown on the maps in this section.

 Explain the general sequence of events in this period and tell from memory the **Famous Years**:

- The Supreme Court ruled segregation illegal in public schools (**1954**).
- John F. Kennedy was elected president (**1960**).
- The first Americans landed on the moon (**1969**).
- Terrorists destroyed the World Trade Center (**2001**).

Take a Practice Test!

(A) (B) (C) (D)

A multiple-choice practice test for this section can be found on the Internet support site at:

www.fasttrackteaching.com

Textbook Page References:

Discuss or write briefly on such questions and topics as these:

1. How did the Cold War affect American life and politics in this period? How did it affect American involvement in conflicts in other parts of the world?

2. Rev. Martin Luther King said the Civil Rights movement was "deeply rooted in the American Dream." What did he mean by that? Explain his strategy of "non-violent civil disobedience."

3. What approach did liberals like President Lyndon Johnson take in the 1960s to reduce poverty in America? What strategies did the "conservative revolution" of President Ronald Reagan favor to improve life for the poor?

4. What have been some of the big changes in American life, including family life, as a result of the Women's Liberation movement of the 1960s and 1970s?

5. Explain why the United States became an increasingly "multi-cultural" society in this period. What benefits and what challenges did this bring?

6. How did America respond to the terrorist attacks of September 11, 2001? How did the attacks change life in the United States?

Timeline 1950 - Present

Find when these events occurred, fill in the blanks, and place them on the main timeline. The thin timeline shows the presidents of this period.

Korean War begins - We went in mainly to stop the spread of _____.

Brown* v. *Board of Ed. - This important case made segregated public schools _____.

Sputnik in space - This first successful satellite was launched by _____.

Cuban missile crisis - For a while, _____ war seemed a real possibility.

March on Washington - Rev. King gave his famous "I Have a _____" speech.

Civil Rights Act of 1964 - It outlawed _____ in public places.

First moon landing - For a brief moment, it _____ all Americans, in spite of deep divisions over the Vietnam War and other issues of the decade.

Woodstock Music Fair - It symbolized the height of the _____ movement.

Nixon resigns - It all started with a break-in at the _____ office building.

South Vietnam falls - American troops had been withdrawn about _____ years earlier.

IBM PC introduced - This computer soon revolutionized _____ offices.

AIDS officially identified - The disease weakens the body's _____ system.

Berlin Wall falls - It was a sure sign that the _____ War was finally ending.

Desert Storm War - America went in to free _____ from occupation by Iraq.

Russia rejects communism - Russians could see their system was just not _____.

Welfare reform passes - This plan won broad support from _____ political parties.

World Trade Center Destroyed - The terrorists, all from the Middle East, also hit the _____ building.

Iraq War - American and British leaders wanted Saddam _____ overthrown because of his involvement with terrorism in Iraq and elsewhere.

Use these terms to fill in the blanks: both, business, Cold, communism, discrimination, Dream, hippie, Hussein, illegal, immune, Kuwait, nuclear, Pentagon, Russia, two, united, Watergate, working

---

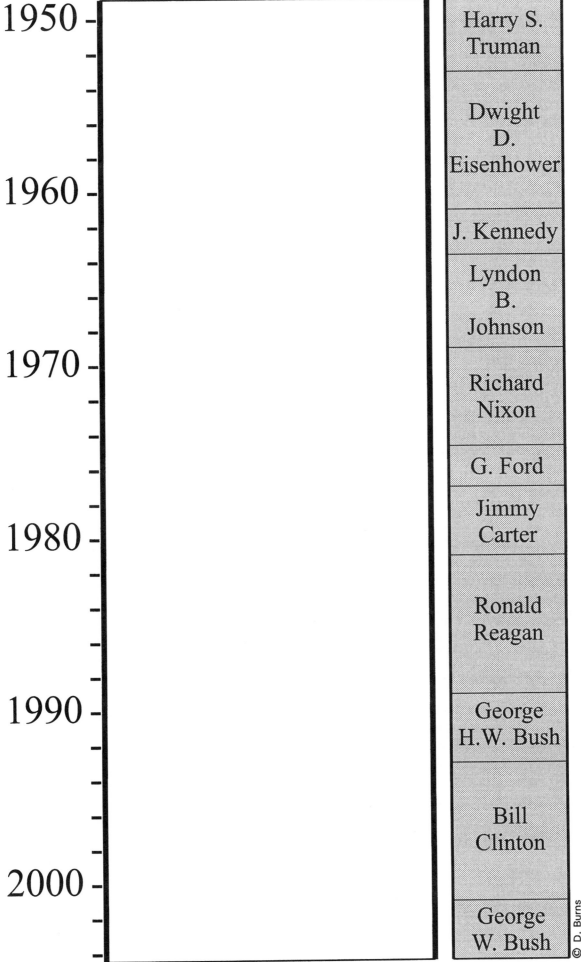

1950 –

1960 –

1970 –

1980 –

1990 –

2000 –

Harry S. Truman

Dwight D. Eisenhower

J. Kennedy

Lyndon B. Johnson

Richard Nixon

G. Ford

Jimmy Carter

Ronald Reagan

George H.W. Bush

Bill Clinton

George W. Bush

TIMELINE: MODERN AMERICA

DECADE: 1950s POST-WAR PROSPERITY

McCarthyism, Korean War, Dwight D. Eisenhower, Levittown, baby boom,

Brown v. *Board of Education*, Rosa Parks, integration, Rev. Martin Luther King, Jr.,

civil disobedience, Sputnik, Intercontinental Ballistic Missile

The end of World War Two in 1945 left America with a much larger federal government, and clearly in the position of world leader. It also left the Soviet Union in a good position to spread its political/economic system of communism. Few doubted that it intended to do so.

China and North Korea became communist after the war ended. In 1950 North Korea invaded South Korea. The U.S. and the United Nations sent troops to help South Korea defend itself. It was one hot spot in the "Cold _____," the common term for the struggle between Russia and the United States for dominance in the decades after 1945.

One aspect of the struggle surfaced in a scare that communists secretly held positions in the U.S. government. Senator Joseph McCarthy created a climate of fear and suspicion for several years with such claims. His accusations were eventually exposed as wildly exaggerated. The term "McCarthyism" grew to describe his tactic of making accusations without real evidence.

During this decade great social changes were underway in America. One sign was the spread of huge new suburban housing tracts like one in Levittown, New York. Millions of young married couples were starting families in the years after World War Two. (Their children would later be called the _____ boom generation.) Some people complained that life in the suburbs was dull, and put too much emphasis on conformity. A song complained of houses and people "made out of ticky-tacky, and they all look just the same." But for most families, the new suburbs seemed a big step _____ in the American Dream.

The work place was also changing. The white collar office worker became much more commonplace as big corporations continued to grow. With names like IBM, GM, and AT&T, the corporations of the 1950s produced and managed a vast expansion of wealth in America. The hard times of the Great Depression and the war years were almost forgotten. "Keeping up with the Joneses" next door became the challenge for many people. Economic growth and strong labor unions helped boost even most _____ workers into the solid middle class.

But the spread of the middle class lifestyle only highlighted the fact that most black Americans were _____ the doors of opportunity. Americans had helped defeat a monstrous system in Europe that preached racial superiority. How, many people asked

Fasttrack to America's Past 8 - 5

themselves, could America continue to allow racial segregation here? But it was here, as "Whites Only" signs and segregated schools made obvious. In this decade the Civil Rights movement geared up to directly challenge this widely accepted pattern.

Some victories came in the courts, such as the case of *Brown* v. *Board of Education of Topeka, Kansas*, in 1954. This Supreme Court decision declared segregated public schools _____. Other victories came as courageous Southern blacks, including women like Rosa Parks, refused to continue taking seats "in the back of the bus."

Most whites knew segregation wasn't right. But many feared that racial integration would bring crime to their neighborhoods and trouble to schools. Cultural differences expressed in behavior and lifestyle meant every step carried the risk of _____ and resentment.

Rev. Martin Luther King, Jr. emerged as a leader by using the tactics of non-violent civil disobedience to appeal to white citizens' sense of American ideals of _____ and equality. Many whites supported the movement. Many others, however, resisted integration and claimed that the federal government had no right to force the issue. Some turned to hate and violence, as was seen in the integration of a high school in Little Rock, Arkansas. President Dwight D. Eisenhower showed he would use troops if necessary to enforce the law. Some schools were integrated, but resistance in many areas often delayed the effort well into the 1960s.

These were also years of great scientific and medical advances. UNIVAC, an early digital computer made for business use, became a familiar name. A vaccine to stop polio was developed. But the launch in Russia of Sputnik, the first space satellite, caused America embarrassment. Rivalry with the Soviet Union intensified. Schools beefed up instruction in math and _____, and education generally became a bigger priority. The space race was on, alongside a far more dangerous arms race. The hydrogen bomb was one of the frightening new atomic weapons that could be hurled across the world on jet bombers, and later, on _____ called Intercontinental Ballistic Missiles.

Through it all, the great new entertainer was television. It soon revealed its potential as a creative medium, but also found criticism as a "vast wasteland" of mediocre programs. Popular music was also changing, with a new style called _____ growing very popular as the first of the baby-boomers reached their teenage years. Its best known performer in this decade was _____ Presley.

Use these terms to fill in the blanks: baby, Elvis, factory, illegal, justice, misunderstanding, outside, rock and roll, rockets, science, up, War

CHARTING THE AFFLUENT SOCIETY

Finish the line graphs below to chart the growth of the economy in these years. Poverty did not vanish, but most Americans shared in a solid prosperity that one writer described with the phrase, "The Affluent Society." The gross national product (GNP) measures the total dollar value of all the goods and services a nation produces in a year.

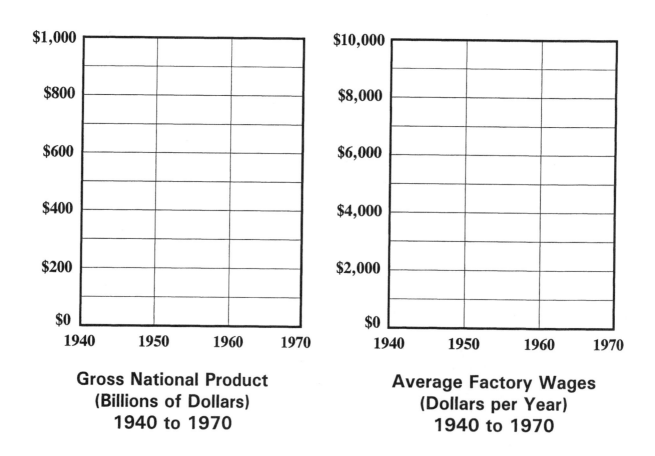

**Gross National Product
(Billions of Dollars)
1940 to 1970**

**Average Factory Wages
(Dollars per Year)
1940 to 1970**

Use the table below to find the information to make the line graphs above.

Year	Gross National Product (Billions of Dollars)	Average Factory Wages (Dollars per Year)
1940	99.7	1,432
1950	285	3,302
1960	504	5,352
1970	977	8,150

source: *Historical Statistics of the United States*

Finish the line graphs below to show more signs of the growing prosperity of this period. The home ownership rate measures the percent of American families that own their own home. Do you think figures like these are a valid way to measure whether or not citizens were achieving "The American Dream" in these decades?

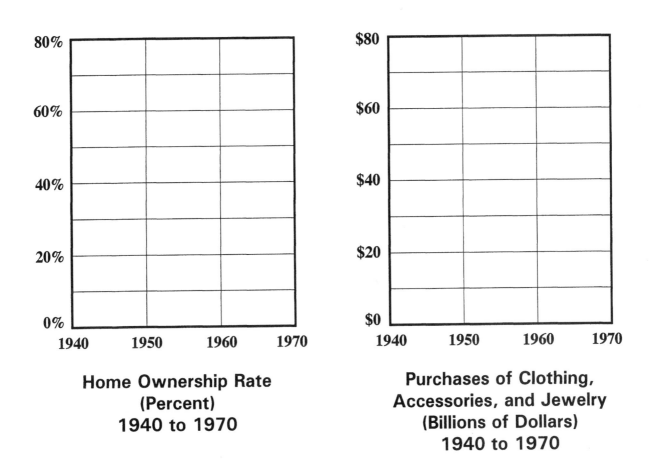

**Home Ownership Rate
(Percent)
1940 to 1970**

**Purchases of Clothing,
Accessories, and Jewelry
(Billions of Dollars)
1940 to 1970**

Use the table below to find the information to make the line graphs above.

Year	Home Ownership Rate (Percent)	Purchases of Clothing, Accessories, and Jewelry (Billions of Dollars)
1940	43.6	8.9
1950	55	23.7
1960	61.9	33
1970	62.4	62.8

source: *Historical Statistics of the United States*

MAP - COLD WAR ALLIANCES

Finish the large map as you complete this page.

THE SUPER-POWERS

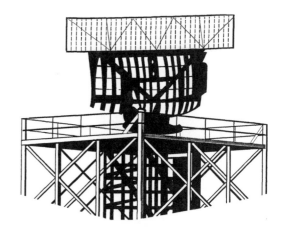

United States - The U.S. emerged from World War Two determined to continue protecting the principles of _____. At the center of this system is the individual citizen, with broad rights to pursue his or her own personal and political goals. These rights include freedom of speech, freedom of religion, and property ownership. All of these were restricted or suppressed in communist societies as unnecessary and _____.

Russia / U.S.S.R. - The Soviet Union and its largest component, Russia, emerged from World War Two determined to protect itself from any future attacks. It was also determined to _____ the system of communism. At the center of this system stood the Communist Party, with wide powers to dictate what citizens could and could not do. Communists claimed that only their system could create true equality, because the central government planned and directed the entire economy. The government provided housing, _____, food, and medical care for all. But constant shortages, shoddy products, forced labor camps, and a massive wall built across **Berlin** by the communist government of East Germany were proof of big problems in the "workers' paradise."

ALLIANCES OF THE COLD WAR ERA

Use green shading to show the U.S. and its allies, red shading to show the communist nations, and yellow shading to show the non-aligned nations. Be sure to complete the key.

U.S. Allies - The most important allies were **Canada** and the nations in **Western Europe.** Other allies included almost all the nations of Central and South America, as well as **Japan.** The U.S. and its allies became involved in _____ to help **South Korea** and **South Vietnam** when they came under attack from communist forces in the 1950s. The map also shows the location of **NORAD**, the North American Defense Command center, and the line of radar stations of the Distant Early Warning (**DEW Line**) system.

Communist Nations - After World War Two, the Soviet Union forced the Eastern European countries on its borders to accept communist governments. These buffer or "satellite" nations, such as Poland and East Germany, took their orders from _____. Russia also kept North Korea under communist control. Later, in 1949, **China** fell to communism under the armies of Mao Zedong. **Cuba** became communist in 1960 under Fidel Castro. **South Vietnam** was conquered by communist North Vietnam in 1975.

Use these terms to fill in the blanks: dangerous, democracy, jobs, Russia, spread, wars

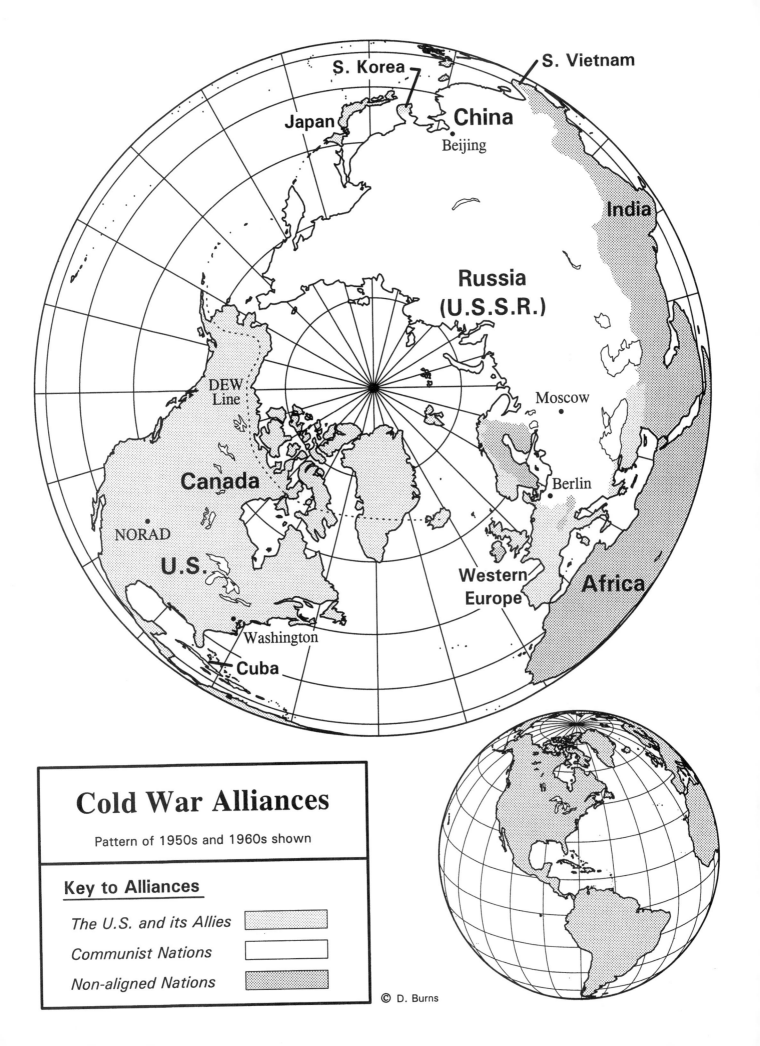

S. Korea

S. Vietnam

Japan

China

Beijing

India

Russia
(U.S.S.R.)

Moscow

DEW
Line

Berlin

Canada

NORAD

Western
Europe

Africa

U.S.

Washington

Cuba

Cold War Alliances

Pattern of 1950s and 1960s shown

Key to Alliances

The U.S. and its Allies

Communist Nations

Non-aligned Nations

© D. Burns

EISENHOWER ON THE ISSUES OF THE 1950s

President Dwight D. Eisenhower supported a strong military to counter the growing strength of the Soviet Union. But he also warned that both sides were being hurt by the Cold War. This is a condensed selection from a famous speech after the death of Joseph Stalin, the leader of the Soviet Union.

The Chance for Peace

Every gun that is made, every warship launched, every rocket fired signifies, in the final sense, a theft from those who hunger and are not fed, those who are cold and are not clothed.

The world in arms is not spending money alone.

It is spending the sweat of its laborers, the genius of its scientists, the hopes of its children.

The cost of one modern heavy bomber is this: a modern brick school in more than 30 cities.

It is two electric power plants, each serving a town of 60,000 population.

It is two fine, fully equipped hospitals.

It is some 50 miles of concrete highway.

We pay for a single fighter plane with a half million bushels of wheat.

We pay for a single destroyer with new homes that could have housed more than 8,000 people.

This is not a way of life at all, in any true sense. Under the cloud of threatening war, it is humanity hanging from a cross of iron.

These plain and cruel truths define the peril and point the hope that comes with this spring of 1953.

The world knows that an era has ended with the death of [the Soviet Union's leader] Joseph Stalin.

The new Soviet leadership now has a precious opportunity to awaken, with the rest of the world, to the point of peril reached, and to help turn the tide of history.

The peace we seek, founded upon decent trust and cooperative effort among nations, can be fortified, not by weapons of war, but by wheat and by cotton, by milk and by wool, by meat and timber and rice. These are the words that translate into every language on earth. These are the needs that challenge this world in arms.

We are prepared to reaffirm, with the most concrete evidence, our readiness to help build a world in which all peoples can be productive and prosperous. We are ready, in short, to dedicate our strength to serving the needs, rather than the fears, of the world.

Group Discussion: *What does President Eisenhower say is the real cost of the Cold War? What does he want both the U.S. and the Soviet Union to do?*

* * *

As schools opened in 1957, President Eisenhower stepped in to resolve a crisis in Little Rock, Arkansas, over the integration of public schools. These are condensed excerpts from his address to the nation explaining the action he was taking.

School Integration in Little Rock

For a few minutes this evening I want to speak to you about the serious situation that has arisen in Little Rock.

In that city, disorderly mobs have deliberately prevented the carrying out of proper orders from a federal court.

This morning the mob again gathered in front of the Central High School of Little Rock, obviously for the purpose of again preventing the carrying out of the court's order relating to the admission of Negro children to that school.

I have today issued an Executive Order directing the use of troops under federal authority to aid in the execution [enforcement] of federal law at Little Rock, Arkansas.

It is important that the reasons for my action be understood by all our citizens. As you know, the Supreme Court of the United States has decided that separate public educational facilities for the races are inherently unequal and therefore compulsory school segregation laws are unconstitutional.

Our personal opinions about the decision have no bearing on the matter of enforcement. The responsibility and authority of the Supreme Court to interpret the Constitution are very clear.

During the past several years, many communities in our Southern states have instituted public school plans for gradual progress in the enrollment and attendance of school children of all races in order to bring themselves into compliance with the law of the land.

They thus demonstrated to the world that we are a nation in which laws, not men, are supreme.

I regret to say that this truth, the cornerstone of our liberties, was not observed in this instance.

Certain misguided persons, many of them imported into Little Rock by agitators, have insisted upon defying the law and have sought to bring it into disrepute. The orders of the court have thus been frustrated.

The very basis of our individual rights and freedoms rests upon the certainty that the president and the executive branch of government will support and insure the carrying out of the decisions of the federal courts.

Mob rule cannot be allowed to override the decisions of our courts.

From intimate personal knowledge, I know that the overwhelming majority of the people in the South - including those of Arkansas and Little Rock - are of good will, united in their efforts to preserve and respect the law even when they disagree with it.

And so, with deep confidence, I call upon the citizens of the State of Arkansas to assist in bringing to an immediate end all interference with the law and its processes.

If resistance to the federal court orders ceases at once, the further presence of federal troops will be unnecessary and the city of Little Rock will return to its normal habits of peace and order, and a blot on the fair name and high honor of our nation in the world will be removed.

Thus will be restored the image of America and of all its parts as one nation, indivisible, with liberty and justice for all.

Group Discussion: *What does President Eisenhower say was blocking efforts by black children to attend Central High School in Little Rock? What was his response as president to try to resolve the situation? What key principle of government did he say was at stake?*

MAP - CIVIL RIGHTS HOT SPOTS

Label and shade lightly with color to highlight the states in which these events occurred.

Topeka, Kansas, where a legal challenge by a black parent to segregated _____ schools led to the historic Supreme Court decision *Brown* v. *Board of Education* in 1954.

Montgomery, Alabama, where Rosa Parks refused to take a seat "in the back of the bus." Her action in 1955 helped launch a successful _____ boycott by black residents that directly challenged segregation.

Little Rock, Arkansas, where the governor of Arkansas tried to use that state's National Guard troops to prevent black students from enrolling in a "white" high school. President Eisenhower put the troops under federal control and sent _____ to escort the black students to school. The year was 1957.

Greensboro, North Carolina, site of a famous "sit-in" in 1960 by four black college students at a lunch counter that had refused to serve blacks. The action prompted hundreds of other students, black and _____, to begin protests against restaurant segregation in other cities.

Jackson, Mississippi, one of many Southern cities where hundreds of black and white "Freedom Riders" traveled to challenge segregation in bus terminals in 1961. In some cities the protesters were attacked. Many were arrested in Jackson and spent that summer in _____.

Birmingham, Alabama, where a major campaign led by Rev. Martin Luther King, Jr. against segregation made headlines in 1963. Pictures of police _____ and water hoses turned on the black protesters shocked the nation. But it was only the most famous of hundreds of protests that spread to scores of cities that year.

Washington, D.C., where the March on Washington for Jobs and Freedom was held in August 1963. Rev. Martin Luther King, Jr. delivered his famous "I Have a _____" speech.

Selma, Alabama, starting point of a famous five day march to Montgomery in 1965. Thousands of people, white and black, joined the march in a show of _____ for the movement.

New York, the city where Malcolm X emerged as a militant critic of American race relations before he was _____ by black gunmen in 1965.

New York, Philadelphia, and **Chicago** were among the big cities where riots linked to racial issues erupted in the "long hot summer" of 1964. The next year, a deadly riot erupted in the Watts area of **Los Angeles**. **Cleveland** was among the big cities hit in 1966. In 1967 dozens of riots struck the country, with those in **Newark** and **Detroit** especially deadly. The pattern gave clear proof that race was not just a _____ issue.

Use these terms to fill in the blanks: bus, dogs, Dream, jail, killed, public, soldiers, support, white, Southern

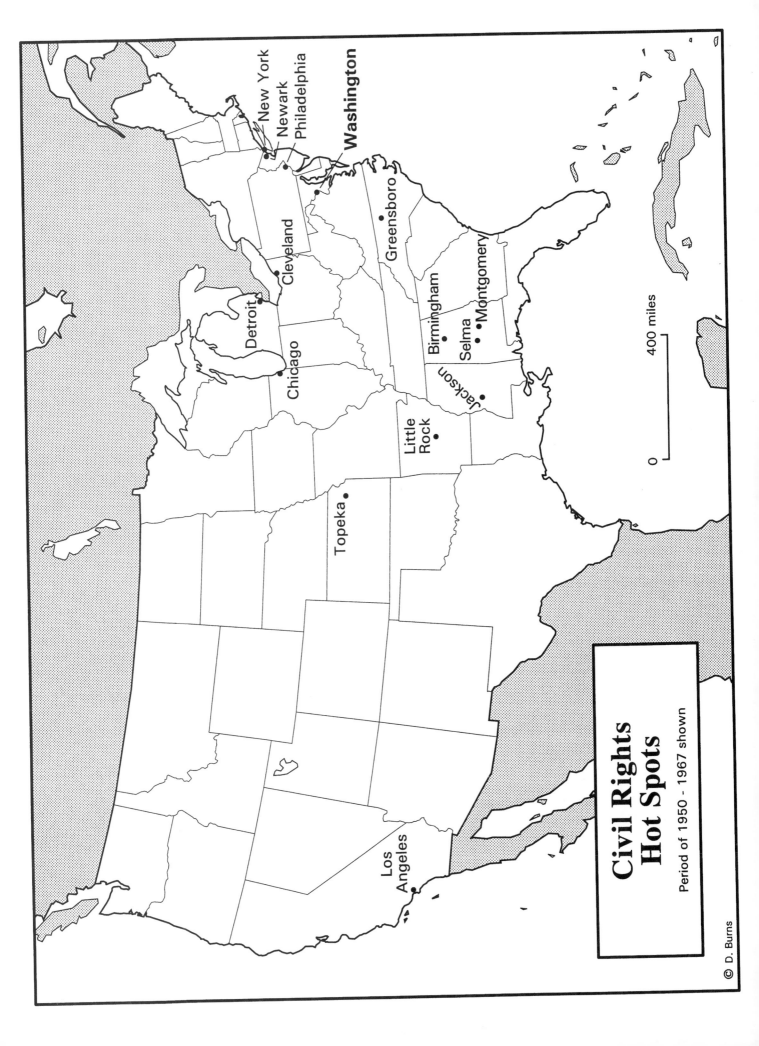

New York
Newark
Philadelphia
Washington
Greensboro
Montgomery
Birmingham
Selma
Jackson
Cleveland
Detroit
Chicago
Little Rock
Topeka
Los Angeles

400 miles

0

Civil Rights Hot Spots

Period of 1950 - 1967 shown

© D. Burns

DECADE: 1960s   NEW FRONTIERS

John F. Kennedy, Peace Corps, Cuban Missile Crisis, March on Washington,

Lyndon Johnson, War on Poverty, Civil Rights Act of 1964, Voting Rights Act of 1965,

Vietnam War, Hippies, Black Power, Women's Liberation, Richard Nixon, Apollo 11

As the 1960s began, two big issues were facing America: first, the Cold War policy of containment of communism, and second, the Civil Rights movement here at home.

John F. Kennedy, a Democrat, was elected in 1960. He projected an image that appealed to many Americans: youthful, educated, and idealistic. He called on Americans to pursue causes like racial equality and world peace. Events in this decade proved that neither goal would be easily achieved.

Cuba was the first big problem for JFK. Revolutionaries led by Fidel Castro, a communist, had taken over the island. The Soviet Union soon built nuclear missile launchers in Cuba. In response, Kennedy ordered American ships to form a blockade around the island to stop any new missiles from being brought in. There was widespread fear that the incident would trigger a _____ war, but Russia backed down.

In another Cold War action, Kennedy sent a much larger number of military advisors to South Vietnam. The government there was desperately trying to fight off communist revolutionaries (the Viet Cong) backed by North Vietnam. It was a step that seemed to commit the U.S. to even greater involvement as things steadily got _____.

Kennedy was assassinated in Dallas, Texas, in 1963. Lyndon Johnson became president. He, too, was concerned with issues of civil rights and poverty. He proposed that Americans fight what he called a War on Poverty to build "The Great Society." His proposals led to a big expansion of government social programs. More money went into public housing projects, for example, and education programs for the poor were expanded.

President Johnson also pushed Congress for approval of the Civil Rights Act of 1964. That law is important because it generally prohibits _____ based on race, color, religion, or sex. A year later he won passage of an important new law designed to protect black citizens' voting rights.

But the growing war in Vietnam demanded more of the nation's _____ and money. Johnson sent more troops to support South Vietnam. The total reached half a million. He ordered bombing attacks on military targets in North Vietnam itself in 1965. He hoped the attacks would force leaders there to negotiate an end to the war. But critics in America denounced the new strategy and said it was only making the war more deadly than before.

Meanwhile, a number of social issues were boiling in America. Riots broke out in black neighborhoods in a number of large cities by the mid-1960s. The Black Power movement, led by people like Malcolm X, pushed a message of black pride and even separatism. Some in the movement were rejecting older civil rights leaders like Rev. Martin Luther King, Jr., who had struggled to bring blacks and whites _____.

Another big issue was Women's Liberation. Its leaders, including Betty Friedan, called for an end to the customs and attitudes that still restricted them from some jobs, or set a double standard for behavior. The newly developed birth control _____ and the mini-skirt became symbols of new attitudes toward sexuality. Some voices were asking what would happen as out-of-wedlock births, divorce, and fatherless homes increased, but few wanted to hear the answers.

In this decade, the _____ boom generation reached high school and college age. This large group of young people born after WW II tilted American culture in many ways. The wild hair, clothing, and _____ of the Hippie movement reflected this. Young people poured energy into many other aspects of the era, including the sexual revolution, drug use, and the anti-war movement. Parents often struggled to _____ why their children seemed in open rebellion to society, when society had given them more advantages than any previous generation. On their side of the generation gap, many young people talked and sang songs about an America that seemed to fall short of its ideals.

By the late 1960s, opposition to the Vietnam war had grown so strong that President Johnson decided not to seek re-election. Many Americans felt society was spinning out of control, especially after the assassinations in 1968 of Rev. Martin Luther King, Jr. and political candidate Robert Kennedy. _____, a Republican who promised more emphasis on "law and order," won the 1968 election.

One pause in this turbulent but exciting time came as America landed astronauts on the moon in 1969. Neil _____ became the first man to leave a footprint on the lunar soil. People around the world watched the Apollo 11 mission on television, and Americans celebrated their pride as one nation.

But as the decade drew to a close, the shouts of the many groups seeking to reshape American society showed _____ was going to stay on the American agenda. No end to the Vietnam war was in sight, and opponents of America's involvement were becoming more vocal than ever in their protests.

Use these terms to fill in the blanks: Armstrong, attention, baby, conflict, discrimination, music, nuclear, pill, Richard Nixon, together, understand, worse

JOHN F. KENNEDY'S INAUGURAL ADDRESS

John F. Kennedy's years as president were cut short by an assassin in 1963. But his influence on American life continued in the idealistic call he sounded in his 1961 inaugural address, condensed below.

Let the word go forth from this time and place, to friend and foe alike, that the torch has been passed to a new generation of Americans - born in this century, tempered by war, disciplined by a hard and bitter peace, proud of our ancient heritage - and unwilling to witness or permit the slow undoing of those human rights to which this nation has always been committed.

Let every nation know, whether it wishes us well or ill, that we shall pay any price, bear any burden, meet any hardship, support any friend, oppose any foe to assure the survival and success of liberty.

To those nations who would make themselves our adversary [enemy], we offer not a pledge but a request: that both sides begin anew the quest for peace, before the dark powers of destruction unleashed by science engulf all humanity in planned or accidental self-destruction.

We dare not tempt them with weakness. For only when our arms are sufficient beyond doubt can we be certain beyond doubt that they will never be used.

But neither can two great and powerful groups of nations take comfort from our present course.

Both sides are overburdened by the cost of modern weapons. Both are rightly alarmed by the steady spread of the deadly atom, yet both are racing to alter that uncertain balance of terror that stays the hand of mankind's final war.

So let us begin anew.

Let both sides seek to invoke the wonders of science instead of its terrors. Together let us explore the stars, conquer the deserts, eradicate [eliminate] disease, tap the ocean depths, and encourage the arts and commerce.

Let both sides unite to heed in all corners of the earth the command of Isaiah [in the Bible] - to "undo the heavy burdens, and let the oppressed go free."

All this will not be finished in the first 100 days, nor even perhaps in our lifetime on this planet. But let us begin.

Now the trumpet summons us again - not as a call to bear arms - but to a struggle against the common enemies of man: tyranny, poverty, disease and war itself.

The energy, the faith, the devotion which we bring to this endeavor will light our country and all who serve it - and the glow from that fire can truly light the world.

And so, my fellow Americans: ask not what your country can do for you - ask what you can do for your country.

With a good conscience our only sure reward, with history the final judge of our deeds, let us go forth to lead the land we love, asking His blessing and His help, but knowing that here on earth, God's work must truly be our own.

Group Discussion: *What warning does Kennedy have about the dangers of the Cold War and arms race? What does he call on America's enemies and Americans themselves to do?*

LBJ CALLS FOR RACIAL JUSTICE

This speech by President Lyndon Johnson (condensed here) was made in 1965 after a famous civil rights march at Selma, Alabama. The marchers wanted better protection of voting rights for blacks.

I speak tonight for the dignity of man and the destiny of democracy.

At times history and fate meet at a single place to shape a turning point in man's unending search for freedom. So it was last week in Selma, Alabama. There, long-suffering men and women peacefully protested the denial of their rights as Americans. Many were brutally assaulted. One good man, a man of God, was killed.

Many of the issues of civil rights are very complex. But about this there can be no argument. Every American citizen must have an equal right to vote. Yet the harsh fact is that in many places in this country men and women are kept from voting simply because they are Negroes.

The Negro citizen may go to register only to be told that the day is wrong, or the hour is late, or the official in charge is absent. He may be asked to recite the entire Constitution, or explain the most complex provisions of State law.

For the fact is that the only way to pass these barriers is to show a white skin.

Experience has clearly shown that the existing process of law cannot overcome systematic discrimination. Wednesday I will send to Congress a law designed to eliminate illegal barriers to the right to vote. This bill will strike down restrictions to voting in all elections - Federal, State, and local - which have been used to deny Negroes the right to vote.

But even if we pass this bill, the battle will not be over. What happened in Selma is part of a far larger movement. It is the effort of American Negroes to secure for themselves the full blessings of American life.

Their cause must be our cause too. Because it is not just Negroes, but really all of us, who must overcome the crippling legacy of bigotry and injustice.

As a man whose roots go deeply into Southern soil, I know how agonizing racial feelings are. But a century has passed, more than a hundred years, since the Negro was freed. And he is not fully free tonight. A century has passed since the day of promise. And the promise is unkept.

The time of justice has now come, and I tell you that I believe sincerely that no force can hold it back. And when it does, I think that day will brighten the lives of every American.

For Negroes are not the only victims. How many white children have gone uneducated, how many white families have lived in stark poverty, because we have wasted our energy to maintain the barriers of hatred and terror?

This great, rich, restless country can offer opportunity and education and hope to all: black and white, North and South, sharecropper and city dweller. These are our enemies: poverty, ignorance, disease. They are the enemies and not our fellow man, not our neighbor.

Group Discussion: *Why does President Johnson believe the federal government must step in to protect black citizens' voting rights? What does he say is the larger issue beyond voting rights?*

MAP - VIETNAM AND SOUTHEAST ASIA

Label and color the map to show these:

North Vietnam   **South Vietnam**

GEOGRAPHICAL FEATURES

Mekong River   **Gulf of Tonkin**

South China Sea   **Ho Chi Minh Trail**

FAMOUS CITIES AND PLACES

Hanoi, the former capital of French Indochina. In this city Ho Chi Minh declared Vietnam independent of France as World War Two ended in 1945. He was determined to see Vietnam _____ of all foreign control. Ho Chi Minh formed a guerrilla army called the Viet Minh to fight for independence. He adopted the communist system for the new government he began forming.

Saigon, where a non-communist semi-independent government was established by the French as an alternative to Ho Chi Minh's communist government. It became the _____ of South Vietnam after the country was divided in 1954. The U.S. supported the government based in Saigon. (Saigon was renamed Ho Chi Minh City when communist troops finally took over all of Vietnam in 1975.)

Dien Bien Phu, where the French army was _____ by Ho Chi Minh's forces in 1954. (The United States, which had been helping the French financially, refused to join the fight itself at that time.)

DMZ line, the "demilitarized zone" or line dividing North and South Vietnam. The split was made in 1954 by an international conference seeking to solve the Vietnam problem. An election was set for 1956 to reunify the country. But the election was _____ by leaders in the U.S. and in South Vietnam when it appeared the communists might win.

Da Nang, an important military base for the U.S. during the 1960s, as Ho Chi Minh began new attacks on South Vietnam to reunify the country by _____.

My Lai, the site of a massacre of an estimated 300 Vietnamese civilians in 1968 by American _____. When the facts about the incident came to light, they shocked and angered Americans at home.

Phnom Penh, capital of Cambodia. As South Vietnam fell in 1975, a communist group also seized power in Cambodia. Its leaders forced the city's population into the countryside, and caused the _____ of perhaps a million or more Cambodians.

Use these terms to fill in the blanks: canceled, capital, deaths, defeated, force, free, soldiers

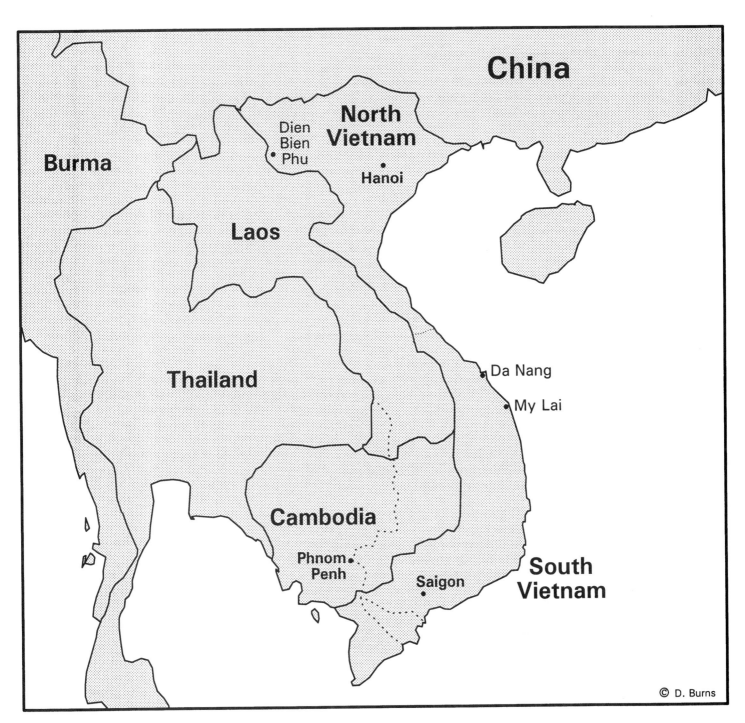

China

North Vietnam

Dien Bien Phu

Hanoi

Burma

Laos

Thailand

Da Nang

My Lai

Cambodia

Phnom Penh

Saigon

South Vietnam

© D. Burns

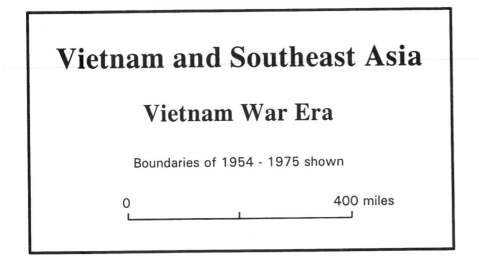

Vietnam and Southeast Asia

Vietnam War Era

Boundaries of 1954 - 1975 shown

0   400 miles

CHARTING WOMEN AND JOBS

The Women's Liberation movement was one of several factors that sent many more women seeking jobs outside the home. Finish the line graph below to see the impact of this trend in recent decades. What are some of the benefits and some of the challenges that this pattern has created for American families?

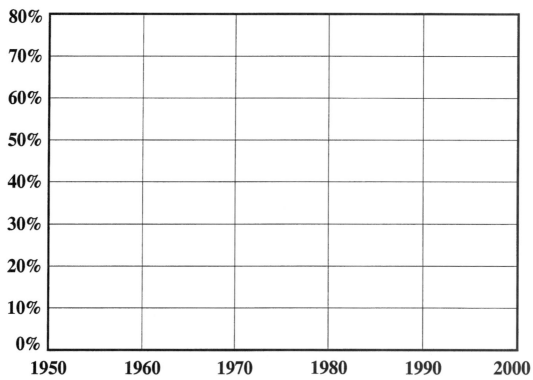

Single Women [   ]
Married Women With Children Under Age 6 [   ]

Percent of Women in Work Force 1950 to 2000

Use the table below to find the information to make the line graph above. Use two different colors to show the trends on the chart. Be sure to complete the color key.

Year	Percent of Single Women in Work Force	Percent of Married Women With Children Under Age 6 in Work Force	Year	Percent of Single Women in Work Force	Percent of Married Women With Children Under Age 6 in Work Force
1950	50.5	11.9	1980	61.5	45.1
1960	44.1	18.6	1990	66.4	58.9
1970	53.0	30.3	2000	68.6	62.8

sources: *Historical Statistics of the United States* and *Statistical Abstract of the United States*

CHARTING THE FIGHT AGAINST POVERTY

In the 1960s, political leaders including President Lyndon Johnson threw the weight - and money - of the federal government behind new programs designed to reduce poverty. That fight has continued, with some variations, to this day. Finish the line graph below to see the results. What factors do you think explain the patterns shown here?

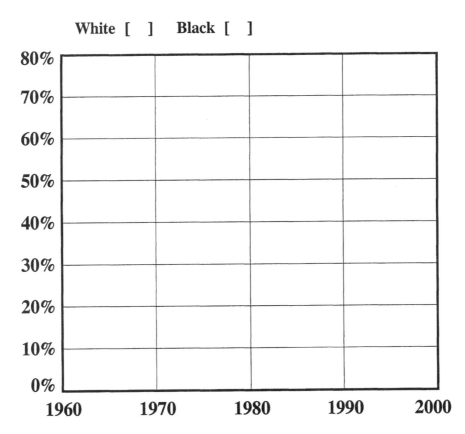

White [   ]   Black [   ]

Percent of Population Below Poverty Level Income
1960 to 2000

Use the table below to find the information to make the line graph above. Use two different colors to show the trends on the chart. Be sure to complete the color key.

Year	Poverty Rate - Percent		Year	Poverty Rate - Percent	
	White	Black		White	Black
1960	17.8	54.0*	1990	10.7	31.9
1970	9.9	33.5	2000	9.4	22.0
1980	10.2	32.5			

*estimated from 1959 data   sources: *Historical Statistics of the United States* and *Statistical Abstract of the United States*

DECADE: 1970s   THE WATERGATE SCANDAL

Environmental Protection Agency (EPA), Vietnamization, Watergate, Gerald Ford,

Jimmy Carter, Organization of Petroleum Exporting Countries (OPEC),

Three Mile Island reactor accident, *Roe* v. *Wade*, white flight

As the 1970s began, the key issue was the continuing war in Vietnam. President Richard Nixon had pledged to end it quickly. But he wanted to avoid an outright defeat for America. He pushed for a process that he called Vietnamization of the war, which meant turning the fighting back over to the South Vietnamese themselves. Meanwhile, anger over the situation was rapidly growing across America. Mass demonstrations against the war were held in Washington and on many _____ campuses.

Nixon felt the protests in America were only encouraging communist North Vietnam to keep up their attacks on South Vietnam. He and his supporters wanted to discredit the anti-war movement. Among other things, a group of Nixon supporters broke into the Washington offices of the Democratic Party in the Watergate building. They intended to place "bugs" (illegal listening devices) on the office telephones. They also wanted to search the office files for documents that might embarrass or discredit the Democrats, who generally _____ Nixon's policies in Vietnam.

But the break-in was discovered. Nixon denied any connection to the incident itself, but investigators turned up convincing evidence that he tried to cover up the crime, and had lied about it to the American people. Congress was soon moving to _____ the president. Rather than face that possibility, he resigned. Vice President Gerald Ford became president, and issued a pardon that protected Nixon from prosecution.

In 1973, as the Watergate scandal was still unfolding, America pulled the last of its troops out of Vietnam. But a shaky cease-fire that had been negotiated did not last long. The North Vietnamese army pushed into Saigon and forcibly reunited the country in 1975. Thousands of Vietnamese risked their _____ and fled in overcrowded boats rather than stay under the rule of the communist government. Many eventually settled in the U.S.

There were other important developments in this decade. In 1970 the first Earth Day was organized. People became more aware of the dangers of air and _____ pollution. The Environmental Protection Agency was created to establish new federal regulations to protect the public. The nation's rivers looked cleaner and smelled better as thousands of sewage treatment plants were upgraded to new EPA standards. Work also began to identify and clean up dump sites where toxic chemical waste had been _____ underground or simply abandoned in old factories.

President Jimmy Carter, who held office in the late 1970s, was especially concerned about the future energy supply. Oil producing countries in the Middle East had formed a group called OPEC, and conspired to raise the price of oil sharply. This increased the price of countless products based on oil, causing severe inflation. Some people said that expanding nuclear energy would solve the problem. But an accident at the Three Mile Island reactor in Pennsylvania convinced many Americans that nuclear power was just too dangerous. Alternative energy sources like solar power and wind power were explored, but no good solution was found to end our _____ on foreign oil.

The nation celebrated its 200th birthday - The Bicentennial - in 1976. Americans had plenty to celebrate. Vast social changes had been made to improve race relations, help the poor, improve education, and _____ the environment. A president had resigned in a scandal, yet the government changed leaders peacefully. Most Americans felt a special pride as they gathered for that year's July 4th festivities.

But America also faced serious challenges. Violent crime and illegal drug use were growing dramatically in many areas. Factories were closing down at an alarming rate as imported cars and other products from overseas grew popular with American shoppers. The Supreme Court decision legalizing abortion (*Roe* v. *Wade*) created sharp divisions of public opinion. Many city residents, white and _____, were becoming fed up with urban problems and moved out to the suburbs. This trend, sometimes called "white flight," left American cities with a shrinking _____ class and a shrinking tax base.

The international situation was mixed. Early in the decade President Nixon pushed successfully for improved relations with Russia and China. President Carter helped persuade Israel and Egypt to sign a historic peace treaty. Even so, the Middle East remained a tinderbox of _____ between Israel and many of the Arab nations. In 1979 a revolution in Iran resulted in an international crisis as American diplomats stationed there were held hostage for more than a year.

President Carter, a Democrat, was dealing with that crisis as he began his re-election campaign. But many Americans were increasingly troubled by the country's lengthening list of problems. Republican candidate Ronald Reagan argued that a new approach was needed. He called for tax reductions to promote the growth of businesses and _____. He said America needed to take a more forceful stand to protect American interests around the world. It was a message that carried him to the White House as the leader of what some called "the conservative revolution."

Use these terms to fill in the blanks: *black, buried, college, conflict, dependence, impeach, jobs, lives, middle, opposed, protect, water*

CHARTING TRENDS OF THE SEVENTIES

The cost of the war in Vietnam and the expense of new social welfare programs both demanded higher spending by the federal government. While progress was made on many social issues, some problems got worse. Complete these line graphs to study the trends.

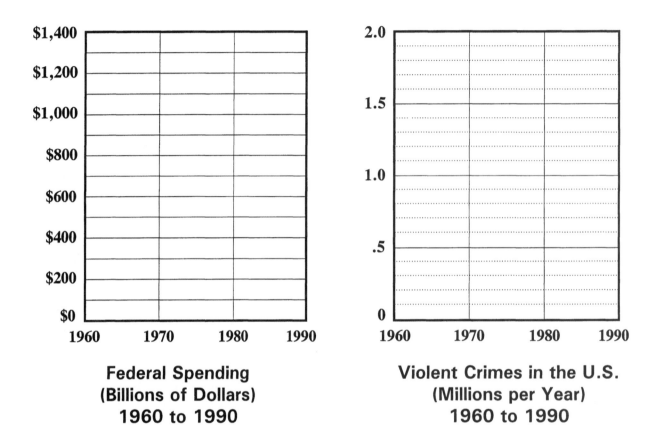

**Federal Spending
(Billions of Dollars)
1960 to 1990**

**Violent Crimes in the U.S.
(Millions per Year)
1960 to 1990**

Use the table below to find the information to make the line graphs above. (You must convert the numbers in the table to make the second graph. For example, 290,000 = .29 million)

Year	Federal Spending (Billions of Dollars)	Violent Crimes in the U.S.
1960	92	290,000
1970	196	730,000
1980	591	1,400,000
1990	1,253	1,800,000

Note: violent crimes data includes reported cases of murder, rape, robbery, and assault.

sources for tables on both pages: *Historical Statistics of the United States* and *Statistical Abstract of the United States*

Finish the line graphs below to show more of the social changes of the 1970s. When you have completed the graphs, develop an explanation for the trends you have shown on these two pages. See if others agree or disagree with your explanation.

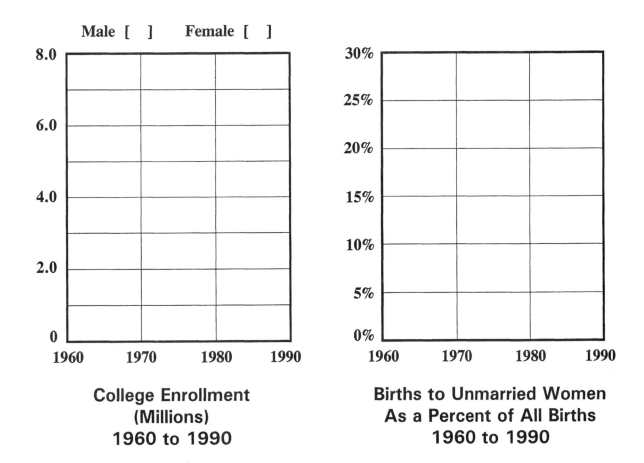

Male [   ]   Female [   ]

**College Enrollment
(Millions)
1960 to 1990**

**Births to Unmarried Women
As a Percent of All Births
1960 to 1990**

Use the table below to find the information to make the line graphs above. Use different colors to show the data on the College Enrollment chart. Be sure to complete the color key.

Year	College Enrollment - Degree Programs (Millions of Students)		Births to Unmarried Women As a Percent of All Births (Percent)
	Male	Female	
1960	2.3	1.3	5.3
1970	4.6	3.3	10.7
1980	5.9	6.2	18.4
1990	6.3	7.5	28.0

MAP - ISRAEL AND THE MIDDLE EAST

Finish labeling and coloring the map to show these places and features. Be sure to complete the key.

GEOGRAPHICAL FEATURES

Mediterranean Sea	Suez Canal
Red Sea	Persian Gulf
Black Sea	Jordan River
Dead Sea	Nile River
Tigris River	Euphrates River

COUNTRIES AND LAND AREAS

Israel, established in 1948 in part as a haven for Jews displaced by _____ persecution. The neighboring Arab states were determined to destroy the new nation until President Carter helped bring Egypt and Israel together to negotiate a peace treaty in 1978.

Egypt, one of the Arab nations that led an _____ on Israel in a 1973 war. By the decade's end, however, Egypt became the first Arab nation to officially recognize Israel, and Israel returned the **Sinai Peninsula** to Egypt.

Syria, another enemy of Israel in the 1973 war. It lies just _____ of **Turkey**.

Jordan and **Lebanon**, both countries with Palestinian Arabs who claim Israel's territory was _____ from them. Many of the Palestinians would like to create their own homeland, perhaps on the land known as the **West Bank**.

Saudi Arabia, a key oil-producing kingdom that joined with other Arab nations in 1973 to _____ oil prices, creating serious economic problems in the U.S. In later years the country moved toward friendlier relations with the United States.

Iran, where religious extremists called Islamic _____ seized control in 1979. The new leaders loudly denounced the U.S. as the "Great Satan," and took 52 American diplomats hostage that same year.

Iraq, which invaded the tiny but oil-rich nation of **Kuwait** in 1990. The U.S. responded with Operation _____ Storm, forcing Iraq's army to withdraw. The dictator Saddam Hussein remained in power in Iraq, however. His efforts to develop chemical, biological, and nuclear weapons led to a new conflict with the United States in 2003.

Use these terms to fill in the blanks: attack, Desert, fundamentalists, Nazi, raise, south, stolen

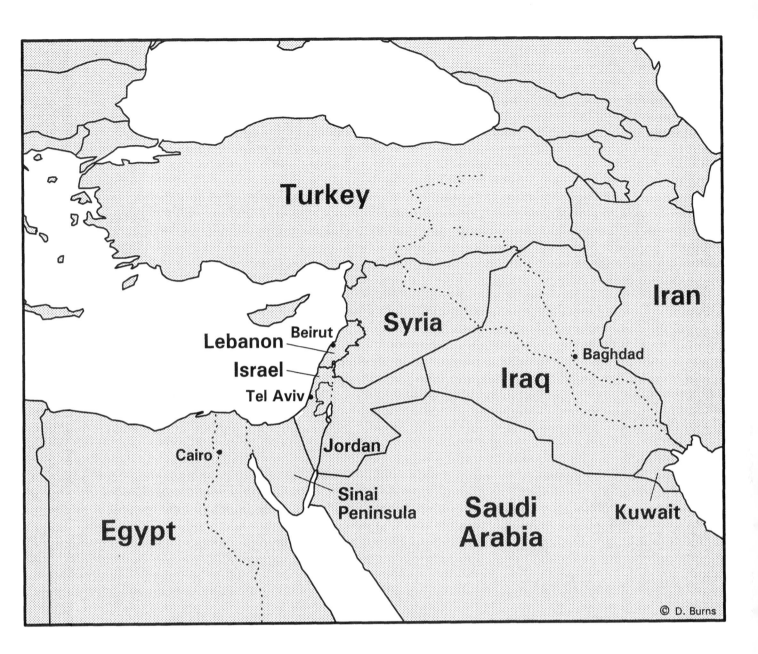

Turkey

Iran

Syria

Lebanon
Beirut

Israel

Tel Aviv

Baghdad

Iraq

Jordan

Cairo

Sinai
Peninsula

Saudi
Arabia

Kuwait

Egypt

© D. Burns

Israel and the Middle East

Boundaries of 1990 shown

Key to Land Areas

Israel

West Bank

0   400 miles

DECADE: 1980s   THE REAGAN YEARS

Ronald Reagan, liberal, conservative, Reaganomics, bureaucracy, Star Wars Defense, post-industrial society, global economy, entrepreneur, federal debt, AIDS

As Ronald Reagan wound up his challenge for the White House in 1980, he had good reason to hope for victory. The economy was stalled. Inflation was running more than 10 percent a year, reducing the purchasing power of people's wages and savings. Interest rates for bank loans and unemployment figures were both high. On top of it all, many of the big American corporations were moving their factories to other _____ where labor costs were lower. Voters were open to new ideas.

Some Democrats argued that America's days of rapid economic growth were over. They said federal government policies should mainly concentrate on making everyone's share of the pie more equal. Reagan, a Republican, said growth was stalled because the government had already become too big and interfered too much in the economy. High taxes and excessive regulations, he argued, were killing the incentive to start _____ businesses. Reagan also said the great expansion of government social programs had created a "welfare trap" that often kept the poor in a life of dependency. Business growth (which creates jobs) would give better opportunities to people of all income levels, he argued.

Reagan's ideas represented a shift away from the views widely held by liberals since the days of Franklin Roosevelt's New Deal programs. The "conservative revolution" of Reagan and his supporters carried a _____ of voters on election day.

Once in office, Reagan pushed for a 30 percent cut in the federal income tax rate. This was balanced in part by _____ the budgets of many federally financed social programs. He and his supporters in Congress said the programs were doing very little to actually help the needy, and were just supporting a large government bureaucracy. Most Democrats criticized the Reagan cuts as "cold-hearted."

The economy did improve dramatically during Reagan's two terms, in part thanks to tax cuts and other pro-business measures. And in spite of budget reductions, the most important social welfare programs _____ in place.

Controversy also surrounded Reagan's Strategic Defense Initiative, sometimes called the Star Wars Defense system. The proposal to create an advanced system of defense against Russian nuclear missiles was criticized by some as technologically impossible. Research and design work began. But the project was dropped, mainly because the Soviet Union and its communist system _____ as the decade ended. (More than 20 years later, the idea was revived as Americans responded to the rising threat of world-wide terrorism.)

In Central America, Reagan's belief in a strong stand against communism was also evident. In both El Salvador and Nicaragua, uprisings against unpopular and abusive governments were spreading. But Reagan believed it was safer in the long run to push for reform of existing governments, rather than risk a victory by revolutionaries with communist leanings. The fighting in Central America sent tens of thousands of _____ from that region to America.

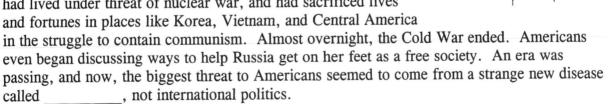

Technology continued changing America in the 1980s. The success of the Space Shuttle was a clear sign of American leadership in high-tech industries. Computers became cheap enough that small businesses and ordinary people began buying them by the _____.

The American economy was shifting to what experts called a new "post-industrial" pattern. Knowledge was becoming the key ingredient in the economy, not coal or iron ore or _____ mills. Another trend was the increasingly global economy created by world-wide trade. Both these trends created many opportunities, but sometimes eliminated jobs as older factories closed or laid off workers. Still, "entrepreneur" became a familiar word in this decade for people who started new businesses, and who sometimes grew very wealthy in the process. Computer wizard Bill Gates is one famous example.

By the end of his second term, even his critics were admitting that Reagan had given back to America a more _____ spirit. But opponents were happy to point out that one his campaign promises, to reduce the federal debt, had not been kept. Another concern, especially in cities, was a rise in the number of homeless people.

In the 1988 elections Democrats challenged Reagan's vice-president, George H.W. Bush, for the White House with a little-known candidate. The strength of the Reagan presidency helped Bush easily win the election.

Soon, however, the biggest political news was out of Russia. That nation, far behind the free nations economically, was beginning attempts to reorganize itself. Within two years, the communists were forced _____ of power in Russia, and the Soviet Union itself was breaking apart. For decades Americans had lived under threat of nuclear war, and had sacrificed lives and fortunes in places like Korea, Vietnam, and Central America in the struggle to contain communism. Almost overnight, the Cold War ended. Americans even began discussing ways to help Russia get on her feet as a free society. An era was passing, and now, the biggest threat to Americans seemed to come from a strange new disease called _____, not international politics.

Use these terms to fill in the blanks: AIDS, collapsed, countries, majority, millions, new, optimistic, out, reducing, refugees, remained, steel

CHARTING THE COMPUTER REVOLUTION

Complete the line graph below to show the spread of computers into American homes. Personal computers became available in the late 1970s, although those early models had a very limited capacity. Why do you think so many families were so eager to buy computers?

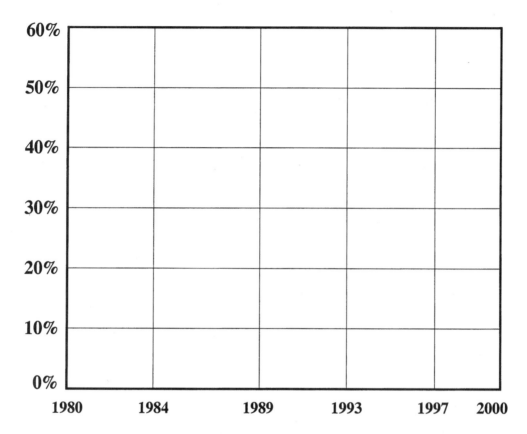

Households With Computers (Percent)
1980 to 2000

Use the table below to find the information to make the line graph above. The Census Bureau did surveys asking about home computers every few years starting in 1984. The graph lines are organized to show the data from the years of those surveys.

Year	Households With Computers (Percent)	Year	Households With Computers (Percent)
1980	1.0 *	1993	22.8
1984	7.9	1997	36.6
1989	14.4	2000	51.0

*estimated   source: *U.S. Census Bureau*

At the heart of every computer is the microprocessor chip. It is a small wafer of silicon, with many thousands of transistor circuits etched on its surface. Complete this bar graph to see the rapid improvement in chip making technology that made the computer revolution possible.

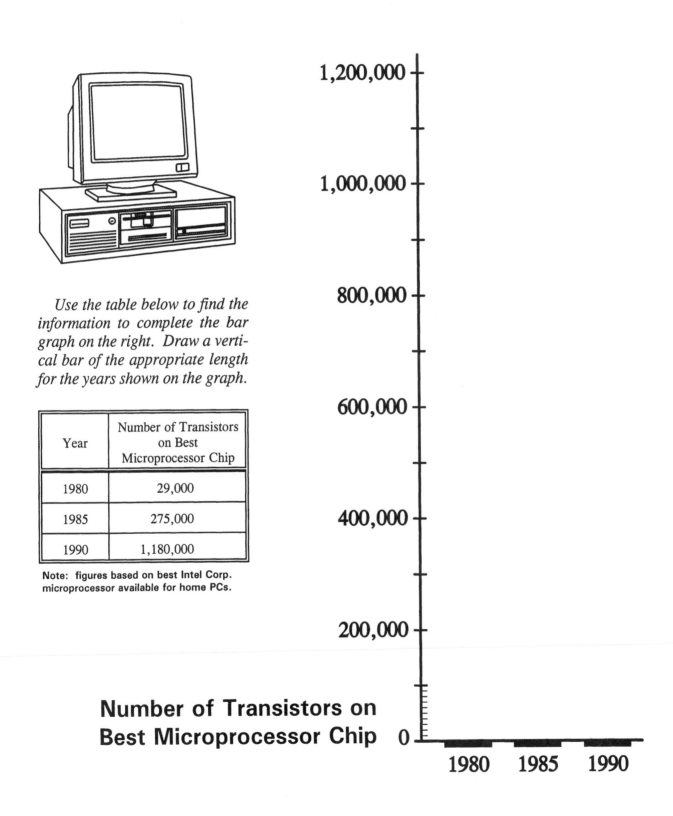

Use the table below to find the information to complete the bar graph on the right. Draw a vertical bar of the appropriate length for the years shown on the graph.

Year	Number of Transistors on Best Microprocessor Chip
1980	29,000
1985	275,000
1990	1,180,000

Note: figures based on best Intel Corp. microprocessor available for home PCs.

Number of Transistors on Best Microprocessor Chip

RONALD REAGAN SPEAKS FOR FREEDOM

One of President Reagan's most famous speeches (condensed here) contained a stunning challenge to the Russian leader of the Soviet Union, Mikhail Gorbachev.

Berlin, like Germany itself, had been divided into sections since the end of World War Two. Russia kept East Germany and half of Berlin under communist rule. In the 1980s those areas were still controlled by the Soviet Union. West Germany was a free democracy allied with the U.S.

The Berlin Wall was built in the early 1960s by the communist leaders of East Germany to stop people there from fleeing to the other side.

Speech at the Berlin Wall - 1987

Behind me stands a wall that encircles the free sectors of this city, part of a vast system of barriers that divides the entire continent of Europe.

From the Baltic, south, those barriers cut across Germany in a gash of barbed wire, concrete, dog runs, and guard towers. Yet it is here in Berlin where the wall emerges most clearly; here, cutting across your city, where the news photo and television screen have imprinted this brutal division of a continent upon the mind of the world.

In this season of spring in 1945, the people of Berlin emerged from their air-raid shelters to find devastation. Where four decades ago there was rubble, today in West Berlin there is the greatest industrial output of any city in Germany - busy office blocks, fine homes and apartments, proud avenues, and the spreading lawns of park land.

From devastation, from utter ruin, you Berliners have, in freedom, rebuilt a city that once again ranks as one of the greatest on Earth.

In the West today, we see a free world that has achieved a level of prosperity and well-being unprecedented in all human history.

In the Communist world, we see failure, technological backwardness, declining standards of health, even want of a most basic kind - too little food. Even today, the Soviet Union cannot feed itself.

After these four decades, then, there stands before the entire world one great and inescapable conclusion: Freedom leads to prosperity. Freedom replaces the ancient hatreds among the nations with comity [courtesy] and peace. Freedom is the victor.

And now the Soviets themselves may, in a limited way, be coming to understand the importance of freedom. We hear much from Moscow about a new policy of reform and openness. Some political prisoners have been released. Certain foreign news broadcasts are no longer being jammed.

Are these the beginnings of profound changes in the Soviet state? Or are they token gestures, intended to raise false hopes in the West?

There is one sign the Soviets can make that would be unmistakable, that would advance dramatically the cause of freedom and peace. General Secretary Gorbachev, if you seek peace, if you seek prosperity for the Soviet Union and Eastern Europe: Come here to this gate. **Mr. Gorbachev, open this gate! Mr. Gorbachev, tear down this wall!**

In Europe, only one nation and those it controls refuse to join the community of freedom. Yet in this age of redoubled economic growth, of information and innovation, the Soviet Union faces a choice: It must make fundamental changes, or it will become obsolete.

As I looked out a moment ago, I noticed words crudely spray-painted upon the wall, perhaps by a young Berliner, "This wall will fall. Beliefs will become reality."

Yes, across Europe, this wall will fall. For it cannot withstand faith; it cannot withstand truth. The wall cannot withstand freedom.

Soviet leader Mikhail Gorbachev did not come to open the Berlin Wall. It was torn down in 1989 and 1990 as people across Germany, Eastern Europe, and Russia itself rose up in rebellion against their Communist Party rulers.

President Reagan completed his second term shortly before the dramatic events that finally brought down the Berlin Wall. These are condensed excerpts from his speech as he returned to private life.

Reagan's Farewell Address - 1989

There are two things that I'm proudest of. One is the economic recovery, in which the people of America created, and filled, 19 million new jobs. The other is the recovery of our morale: America is respected again in the world, and looked to for leadership.

Common sense told us that when you put a big tax on something, the people will produce less of it. So we cut the people's tax rates, and the people produced more than ever before.

Our economic program brought about the longest peacetime expansion in our history: family income up, the poverty rate down, entrepreneurship booming, and an explosion in research and new technology.

And something else we learned: once you begin a great movement, there's no telling where it will end.

Countries across the globe are turning to free markets and free speech, and turning away from the ideologies of the past. For them, the Great Rediscovery of the 1980s has been that the moral way of government is the practical way of government. Democracy, the profoundly good, is also the profoundly productive.

Back in the 1960s when I began, it seemed to me that we had begun reversing the order of things, that through more and more rules and regulations and taxes, the government was taking more of our money, more of our options, and more of our freedom.

I went into politics in part to put up my hand and say, "Stop!"

I think we have stopped a lot of what needed stopping. And I hope we have once again reminded people that man is not free unless government is limited. There's a clear cause and effect here that is as neat and predictable as a law of physics: as government expands, liberty contracts.

Group Discussion: *In the first speech, what contrast does Reagan make between life on the two sides of the Berlin Wall? What point does he want to make with his challenge to Soviet leader Gorbachev?*

In the second speech, what does Reagan count as the accomplishments of his years in office? What point does Reagan want to leave with his audience about government power?

DECADE: 1990s   THE COLD WAR ENDS

George H.W. Bush, Desert Storm, Rodney King case, affirmative action, multi-culturalism,

Cesar Chavez, Bill Clinton, welfare reform, Monica Lewinsky scandal

Looking over newspaper headlines, most Americans would probably rank 1990 as a very good year. The Cold War ended as communist leaders lost their grip on the Soviet Union. The struggle had been a dark streak running through American life for more than forty years. McCarthyism, the arms race, fallout shelters, Vietnam - they were all a part of it. Now, incredibly, the Russians were admitting openly that communism had led them not to a workers' paradise, but into poverty and _____.

The collapse of the Soviet Union and communism had an enormous impact on America. American armed forces were told to begin cutting back, as the old enemy began acting more like a _____. Politicians including President George H.W. Bush began talking about the "Peace Dividend," that is, the money that could be switched from defense needs to help solve other problems.

Another sign of the change came as American troops moved into the Middle East to free Kuwait in early 1991, after it was invaded by Iraq. In earlier times Russia would have played its hand against America's intervention. Now it cooperated with the multi-national effort of Operation Desert Storm. The American-led military action was a big success. But some people grumbled that the whole affair seemed more about _____ supplies than liberty. Kuwait, quickly freed, was still no democracy.

Overall, Desert Storm and the changes in Russia seemed to most citizens a sign of the strength of America's basic principles. Yet as the 1992 presidential campaign got underway,

it was clear that beyond the basics there was considerable disagreement. Conservatives claimed America's culture was rapidly falling apart. They pointed to the growth of violence, the spread of single parent families, and young people unwilling or unable to take responsible roles in society. Liberals saw the same problems, but claimed they were evidence of racism, sexism, or _____ of opportunity for the poor.

Race and ethnicity remained troublesome issues. African-Americans had successfully moved into the highest levels of society. Virginia, once part of the old Confederacy, had elected a black governor. But in Los Angeles a deadly _____ erupted when police accused of brutality during the arrest of a speeding black motorist named Rodney King were declared "not guilty" by a mostly white jury. Race relations were also strained by complaints that affirmative action programs designed to help minorities amounted to "reverse discrimination" against whites.

At the same time, other ethnic groups, especially Hispanics, were becoming more prominent parts of the American picture. As a union leader, Cesar Chavez became famous for his work to improve conditions for Hispanic farm workers. Big city school districts struggled to cope with children speaking dozens of languages. Some leaders argued that America should simply embrace the new spirit of "multi-culturalism." Others, however, warned that without a common culture and language shared by _____ Americans, the country would fall apart in endless squabbling among different groups.

Many of these issues became part of the 1992 election. Democrat Bill Clinton, a former governor of Arkansas, won the White House. He had come of age during the turbulent 1960s and embraced many of the liberal views that had grown in that era.

President Clinton and his wife, Hillary, were eager to create a National Health Care system. Canada, England, and a number of other countries had such plans in place for years. The proposal would put the federal government in charge of providing medical care to all. The idea was very attractive to the millions of Americans who could not afford the cost of health _____. But critics said turning over control of the nation's hospitals and doctors to the federal government would result in _____ quality medical care for everyone. The plan was defeated by Congress.

The 1994 elections tipped _____ houses of Congress to Republican majorities for the first time in many years. It seemed a clear signal that the shift to more conservative views that started in the 1980s was still very much alive. Welfare reform was one result. Congress wrote, and the president approved, changes that allowed states to set time _____ and work requirements for welfare recipients. Budget compromises were also reached to bring federal spending in better balance with the government's income from taxes. A rapidly growing economy in the last half of this decade helped bring success to both these efforts.

President Clinton was reelected in 1996, keeping the White House in the hands of the _____. Before the decade was over, however, the president was impeached when allegations were made of personal misconduct involving a young woman working at the White House. The president was convicted by the Senate of some charges related to the scandal. But the Senate voted _____ removing Clinton from office. As the Monica Lewinsky scandal faded from headlines, most Americans were thankful that the nation was ending the decade on a prosperous and mostly peaceful note.

Use these terms to fill in the blanks: *against, all, both, Democrats, friend, insurance, lack, limits, lower, oil, oppression, riot*

THE FEDERAL BUDGET & THE FEDERAL DEBT

One of the biggest issues in the 1980s and 1990s was the increasing size of the federal debt. The debt is a result of the fact that in most years in recent decades, the government spent more than it collected in taxes. The government must borrow money (by selling savings bonds and other means) to make up the gap. To help understand basic budget issues, use the table below to answer the questions on the next page.

Year	Income Billions of Dollars	Spending Billions of Dollars	Budget Surplus (+) or Deficit (-) Billions of Dollars	Spending As a Percent of the GDP	Federal Debt Billions of Dollars
1970	192.8	195.6	- 2.8	19.3	380.9
1975	279.1	332.3	- 53.2	21.3	541.9
1980	517.1	590.9	- 73.8	21.6	909.1
1985	734.1	946.4	- 212.3	22.9	1,817.5
1990	1,032.0	1,253.2	- 221.2	21.8	3,206.6
1995	1,351.8	1,515.8	- 164.0	20.7	4,921.0
2000	2,025.2	1,788.8	+ 236.4	18.2	5,629.0

source: *Statistical Abstract of the United States*

Income - The amount of money the federal government collects in a year, mainly from taxes.

Spending - The amount of money the federal government spends in a year on social programs, defense, research, etc.

Surplus or Deficit - The difference between the government's income and spending in a given year. If the federal government spends more than it collects, there is a deficit; if less, there is a surplus.

Spending as a Percent of the GDP - Compares federal government spending to the size of the nation's overall economy. The GDP is the Gross Domestic Product, an estimate in dollars of the total value of all goods and services produced by the nation's economy in a year.

Federal Debt - The total amount of money the federal government owes on money it has borrowed to cover deficits in the federal budget. The debt is now in the trillions of dollars.

| 1,000,000,000 = 1 billion | 1,000 billion = 1 trillion = 1,000,000,000,000 |

Mark each statement below true or false. If it is false, rewrite the <u>underlined word or phrase</u> on the blank line to make the statement true. Check the figures carefully!

1. The federal government's income from taxes and other sources in 1990 was <u>more than five times</u> as large as it was in 1970.

True   **False**

_____

2. Spending by the federal government <u>grew rapidly</u> from 1970 to 2000.

True   **False**

_____

3. In <u>all of the years</u> shown, the federal government had a deficit in its budget.

True   **False**

_____

4. In 2000 the federal government had a total income just over <u>two billion</u> dollars.

True   **False**

_____

5. Federal spending has been a <u>fairly steady</u> proportion of the nation's total economy since 1970, generally staying between 18 and 23 percent.

True   **False**

6. President Ronald Reagan and Congress <u>reduced</u> federal spending from 1980 to 1985.

True   **False**

_____

7. Under President Clinton in the 1990s, federal spending increased, but the government's income grew even faster, resulting in a <u>budget surplus</u> in 2000.

True   **False**

_____

8. The size of the federal debt <u>fell steadily</u> from 1970 to 2000.

True   **False**

_____

9. In 1990, the federal debt was a bit over <u>three trillion</u> dollars.

True   **False**

_____

10. Written out completely, the federal debt in 2000 was <u>$ 5,629,000,000</u>.

True   **False**

_____

CHARTING WELFARE REFORM

Complete the line graph below to show the growth of welfare and the results of the 1996 welfare reform law. The figures show the number of people in the U.S. receiving aid under the most common welfare program. How effective was the welfare reform law?

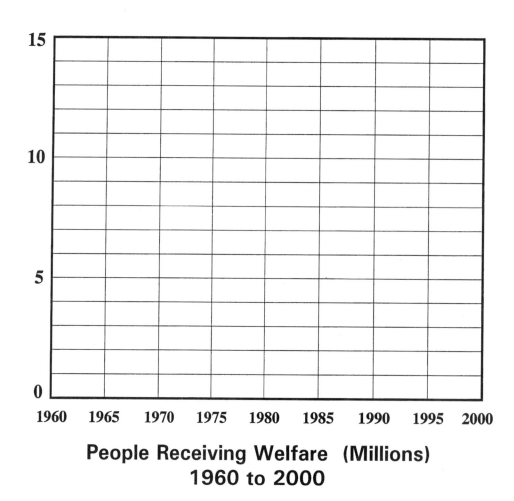

People Receiving Welfare (Millions)
1960 to 2000

Use the table below to find the information to make the line graph above.

Year	Welfare Recipients* (Millions)	Year	Welfare Recipients (Millions)	Year	Welfare Recipients (Millions)
1960	3,005,000	1975	11,165,000	1990	11,460,000
1965	4,329,000	1980	10,597,000	1995	13,652,000
1970	8,466,000	1985	10,813,000	2000	5,781,000

*figures are for AFDC and TANF recipients

sources: *Historical Statistics of the United States* and *Statistical Abstract of the United States*

HILLARY CLINTON ON CHILD CARE

Hillary Clinton was an active First Lady and later, a U.S. Senator. Child care issues remained one of her concerns, as this condensed speech shows.

I wanted to come and tell you why this is an issue that deserves White House attention, deserves the attention of our nation, and one that we hope will raise awareness of these issues around the country.

More and more families are seeking child care. Over half of all the infants under age one are in day care. Twelve million children under the age of six, and 17 million more age six through 13, have both parents or their only parent in the work force.

The plain fact is that there is simply not enough quality care for the children who need it. Quality care is financially out of reach for the hard-working American families whose children deserve the best attention they can receive.

Now, there are many reasons to put our children's needs first. One reason is because we know that how we care for our children is critical to their intellectual and emotional development. Just 15 years ago, even scientists thought that a baby's brain structure was virtually complete at birth.

Now, neuroscience tells us that it is a work in progress, and that everything we do with a child has some kind of potential physical influence on that rapidly forming brain.

Experiences in those first three years of life can also determine how well a child learns. When someone speaks, reads, or plays with an infant or toddler, he or she, whether it is a parent, a grandparent, an older sibling or care-giver, is activating the connections in that child's brain that will one day enable her to think and read and speak and solve problems herself.

Now, what that means is that sub-par care, whether in the home or in a child care setting, means that a young brain is being deprived of what it needs to live up to its natural potential.

Another reason we need to act is that we now have evidence that child care is too often inadequate.

A recent national study of child care centers found that 70 percent of children are in care that is barely adequate. Ten percent are in care that is dangerous to their health and safety.

That means that they spend hours of their days with care givers who do not follow basic sanitary practices, who rarely cuddle, talk to or play with these infants and toddlers, in rooms that lack toys and other materials to encourage development, and in places where the ratio of children to adults is too high for individual attention.

Now, there's no doubt that the most important, lasting influence on any child is that child's family. But we know that good, quality child care can improve a child's chances, if that child is in a difficult family situation. So turning to child care is not just something that is a nice issue to talk about.

It is, as the President calls it, the next great frontier of public policy. To build up and strengthen our families, to give them more support so they can do their jobs both at home and in the workplace, will help us chart that frontier for generations of American children to come.

Group Discussion: *What are the main points Hillary Clinton makes about the need for better day care for children? What does she mean when she says the issue is "the next great frontier of public policy"?*

DECADE: 2000s   A NEW MILLENNIUM

George W. Bush, 9-11 attacks, Osama bin Laden, Saddam Hussein

The start of the year 2000 appeared to most Americans as a milestone deserving a great celebration. The United States and its open, democratic society stood as one of the world's greatest _____ stories. The tyrannical systems that bloodied the earth in the previous century - fascism and communism - had failed in their challenge.

America's system of democracy and capitalism had itself steadily been improving. Federal and state governments had achieved a balance of regulations that kept business growing but also protected workers and consumers. Government social welfare programs created a "safety net" to help those in need. The political parties might debate the details of these policies, but there was more _____ than disagreement about America's recipe for success.

One result was that the 2000 presidential election was among the closest in history. Running for the Republicans was a former Texas governor, George W. Bush. (He is also a son of former President George H.W. Bush.) Vice President Al Gore carried the Democratic party banner. Election results showed that Al Gore won a slight _____ of the popular vote, but George W. Bush appeared to have a slight majority in the crucial Electoral College vote total.

A feverish struggle began over the vote count in Florida, where a few hundred ballots one way or the other could determine the outcome of the election. Charges of fraud and unfair counting of ballots flew from both sides. In the end the _____ Court was called in to rule on the legality of the counting and recounting. Weeks after the election, Bush was declared the winner of the popular vote in Florida, and with that state's Electoral College votes, he was declared the official winner.

President Bush's first big concern was the economy. Even before the election the bubble of rapid business growth and investment of the late 1990s was showing signs of trouble. Soon a mild recession set in, although to anyone who lost their _____ or to businesses thrown into bankruptcy, it seemed anything but mild.

A far more tragic event united the country as the year 2001 moved into autumn. Americans watched in horror on September 11 as two hijacked jetliners full of passengers were deliberately crashed into the World Trade Center towers in New York City. The hijackers - all terrorists from the Middle East - crashed another jetliner into the Pentagon building just outside Washington, D.C.

Over 3,000 people were killed in the attacks, including those on a fourth jetliner driven into the ground when _____ on board mounted a heroic fight to stop the terrorists' plan to destroy the White House or Capitol building.

The attacks were organized by Osama bin Laden, a wealthy Saudi Arabian who established terrorist training camps in Afghanistan. He and his organization, called al Qaeda, followed a fanatical form of Islam that preached a *jihad*, or holy war, against the United States.

Bin Laden's organization saw the U.S. as a threat precisely because of the values that made America a success: personal freedom, religious _____, free speech, and free enterprise. None of these could be found in the bizarre world the terrorists dreamed of creating. Americans quickly began learning about the beliefs of Islam, and wondered how its teachings could become so twisted into a message of terrorism.

Within hours of the attacks reports of incredible heroism began spreading. Hundreds of firefighters, police, emergency workers, and ordinary citizens had begun rescue attempts in the burning buildings. As the buildings collapsed, many were still inside, still trying to save lives. American flags suddenly began appearing outside millions of homes all across the country in a display of _____ and unity.

President Bush called the attacks an act of war. He declared that America wanted bin Laden "Dead or Alive." The terrorist was hiding in Afghanistan, where he had the support of that country's ruling group, called the Taliban. The Taliban itself was based on extreme Islamic beliefs and a brutal style of government that considered listening to _____ a crime.

Many other nations pledged to _____ in the fight against terrorism. As American troops entered Afghanistan to search for bin Laden, even some Afghan groups that opposed the Taliban agreed to help. The Taliban government was quickly _____, but bin Laden avoided capture.

The determination of the United States to track down the sources of terrorism brought new attention to the brutal ruler of Iraq, Saddam Hussein. President Bush demanded that Iraq destroy any biological, chemical, or _____ weapons it held. Saddam Hussein denied having such weapons. But U.S. officials said there was solid evidence that his regime had worked for years to develop nerve gas and deadly biological agents like anthrax. Early in 2003 American and British forces moved into Iraq and quickly forced Hussein from power. Their goal in the military action was to help the Iraqi people create a new democratic government free from force and terror.

Use these terms to fill in the blanks: agreement, job, join, majority, music, nuclear, overthrown, passengers, pride, success, Supreme, tolerance

GEORGE W. BUSH AND THE WAR ON TERRORISM

President Bush used his State of the Union address in January, 2002, to outline the status of the war on terrorism. The U.S. had already formed a coalition, or alliance, of nations willing to fight against terrorism. These are condensed excerpts.

As we gather tonight, our nation is at war, our economy is in recession, and the civilized world faces unprecedented dangers. Yet the state of our Union has never been stronger.

We last met in an hour of shock and suffering. In four short months, our nation has comforted the victims, begun to rebuild New York and the Pentagon, rallied a great coalition, captured, arrested, and rid the world of thousands of terrorists, destroyed Afghanistan's terrorist training camps, saved a people from starvation, and freed a country from brutal oppression.

Our cause is just, and it continues. Our discoveries in Afghanistan confirmed our worst fears, and showed us the true scope of the task ahead. We have seen the depth of our enemies' hatred in videos, where they laugh about the loss of innocent life. And the depth of their hatred is equaled by the madness of the destruction they design.

We have found diagrams of American nuclear power plants and public water facilities, detailed instructions for making chemical weapons, surveillance maps of American cities, and thorough descriptions of landmarks in America and throughout the world.

What we have found in Afghanistan confirms that, far from ending there, our war against terror is only beginning. Most of the 19 men who hijacked planes on September the 11th were trained in Afghanistan's camps, and so were tens of thousands of others. Thousands of dangerous killers, schooled in the methods of murder, often supported by outlaw regimes [governments], are now spread throughout the world like ticking time bombs, set to go off without warning.

Our nation will continue to be steadfast and patient and persistent in the pursuit of two great objectives. First, we will shut down terrorist camps, disrupt terrorist plans, and bring terrorists to justice.

Our military has put the terror training camps of Afghanistan out of business, yet camps still exist in at least a dozen countries. A terrorist underworld operates in remote jungles and deserts, and hides in the centers of large cities.

Our second goal is to prevent regimes that sponsor terror from threatening America or our friends and allies with weapons of mass destruction. Some of these regimes have been pretty quiet since September the 11th. But we know their true nature.

North Korea is a regime arming with missiles and weapons of mass destruction, while starving its citizens.

Iran aggressively pursues these weapons and exports terror, while an unelected few repress the Iranian people's hope for freedom.

Iraq continues to flaunt its hostility toward America and to support terror. The Iraqi regime has plotted to develop anthrax, and nerve gas, and nuclear weapons for over a decade. This is a regime that has already used poison gas to murder thousands of its own citizens - leaving the bodies of mothers huddled over their dead children.

States like these, and their terrorist allies, constitute an axis of evil, arming to threaten the peace of the world. By seeking weapons of mass destruction, these regimes pose a grave and growing danger. They could provide these arms to terrorists, giving them the means to match their hatred. They could attack our allies or attempt to blackmail the United States. In any of these cases, the price of indifference [doing nothing] would be catastrophic.

During these last few months, I've been humbled and privileged to see the true character of this country in a time of testing. Our enemies believed America was weak and materialistic, that we would splinter in fear and selfishness. They were as wrong as they are evil.

The American people have responded magnificently, with courage and compassion, strength and resolve. As I have met the heroes, hugged the families, and looked into the tired faces of rescuers, I have stood in awe of the American people.

We have a great opportunity during this time of war to lead the world toward the values that will bring lasting peace.

All fathers and mothers, in all societies, want their children to be educated, and live free from poverty and violence. No people on Earth yearn to be oppressed, or aspire to servitude, or eagerly await the midnight knock of the secret police.

If anyone doubts this, let them look to Afghanistan, where the Islamic "street" greeted the fall of tyranny [the Taliban rulers] with song and celebration. Let the skeptics look to Islam's own rich history, with its centuries of learning, and tolerance and progress.

America will lead by defending liberty and justice because they are right and true and unchanging for all people everywhere.

No nation owns these aspirations [ideals], and no nation is exempt from them. We have no intention of imposing our culture. But America will always stand firm for the non-negotiable demands of human dignity: the rule of law; limits on the power of the state; respect for women; private property; free speech; equal justice; and religious tolerance.

America will take the side of brave men and women who advocate [support] these values around the world, including the Islamic world, because we have a greater objective than eliminating threats and containing resentment. We seek a just and peaceful world beyond the war on terror.

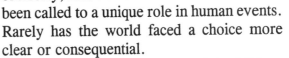

In a single instant, we realized that this will be a decisive decade in the history of liberty, that we've been called to a unique role in human events. Rarely has the world faced a choice more clear or consequential.

Our enemies send other people's children on missions of suicide and murder. They embrace tyranny and death as a cause and a creed. We stand for a different choice, made long ago, on the day of our founding. We affirm it again today. We choose freedom and the dignity of every life.

Steadfast in our purpose, we now press on. We have known freedom's price. We have shown freedom's power. And in this great conflict, my fellow Americans, we will see freedom's victory.

Group Discussion: *What does President Bush say are the main objectives or goals of America in the war on terrorism? What principles does he think will unite people, including many in the Islamic world, in the fight against terrorism?*

Appendix

The appendix pages contain these additional resources:

The Declaration of Independence

Blank Map - U.S.A.

Blank Map - U.S.A. Contiguous 48 states only

Blank Map - The World

Use the blank maps to develop your own custom projects. For example, you may want to study state-by-state voting in an important election. The world map might be useful to show recent sources of immigration or other global trends.

Recommended Reading

This study guide will be most helpful if used in conjunction with other sources of information about America's past. Many topics can be easily researched in encyclopedias and atlases available in libraries or on-line. Other books and atlases you may find useful include:

Hammond Atlas of United States History, (Union, N.J.: Hammond World Atlas Corp., 2002), is an inexpensive atlas with scores of useful and interesting historical maps.

The American Reader, edited by Diane Ravitch (N.Y.: HarperCollins Publishers, 1990), is a multi-cultural anthology of speeches, poems, songs, and photographs that document America's story.

The World's Great Speeches, edited by Lewis Copeland and Lawrence W. Lamm (Mineola, NY: Dover Publications, Inc., 1973), contains many of the most famous speeches in American history, including many condensed in this publication.

A New Age Now Begins, by Page Smith (N.Y.: McGraw-Hill Book Company, 1976), is the first in a multi-volume narrative history of the United States by Prof. Smith. The books in the series are widely available in libraries. Search by the author's name. Ideal for adults and older high school students, the series gives insightful and balanced accounts of almost any topic in American history.

A History of US, by Joy Hakim (N.Y.: Oxford University Press, 1995), is also a multi-volume narrative history of America. The series features well-illustrated easy-to-read pages ideal for younger readers. Available in libraries and in paperback in many bookstores.

The Declaration of Independence

In CONGRESS, July 4, 1776,

The unanimous Declaration of the thirteen united States of America,

When in the Course of human events, it becomes necessary for one people to dissolve the political bands which have connected them with another, and to assume among the powers of the earth, the separate and equal station to which the Laws of Nature and of Nature's God entitle them, a decent respect to the opinions of mankind requires that they should declare the causes which impel them to the separation.

We hold these truths to be self-evident, that all men are created equal, that they are endowed by their Creator with certain unalienable Rights, that among these are Life, Liberty, and the pursuit of Happiness.

That to secure these rights, Governments are instituted among Men, deriving their just powers from the consent of the governed,

That whenever any Form of Government becomes destructive of these ends, it is the Right of the People to alter or to abolish it, and to institute new Government, laying its foundation on such principles and organizing its powers in such form, as to them shall seem most likely to effect their Safety and Happiness.

Prudence, indeed, will dictate that Governments long established should not be changed for light and transient causes; and accordingly all experience hath shewn, that mankind are more disposed to suffer, while evils are sufferable, than to right themselves by abolishing the forms to which they are accustomed.

But when a long train of abuses and usurpations, pursuing invariably the same object evinces a design to reduce them under absolute Despotism, it is their right, it is their duty, to throw off such Government, and to provide new Guards for their future security.

Such has been the patient sufferance of these Colonies; and such is now the necessity which constrains them to alter their former Systems of Government. The history of the present King of Great Britain is a history of repeated injuries and usurpations, all having in direct object the establishment of an absolute Tyranny over these States. To prove this, let Facts be submitted

---

Notes and definitions for students:

station: *position or rank*
impel: *force*

endowed: *provided*
unalienable: *cannot be taken away (also, inalienable)*

transient: *brief*
hath shewn: *has shown*
disposed: *willing*

usurpations: *improper takings of political power*
evinces: *reveals*
despotism: *a government that abuses power*
constrains: *forces*

tyranny: *cruel or abusive government*

to a candid world.

He has refused his Assent to Laws, the most wholesome and necessary for the public good.

He has forbidden his Governors to pass Laws of immediate and pressing importance, unless suspended in their operation till his Assent should be obtained, and when so suspended, he has utterly neglected to attend to them.

He has refused to pass other Laws for the accommodation of large districts of people, unless those people would relinquish the right of Representation in the Legislature, a right inestimable to them and formidable to tyrants only.

He has called together legislative bodies at places unusual, uncomfortable, and distant from the depository of their public Records, for the sole purpose of fatiguing them into compliance with his measures.

He has dissolved Representative Houses repeatedly, for opposing with manly firmness his invasions on the rights of the people.

He has refused for a long time, after such dissolutions, to cause others to be elected; whereby the Legislative powers, incapable of Annihilation, have returned to the People at large for their exercise; the State remaining in the meantime exposed to all the dangers of invasion from without, and convulsions within.

He has endeavoured to prevent the population of these States; for that purpose obstructing the Laws for Naturalization of Foreigners; refusing to pass others to encourage their migrations hither, and raising the conditions of new Appropriations of Lands.

He has obstructed the Administration of Justice, by refusing his Assent to Laws for establishing Judiciary powers.

He has made Judges dependent on his Will alone, for the tenure of their offices, and the amount and payment of their salaries.

He has erected a multitude of New Offices, and sent hither swarms of Officers to harass our people, and eat out their substance.

He has kept among us, in times of peace, Standing Armies, without the consent of our legislatures.

He has affected to render the Military independent of and superior to the Civil power.

He has combined with others to subject us to a jurisdiction foreign to our constitution and unacknowledged by our laws; giving his Assent to their Acts of pretended Legislation:

For quartering large bodies of troops among us:

assent: *approval*

("He," of course, is King George III)

relinquish: *give up*
inestimable: *of very high value*
formidable: *threatening*

fatiguing: *tiring*

dissolved: *closed down (here, meetings of elected colonial leaders)*

endeavoured: *attempted*

tenure: *length of employment*
hither: *to here (These are references to the British troops and their officers sent to the colonies.)*

jurisdiction: *political rule (here, by the Parliament)*
pretended: *invalid*
quartering: *lodging*

For protecting them by a mock Trial from punishment for any
    Murders which they should commit on the Inhabitants of
    these States:

For cutting off our Trade with all parts of the world:

For imposing Taxes on us without our Consent:

For depriving us in many cases of the benefits of Trial by Jury:

For transporting us beyond Seas to be tried for pretended
    offences:

For abolishing the free System of English Laws in a
    neighbouring Province, establishing therein an Arbitrary
    government, and enlarging its Boundaries so as to render
    it at once an example and fit instrument for introducing
    the same absolute rule into these Colonies:

For taking away our Charters, abolishing our most valuable
    Laws and altering fundamentally the Forms of our
    Governments:

For suspending our own Legislatures, and declaring themselves
    invested with power to legislate for us in all cases
    whatsoever.

(These are all references to laws passed by the British Parliament, and approved by the King. The colonists are declaring that the laws never had any real legal basis.)

(This refers to the Quebec Act of 1774.)

He has abdicated Government here by declaring us out of his Protection and waging War against us.

He has plundered our seas, ravaged our Coasts, burnt our towns, and destroyed the lives of our people.

He is at this time transporting large Armies of foreign Mercenaries to complete the works of death, desolation and tyranny, already begun with circumstances of cruelty and perfidy scarcely paralleled in the most barbarous ages, and totally unworthy the Head of a civilized nation.

He has constrained our fellow Citizens taken Captive on the high Seas to bear Arms against their Country, to become the executioners of their friends and Brethren, or to fall themselves by their Hands.

He has excited domestic insurrections amongst us, and has endeavoured to bring on the inhabitants of our frontiers, the merciless Indian Savages, whose known rule of warfare is an undistinguished destruction of all ages, sexes and conditions.

abdicated: *given up*

(Some British attacks had already been made by this time.)
mercenaries: *hired soldiers (here, the German Hessians)*
perfidy: *treachery*

(By law, British ships could force sailors to serve on warships)

insurrections: *violent uprisings (here, by Loyalists and Indians)*

In every stage of these Oppressions We have Petitioned for Redress in the most humble terms. Our repeated Petitions have been answered only by repeated injury. A Prince, whose character is thus marked by every act which may define a Tyrant, is unfit to be the ruler of a free people.

Nor have We been wanting in attentions to our British brethren. We have warned them from time to time of attempts by their legislature to extend an unwarrantable jurisdiction over us.

redress: *setting things right*
tyrant: *a cruel or abusive ruler*
wanting: *lacking*
unwarrantable: *unjustified*

We have reminded them of the circumstances of our emigration and settlement here. We have appealed to their native justice and magnanimity, and we have conjured them by the ties of our common kindred to disavow these usurpations, which would inevitably interrupt our connections and correspondence. They too have been deaf to the voice of justice and of consanguinity. We must, therefore, acquiesce in the necessity, which denounces our Separation, and hold them, as we hold the rest of mankind, Enemies in War, in Peace Friends.

We, therefore, the Representatives of the United States of America, in General Congress, Assembled, appealing to the Supreme Judge of the world for the rectitude of our intentions, do, in the Name, and by the authority of the good People of these Colonies, solemnly publish and declare, That these United Colonies are, and of Right ought to be Free and Independent States; that they are Absolved from all Allegiance to the British Crown, and that all political connection between them and the State of Great Britain is and ought to be totally dissolved; and that as Free and Independent States, they have full Power to levy War, conclude Peace, contract Alliances, establish Commerce, and to do all other Acts and Things which Independent States may of right do.

And for the support of this Declaration, with a firm reliance on the protection of Divine Providence, we mutually pledge to each other our Lives, our Fortunes, and our sacred Honor.

magnanimity: *generous spirit*
conjured: *begged*
kindred: *ancestry*
disavow: *reject*
consanguinity: *common blood or ancestry*
acquiesce: *agree reluctantly*

rectitude: *rightness*

absolved: *released*

levy: *officially declare*

mutually: *together*

John Hancock, *President from Massachusetts*
Georgia: *Button Gwinnett, Lyman Hall, George Walton*
North Carolina: *William Hooper, Joseph Hewes, John Penn*
South Carolina: *Edward Rutledge, Thomas Heyward, Jr., Thomas Lynch, Jr., Arthur Middleton*
Maryland: *Samuel*

Chase, William Paca, Thomas Stone, Charles Carroll of Carrollton
Virginia: *George Wythe, Richard Henry Lee, Thomas Jefferson, Benjamin Harrison, Thomas Nelson, Jr., Francis Lightfoot Lee, Carter Braxton*
Pennsylvania: *Robert Morris, Benjamin Rush, Benjamin Franklin, John Morton, George Clymer, James Smith,*

George Taylor, James Wilson, George Ross
Delaware: *Caesar Rodney, George Read, Thomas McKean*
New York: *William Floyd, Philip Livingston, Francis Lewis, Lewis Morris*
New Jersey: *Richard Stockton, John Witherspoon, Francis Hopkinson, John Hart, Abraham Clark*
New Hampshire: *Josiah*

Bartlett, William Whipple, Matthew Thornton
Massachusetts: *John Hancock, Samual Adams, John Adams, Robert Treat Paine, Elbridge Gerry*
Rhode Island: *Stephen Hopkins, William Ellery*
Connecticut: *Roger Sherman, Samuel Huntington, William Williams, Oliver Wolcott*

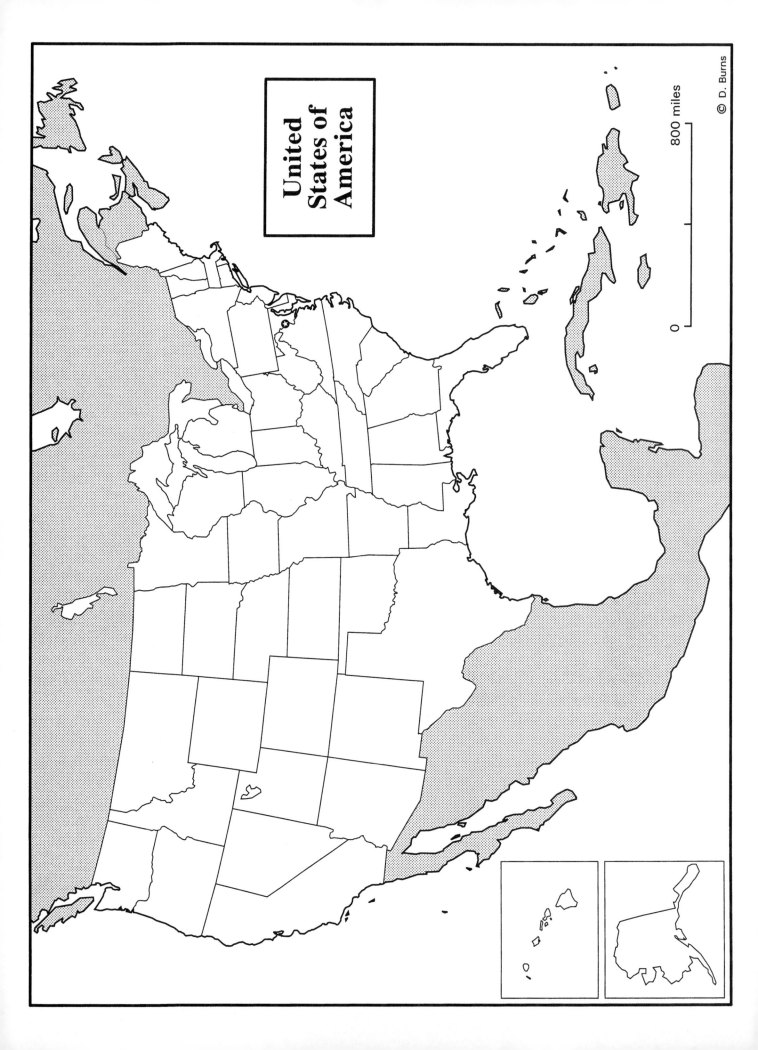

United States of
America

© D. Burns

800 miles

0

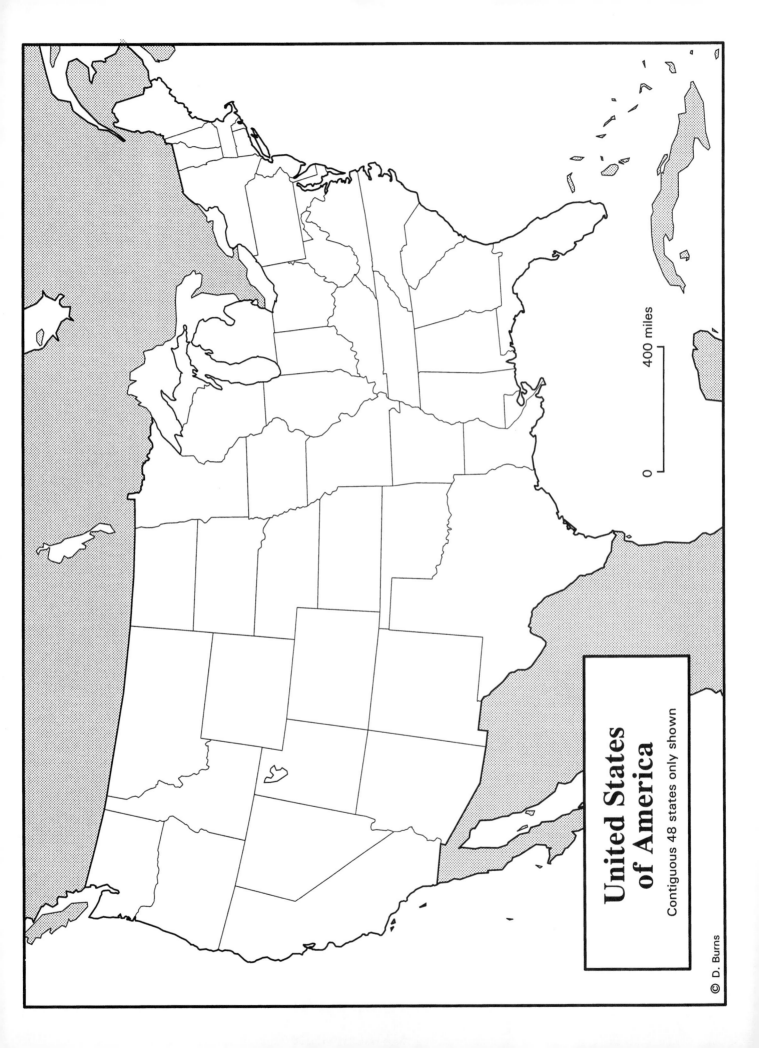

United States
of America

Contiguous 48 states only shown

400 miles

0

© D. Burns

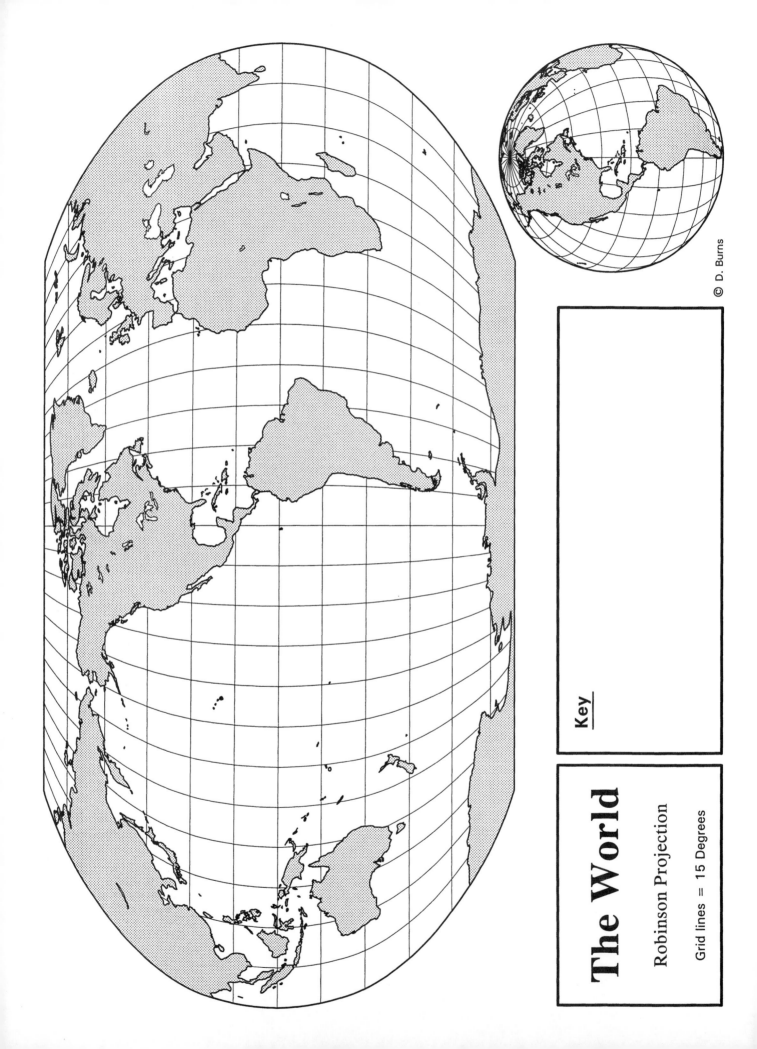

The World

Robinson Projection

Grid lines = 15 Degrees

Key

© D. Burns